PHYSICALLY BASED REAL-TIME AURALIZATION OF INTERACTIVE VIRTUAL ENVIRONMENTS

Von der Fakultät für Elektrotechnik und Informationstechnik der
Rheinisch-Westfälischen Technischen Hochschule Aachen
zur Erlangung des akademischen Grades eines
Doktors der Ingenieurwissenschaften
genehmigte Dissertation

vorgelegt von

Diplom-Ingenieur
Dirk Schröder
aus Köln

Berichter: Univ.-Prof. Dr. rer. nat. Michael Vorländer
Prof. U. Peter Svensson, Ph.D., NTNU Trondheim

Tag der mündlichen Prüfung: 04. Februar 2011

Diese Dissertation ist auf den Internetseiten der Hochschulbibliothek online verfügbar.

Dirk Schröder

Physically Based Real-Time Auralization of Interactive Virtual Environments

Logos Verlag Berlin GmbH

λογος

Aachener Beiträge zur Technischen Akustik

Editor:
Prof. Dr. rer. nat. Michael Vorländer
Institute of Technical Acoustics
RWTH Aachen University
52056 Aachen
www.akustik.rwth-aachen.de

Bibliographic information published by the Deutsche Nationalbibliothek

The Deutsche Nationalbibliothek lists this publication in the Deutsche Nationalbibliografie; detailed bibliographic data are available in the Internet at http://dnb.d-nb.de .

D 82 (Diss. RWTH Aachen University, 2011)

ISBN 978-3-8325-3031-0
ISSN 1866-3052
Vol. 11

Logos Verlag Berlin GmbH
Comeniushof, Gubener Str. 47,
D-10243 Berlin
Tel.:   +49 (0)30 / 42 85 10 90
Fax: +49 (0)30 / 42 85 10 92
http://www.logos-verlag.de

~ To my beloved parents, Ursula and Friedhelm Schröder ~

Abstract

Over the last decades, Virtual Reality (VR) technology has emerged to be a powerful tool for a wide variety of applications covering conventional use, e.g., in science, design, medicine and engineering, as well as in more visionary applications such as the creation of virtual spaces that aim to act real. However, the high capabilities of today's VR-systems are mostly limited to first-class visual rendering. In order to boost the range of applications, state-of-the-art systems aim to reproduce virtual environments as realistically as possible for the purpose of maximizing the user's feeling of immersion, presence and acceptance. Such immersive systems deliver multiple sensory stimuli and provide an opportunity to act interactively, as reality is neither mono-modal nor static.

Analogous to visualization, the auralization of virtual environments describes the simulation of sound propagation inside enclosures where methods of Geometrical Acoustics are mostly applied for a high-quality synthesis of aural stimuli that go along with a certain realistic behavior. Here, best results are achieved by combining deterministic methods for the computation of early specular sound reflections with stochastic approaches for the computation of the reverberant sound field. By adapting acceleration algorithms from Computer Graphics, current implementations can manage the computational load of moving sound sources around a moving receiver in real-time – even for complex but static architectural scenarios.

In the course of this thesis, the design and implementation of the real-time room acoustics simulation software RAVEN will be described, which is a vital part of the implemented 3D sound-rendering system of RWTH Aachen University's immersive VR-system. RAVEN relies on present-day knowledge of room acoustical simulation techniques and enables a physically accurate auralization of sound propagation in complex environments including important wave effects such as sound scattering, airborne sound insulation between rooms and sound diffraction. Despite this realistic sound field rendering, not only spatially distributed and freely movable sound sources and receivers are supported at runtime but also modifications and manipulations of the environment itself. All major features are evaluated by investigating both the overall accuracy of the room acoustics simulation and the performance of implemented algorithms, and possibilities for further simulation optimizations are identified by assessing empirical studies of subjects operating in immersive environments.

Zusammenfassung

In den letzten Jahrzehnten hat sich die Virtual Reality (VR) Technologie zu einem leistungsfähigen Werkzeug entwickelt, das in einer Vielzahl von herkömmlichen Anwendungen Einzug gehalten hat. Hierzu gehören Bereiche aus Forschung, Design, Medizin und Entwicklung, in denen neue Wege über die Verwendung von VR eingeschlagen werden, wie z.B. die Erstellung virtueller Umgebungen, in denen versucht wird ein möglichst plausibles Abbild der Wirklichkeit zu schaffen. Die theoretisch hohe Leistungsfähigkeit heutiger VR-Systeme ist allerdings meist beschränkt auf eine qualitativ hochwertige visuelle Darstellung, obwohl deren Anwendungsbereich signifikant erweitert werden kann durch den Einsatz multi-modaler Systeme. Multimodale Systeme können mehrere Sinnesreize gleichzeitig stimulieren und bieten dem Benutzer die Möglichkeit mit der virtuellen Welt direkt zu interagieren – denn in den meisten Fällen sind reale Situationen weder mono-modal noch statisch. Diese sogenannten immersiven Systeme sind dafür konzipiert ein virtuelles Abbild einer Umgebung so realistisch wie möglich wiederzugeben, um so beim Benutzer das Gefühl der Immersion, Präsenz und Akzeptanz zu verstärken.

In Analogie zur Visualisierung beschreibt die Auralisierung von virtuellen Umgebungen die Simulation von Schallausbreitung innerhalb von Räumen oder anderen begrenzten Gebieten. Methoden der Geometrischen Akustik kommen hier meistens zum Einsatz, da sie eine qualitativ hochwertige und physikalisch basierte Schallfeld-Synthese ermöglichen. Die besten Ergebnisse werden hierbei mit Hilfe von hybriden Verfahren erreicht, die deterministischen Methoden für die Berechnung von frühen spiegelnden Schallreflexionen mit stochastischen Simulationsverfahren für eine adäquate Nachbildung des Nachhalls in Räumen kombinieren. Durch die Adaption von Beschleunigungs-Algorithmen aus der Computergrafik sind aktuelle Implementierungen in der Lage bewegte Schallquellen und Empfänger in komplexen, aber statischen architektonischen Szenarien in Echtzeit zu simulieren.

Im Zuge dieser Arbeit wird das Konzept und die Umsetzung der echtzeitfähigen Raumakustik-Simulationssoftware RAVEN beschrieben, die ein wesentlicher Bestandteil des immersiven VR-Systems an der RWTH Aachen ist. RAVEN basiert auf dem heutigen Wissen von raumakustischen Simulationsverfahren und ermöglicht eine physikalisch korrekte Simulation der Schallausbreitung in komplexen Umgebungen, einschließlich wichtiger Welleneffekte wie Schallstreuung, Luftschalldämmung zwischen Räumen und Schallbeugung. Die angewandten Simulationsverfahren werden hinsichtlich ihrer Genauigkeit und Grenzen ihrer Echtzeitfähigkeit untersucht, wobei gezeigt werden wird, dass RAVEN trotz der realistischen Klangfeldsynthese nicht nur die Echtzeit-Simulation von räumlich verteilten und frei beweglichen Schallquellen und Empfängern ermöglicht, sondern auch die direkte Änderung und Manipulation der virtuellen Umgebung selbst. Des weiteren werden Möglichkeiten für die weitere Optimierung der Simulationsparametrierung aufgezeigt, die durch die Beurteilung empirischer Studien von Versuchspersonen identifiziert werden konnten.

Preface

"Whereas film is used to show reality to an audience, cyberspace is used to give a virtual body, and a role, to everyone in the audience. Print and radio tell; stage and film show; cyberspace embodies. [...]. A spacemaker sets up a world for an audience to act directly within, and not just so the audience can imagine they are experiencing an interesting reality, but so they can experience it directly. [...]. The filmmaker says, 'Look. I'll show you'. The spacemaker says, 'Here, I'll help you discover'."

(*Elements of a Cyberspace Playhouse*, Randal Walser)

I remember that I had my first contact with the term "Virtual Reality" at the age of 17, that was in 1992, when I saw the movie "The Lawnmower Man" directed by Brett Leonard. In this movie, Pierce Brosnan plays Dr. Lawrence Angelo, a visionary computer scientist who was dreaming of the possibility to excite, train and even improve a subject's brain/mind capabilities by using sophisticated Virtual Reality technology. Angelo was convinced that "Virtual Reality holds a key to the evolution of the human mind". According to his theory, a ground-breaking man-machine interconnection could be established by completely immersing subjects to cyberspace – a term that was coined in the 80s by William F. Gibson who described in his debut novel "Neuromancer" cyberspace as a

"[...] representation of data abstracted from banks of every computer in the human system. Unthinkable complexity. Lines of light ranged in the non-space of the mind, clusters and constellations of data. Like city lights, receding.".

By using such an interface, Angelo hoped to enable a direct link to the human consciousness for altering both the perception and reception. His first subject was his lawnmower man, Jobe Smith, who was retarded. Angelo successfully improved his intelligence by sending him to cyberspace, but major side-effects evolved since Smith got addicted to *information*. To keep it short: After developing supernatural psychic power that went along with a God psychosis, Smith left his physical body and uploaded his mind to cyberspace making him virtually immortal. He became "Cyber Christ".

Although I hope that "The Lawnmower Man" is not Brett Leonard's masterpiece, the core idea of this movie has fascinated me until today. It was even my main motivation to study communication and information technology at RWTH Aachen University. I wanted to face immersive technology from a professional side and see how close we really are to the claim of *Simulism*. Simulism postulates that reality can be simulated (for example by computers) to a degree indistinguishable from the "true" ontic reality and can contain conscious minds who are not aware whether they are living inside a simulation.

Today, technologically-achieved Virtual Reality does not entirely satisfy the experience of actuality, i.e., participants are not yet in doubt about the nature of what they experience. However, computing power and simulation techniques have improved drastically during the last 20 years and first prototypes of real-time immersive environments have already been built. Quite limited in their capabilities though, but good effort is made in improving such systems. Is it then too far-fetched to raise the question if Virtual Reality technology is perhaps only some steps away from fulfilling mankind's dream to make us become God-like creators of our *own* reality? A *simulated* reality, generated by a human-machine interface that makes the transcending medium disappear and enables an imagination beyond belief. Heim even went a step further and claimed that Virtual Reality is not necessarily bound to what we know from our own experiences of reality with all of its anchoring elements of stability such as time and space. In his book "The Metaphysics of Virtual Reality" he argued that

"*[...] The ultimate Virtual Reality is a philosophical experience, probably an experience of the sublime or awesome. The sublime, as Kant defined it, is the spine-tingling chill that comes from the realization of how small our finite perceptions are in the face of the infinity of possible, virtual worlds we may settle into and inhabit. The final point of a virtual world is to dissolve the constraints of the anchored world so that we can lift anchor – not to drift aimlessly without point, but to explore anchorage in ever-new places and, perhaps, find our way back to experience the most primitive and powerful alternative embedded in the question posed by Leibniz: Why is there anything at all rather than nothing?*".

What does "reality" then mean? If we were able to fake it through mediated hallucinations, is our subjective reality just a manipulable cognitive process of the human brain? This is still a highly controversial question in epistemology until today. According to Coyne there are basically two schools of thought on how reality is subjectively perceived and how it should be represented to create its virtual counterpart. Here, the *data-oriented view* regards reality as a matter of data input stating that only a greater quantity of data and a higher quality of detail effects a sense of the real since the human body is considered to be just an elaborate input device. On the contrary, the *constructivist view* claims that

"*We rely on simple cues and clues from the environment. We can be immersed in any environment. Depending on our state of mind, our interest, what we have been taught to experience, our personal and collective expectations, and our familiarity with the medium.*"[1]

The probably most uncompromising constructivist view – that I like the most – is called *Radical Constructivism*, which was mainly advocated by Von Glasersfeld and describes reality as

"*[...] the world we experience; from it alone we deduce, in our own ways, ideas and things as well as the concepts of the relations with which we create links and build up theories that allow us to formulate more or less viable explanations and predictions in our life world.*",

---

[1]Richard Coyne, *Heidegger and Virtual Reality: The Implications of Heidegger's Thinking for Computer Representations*.

and further

"We never use all existing signals[2] but select a relatively small number and, if needed, complement this selection with perceptions recalled (which are not produced spontaneously by the senses). The need is established by the context of the action in which we find ourselves; and this context never requires us seeing the 'environment' as it is 'in reality' [...]. From the perspective of acting it is irrelevant whether one's idea of the environment is a 'true' picture of ontic reality.".

In other words, the Radical Constructivism postulates that our reality is constructed from individual sensory performance and limited memory capacity. An objective perception and complete knowledge of the ontic reality is therefore impossible and, thus, reality is reduced to a subjective experience of our 'true' world. Moreover, we can *learn* to accept any immersive virtual reality system as *real* without the need of a complete representation of ontic reality in its entire complexity. Thus, ignoring this constructed nature of perception, as it is done in data-oriented approaches, implies that a Virtual Reality system for a fly does not differ much to that for a human. But is this really feasible? From my point of view, it is definitely not.

For the next roughly two hundred pages, I will describe the concept and implementation details of a software framework for the human-centered real-time auralization of dynamic and interactive virtual environments. RAVEN, as I entitled this framework, was born during my master thesis at the Institute of Technical Acoustics (ITA), RWTH Aachen University, and became quite mature during my Ph.D. studies. Today it offers features that I could not even think of on the day when RAVEN was born. I wish I could claim the credits for this work all by myself, but I truly had immense support and would like to take the opportunity to thank some very special people for their trust, effort, collaboration and friendship during my doctoral studies.

I want to start with Michael Vorländer who not only served as my doctoral advisor but also encouraged and guided me throughout my entire time as Ph.D. student. I feel tremendously lucky that Michael gave me the chance to carry out my research at his institute with almost unlimited support in every perspective. Tobias Lentz definitely drew me to the research area of Virtual Acoustics by supervising my master thesis and later working with me side by side. Together with Ingo Assenmacher, who was working at the Virtual Reality Group (VRG) at the Center for Computing and Communication of RWTH Aachen University, I had the honor to be part of a work group of professional and reliable experts who always poured their heart and soul into our mutual goal of building a cutting-edge Virtual Reality system. The work group was gradually enforced through the Ph.D. students Frank Wefers (ITA) and Dominik Rausch (VRG), who both turned out to be valuable team members working out their hearts to make the impossible possible. It was an exciting time for all of us – so full of frustration, but also so full of joy and glory. Special thanks to Torsten Kuhlen, head of the VRG at RWTH Aachen University, who supported and encouraged our work throughout the years.

Apart from this work group, I am grateful for having had so many helping hands. Doubtlessly, two important names are hereby Alexander Pohl and Sönke Pelzer who have always accompanied me during my entire Ph.D. time, either as student workers, master students, colleagues or friends. Even when their own time schedule was

---

[2] *Stimuli of the ontic reality.*

extremely tight, they were always working through illness to help me meet publication deadlines. You have my deepest gratitude. Furthermore, I would like to thank my former student workers Lukas Aspöck, Jochen Giese and Martin Landt – reliable persons who were always doing their assigned work in a very passionate way. Thanks also to Philipp Dross, Stefan Reuter, Alexander Ryba, Marc Schlütter, Björn Starke, Moritz Fricke, Philipp Schmidt, Stephan Gsell, Umberto Palmieri, Elzbieta Nowicka, David Kolf and Lukas Jauer for their exceptional work either in the scope of their Master thesis and/or student research project. I would also like to thank Uwe Stephenson for his many valuable advices on the secrets of stochastic models for the simulation of edge diffraction. Paula Niemietz was the charming voice in my demonstration videos and I'm very grateful for her time, commitment and great personality. I also want to express my deepest gratitude to the German Research foundation who have supported my research over the last three years. Their scholarship doubtlessly gave me the freedom to think more broadly about my graduate work.

Special thanks to all my colleagues at ITA for the interesting, often funny and never-ending discussions during our legendary coffee breaks. Especially Gottfried Behler, Andreas Franck, Rainer Thaden, Rolf Kaldenbach, Ingo Witew, Michael Makarski, Anselm Goertz, Janina Fels, Pascal Dietrich, Markus Müller-Trapet, Renzo Vitale, Jan Köhler, Bruno Sanches Masiero, João Henrique Diniz Guimarães, Martin Pollow, Matthias Lievens, Sebastian Fingerhuth, Marc Aretz, Martin Guski and Elena Shabalina had always a sympathetic ear and solutions for my problems. They were an unfailing source of encouragement during my ITA time and I can think of no finer individuals to work with. Special thanks to Uwe Schlömer and the members of the mechanical workshop for their time and expertise to help design and assemble several prototypes with unbelievable accuracy. I had a great time with my ITA family and I will miss all of you.

During my Ph.D. studies, I was also tremendously lucky to spend some months in Trondheim, Norway, at NTNU's Centre for Quantifiable Quality of Service in Communication Systems (Q2S) under the supervision of Peter Svensson. Peter instilled in me a love for simulating edge diffraction of sound and I'm very grateful for his patient advice. He also agreed on becoming my second mentor of my graduate work and I truly can think of no one better. Nima Darabi and Jordi Puig were definitely a source of inspiration for me with their infectious enthusiasm and outlook on life that resurrected my almost forgotten passion for art and philosophy. It was an amazing time at office E-228 in any perspective.

Finally, I would like to thank my parents, Ursula and Friedhelm Schröder. Words can hardly express my deepest gratitude for their everlasting love, sacrifice, guidance and encouragement. This dissertation is dedicated to them.

Contents

IV Evaluation   127

V Summary & Outlook   163

VI Appendix   175

Acronyms

AABB	Axis-Aligned Bounding Box
AFC	Alternative Forced Choice
ASG	Acoustic Scene Graph
ACG	Audio Communication Group
BEM	Boundary Element Method
BCI	Brain Computer Interface
BF	Brute Force
BRIR	Binaural Room Impulse Response
BRTF	Binaural Room Transfer Function
BSP	Binary Space Partitioning
BTME	Biot-Tolstoy-Medwin Expression
BVH	Bounding Volume Hierarchy
CAVE	Cave Automatic Virtual Environment
CG	Computer Graphics
CTC	Cross-Talk Cancellation
DAPDF	Deflection Angle Probability Density Function
DC	Deflection Cylinder
DG	Directivity Group
DIS	Diffraction Image Source
DS	Diffraction Source
FEM	Finite Element Method
GA	Geometrical Acoustics
GPU	Graphics Processing Unit
GUI	Graphical User Interface
HRIR	Head Related Impulse Response
HRTF	Head Related Transfer Function
ILD	Interaural Level Difference
IS	Image Source
IST	Image Source Tree
ITA	Institute of Technical Acoustics, RWTH Aachen University
ITD	Interaural Time Difference
JND	Just Noticeable Difference
LIFO	Last-In-First-Out
LTI	Linear Time-Invariant
MPI	Message Passing Interface
NTNU	Norges Teknisk-Naturvitenskapelige Universitet
OpenDAFF	Open Directional Audio File Format
OpenMP	Open Multi-Processing

PPM	Plane-Polygon Map
PST	Path Search Tree
PT	Parameter Threshold
PPG	Propagation Path Graph
PS	Primary Source
RAVEN	Room Acoustics for Virtual Environments
RIR	Room Impulse Response
RT	Ray Tracing
RTF	Room Transfer Function
RWTH	Rheinisch-Westfälische Technische Hochschule
SEA	Statistical Energy Analysis
SH	Spatial Hashing
SS	Secondary Source
UTD	Uniform Theory of Diffraction
VA	Virtual Acoustics
VC	Voxel Candidates
ViSTA	Virtual Reality for Scientific Technical Applications
VT	Voxel Tracing
VR	Virtual Reality
VRG	Virtual Reality Group, RWTH Aachen University

Part I

Introduction

Chapter 1

Introduction

'Our argument is that experiencing presence in a remote operations task or in a virtual environment (VE) requires the ability to focus on one meaningfully coherent set of stimuli (in the VE) to the exclusion of unrelated stimuli (in the physical location). To the extent that the stimuli in the physical location fit in with the VE stimuli, they may be integrated to form a meaningful whole.'

(*Measuring Presence in Virtual Environments: A Presence Questionaire*, Bob G. Witmer and Michael J. Singer, American scientists)

1.1 Virtual Environments

In 1956, Morton L. Heilig started with the development of a one-person theater, which he later called the *Sensorama*. The Sensorama combined projected film, audio, vibration, wind, and odors, in order to create a plausible set of stimuli that made the user rather feel the presented scenery, such as a motorcycle ride through New York, instead of just observing it as on television (see Fig. 1.1). As the age of computers was still about to begin at that time, the entire experience was prerecorded and played back on demand. Nonetheless, Heilig's machine can be regarded today as the first multi-modal immersive virtual experience – at least in the modern interpretation of Virtual Reality (VR)-systems, as the idea of creating the *ultimate medium* that perfectly matches reality has always fascinated mankind since the dawn of time. Ever since Heilig's pioneering work, considerable effort has been put into the development of improved VR-systems, where the term VR refers from a technical point of view to the representation and simultaneous perception of reality and its physical attributes in an interactive computer-generated virtual environment. Today, VR-technology is used in numerous applications, for instance, engineering, science, design, medicine, art and architecture. The focus of these applications lies usually on the visual component of the virtual environment, and other modalities, if present at all, are often added just as an effect without any plausible reference to the physical aspects of the presented scenery. However, VR-systems that aim at enabling immersive applications should address at least the hearing, too, since it is a well-known fact that the visual perception

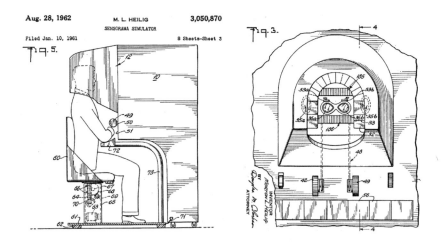

(a) Side view.   (b) Frontal view.

Figure 1.1: Construction plans of Heiliger's Sensorama, taken from the corresponding U.S. Patent 3050870 [Hei62] published in 1962.

is significantly augmented by matching sound stimuli – especially in architectural applications such as a virtual walk through a complex of buildings. Here, auditory information helps to assign meaning to visual information and the user evaluates these events on attributes such as spaciousness, coloration, and source localization, which significantly boosts the feeling of actual presence in the simulated scene. In general, the quality of a VR-system is assessable by the user's degree of immersion, which improves with the number of simulated coherent stimuli and provided level of user interactivity.

Analogous to visualization, the term *auralization* describes the generation of aural stimuli that correspond to the current sound propagation throughout the simulated scene. In recent years, the development of room acoustics prediction tools and auralization techniques has made a major leap forward, thereby enabling a physically based simulation of virtual environments in real-time. The speed-up is usually achieved by adapting acceleration techniques from Computer Graphics (CG), since most simulation methods are based on the basic principles of Geometrical Acoustics (GA). In GA, the sound field is reduced to the dispersion of incoherent sound particles with a dictated frequency and amount of energy, which perfectly matches simulation methods from CG. However, the frequency range in acoustics involves three orders of magnitude (ranging from 20 Hz to 20 kHz and wavelengths from about 20 m to 2 cm), where neither approximations of small wavelengths nor large wavelengths can be assumed with general validity. Important wave phenomena, such as diffraction at low frequencies, scattering at high frequencies, and specular reflections have to be considered to enable a physically based sound field modeling. Hence, from the physical point of view (not to mention the challenge of implementation), the question of modeling and simulation of an exact virtual sound is by orders of magnitude more difficult than the task of creating visual images, which might be the reason for the delayed implementation of physically based 3D audio rendering engines for virtual environments.

Whereas low-reflective outdoor scenarios can be simulated rather fast and accurately today, the determination of the spatial sound field in enclosures is still a difficult task, especially under real-time constraints. In indoor scenarios, even rather simple situations require quite complex acoustic models, and the more the user is allowed to interact with the scenery, the more this complexity increases. Flexible simulation models are therefore required that describe directional patterns of sound-emitting sources and the receiver, as well as the wave phenomena of sound diffraction, sound scattering and sound transmission, without leading to an explosion of computation time. Especially complete dynamic environments become quite challenging, where the user is not only allowed to move freely in all three dimensions and interact with sound sources in any order, but also to modify the scene geometry itself and directly perceive the impact on the sound field in real-time. Unfortunately, a change of the scene geometry significantly affects the whole auralization chain and, therefore, making a number of approximations is inevitable to keep the computational workload in such demanding situations within the given real-time constraints. However, the resulting sound is not intended to be physically absolutely correct, but perceptively plausible, whereby knowledge of the human sound perception and the field of psychoacoustics are essential to find the optimal balance between simulation accuracy and available computation power.

1.2 Related Work

Real-time auralization systems have been investigated by many groups. Notable here is the pioneering work by Lauri Savioja et al. at the TKK Helsinki University, Finland, who presented the first audio-visual virtual environment called Experimental Virtual Environment (EVE) that featured a physically based auralization engine known as Digital Interactive Virtual Acoustics (DIVA) [Sav99, SHLV99]. Some years later, Thomas Funkhouser et al. introduced a very fast simulation method that first enabled the real-time simulation of sound propagation paths in complex architectural scenarios by means of so-called beam trees that encode specular reflection paths of a static sound source in a very efficient manner [FTC+04]. At the same time, Nicolas Tsingos et al. introduced a concept for the perceptual audio rendering of complex virtual environments [TGD04] in connection with the 'REVES' research project at INRIA, France. Lately, quite advanced simulation frameworks were presented such as the work by Christian Lauterbach et al. [CLT+08] at the University of North Carolina, USA as well as the Open Source projects 'UNI-VERSE' [Lun08] and the auralization framework by Noisternig et al. [NKSS08].

The aim of the VR activities at Rheinisch-Westfälische Technische Hochschule

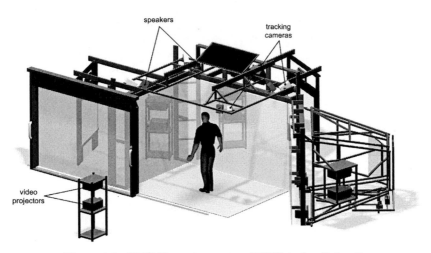

Figure 1.2: CAVE-like environment at RWTH Aachen University.

(RWTH) Aachen University is to create a reference platform for developing and applying multi-modal environments including high-quality acoustics. Such a system can be used for scientific research and testing as well as for the development of complexity-reduced surround-sound systems for professional audio or home entertainment. The group working on the acoustic VR-system is supported by the German Research Foundation in a series of funded projects, where the Institute of Technical Acoustics, RWTH Aachen University (ITA) jointly worked with the Virtual Reality Group, RWTH Aachen University (VRG), which is the core group of a consortium of several institutes at RWTH Aachen University and external partners covering the disciplines of computer science, architecture, civil engineering, mechanical engineering, electrical engineering and information technology, psychology and medicine [VRC].

1.3   Interactive Virtual Environments at RWTH Aachen University

Shortly after the establishment of the first VR developments at RWTH Aachen University, the activities in computer science were joined with those in acoustics. The advantage was that both groups had deep knowledge in their specific field so that the competences could be combined with high synergy. The initial step was to integrate interactive VR technology (visual and haptic) with headphone-free audio reproduction. At that time the decision was made in favor of a stereo loudspeaker setup for an adaptive Cross-Talk Cancellation (CTC). The first task was to integrate tracking and adaptive filtering into a CTC-system which turned out to be a flexible solution for various display environments.

(a) Virtual exploration of a concert hall.   **(b)** Object manipulation.

(c) Sound source manipulation.   **(d)** Virtual exploration of a sound source.

Figure 1.3: Users operating in an example application of a virtual concert hall that is run by the immersive virtual environment at RWTH Aachen University.

In 2004 a Cave Automatic Virtual Environment (CAVE)[1]-like five-sided surround-screen projection system was installed at RWTH Aachen University (see Fig. 1.2 and Fig. 1.3). Having dimensions of 3.6 m x 2.7 m x 2.7 m, it can be reconfigured using a slide door and a movable wall. Stereoscopic images are produced by two images per screen with a resolution of 1600x1200 pixels each and are separated by polarized glasses. The system uses several infrared cameras for tracking various input devices and the user's head position/orientation. All VR-applications are based on the Open Source software framework called Virtual Reality for Scientific Technical Applications (ViSTA) which is a flexible and efficient platform for realizing complex

---

[1]The term CAVE relates to project name of the first room-mounted installation system based on a combination of large projection screens that surrounded the user, developed by Cruiz-Nera et al. in 1992 [CNSD+92].

scientific and industrial applications [AK08]. One of ViSTA's key feature comprises functionality for creating multi-modal interaction metaphors including visual, haptic and acoustic stimuli. For such elaborate multi-modal interfaces, flexible sharing of different types of data with low latency access is needed while maintaining a common temporal context. Therefore, ViSTA has an inherent high-performance device driver architecture. It provides a novel approach for history recording of input data by means of a ring buffer concept that guarantees both a low latency and a consistent temporal access to device samples at the same time [Ass09]. Furthermore, a compensation scheme for tracking data is integrated in ViSTA that, based on current tracking samples, can predict the state of the human head position and orientation for the time of application.

For reproducing acoustic signals, the dynamic CTC-system has been upgraded to four loudspeakers that are installed at the top of the CAVE (see Fig. 1.2). This setup was chosen over a simple stereo system in order to achieve a good binaural reproduction that is independent of the user's orientation, where the best current speaker configuration is determined by minimizing the overall compensation energy [Len07]. Audio streaming is conducted using Steinberg's ASIO professional audio architecture at a sampling rate of 44.1 kHz and a streaming buffer size (block length) of 512 samples, whereby a dedicated low-latency convolution engine is applied that implements a parallelized and highly optimized non-uniformly partitioned convolution in the frequency domain. Here, a smooth filter transition is realized by cross-fading in the time domain. This engine manages to convolve 88200 filter coefficients, which relates to a filter length of 2 s at 44.1 kHz sampling rate, with signals of more than 50 sound sources in real-time [Wef07, WB10].

1.4   Aim of this Work

Another vital part of the VR-system at RWTH Aachen University yields the hybrid real-time room acoustics simulation software Room Acoustics for Virtual Environments (RAVEN), where the concept and implementation will be completely described in the course of this thesis. After only 6 years of intensive development, today RAVEN provides an open and flexible real-time simulation framework that is fully integrated in the exisiting ViSTA framework as a network service and which is unique in the large number of simulation features (a brief overview is given in Appx. B). RAVEN relies on present-day knowledge of room acoustical simulation techniques based on GA and enables a physically accurate auralization of sound propagation in complex environments in real-time, including important wave effects such as sound scattering, airborne sound insulation between rooms and sound diffraction. Despite this realistic sound field rendering, not only are spatially distributed and freely movable sound sources and receivers supported at runtime but also modifications and manipulations of the environment itself.

All major features will be evaluated by investigating both the overall accuracy of the room acoustics simulation and the performance of implemented algorithms, where it will be shown that RAVEN is able to handle simulation events at interactive rates with an overall simulation accuracy that can compete with state-of-the-art (commercial) software solutions. In addition, possibilities for further simulation optimizations are identified by assessing empirical studies of subjects operating in immersive environments.

Part II

Concept

Chapter 2

Sound Propagation in Rooms

'Darkness is to space what silence is to sound, i.e., the interval.'

Marshall McLuhan, Canadian media theorist

To auralize the acoustical characteristics of an architectural virtual scenario, proper physical models are required that capture the complex process of sound propagation within enclosures, i.e., rooms. The reverberation caused by sound reflections is an essential acoustical attribute of a room, as it gives the room its very individual sound. In this chapter, models for the description of a sound source, sound absorption, sound scattering, sound transmission, and sound diffraction will be briefly introduced, which allow the computation of the alteration of sound intensity at a certain position for a certain time. They are the basis for almost any room acoustical simulation methods and, thus, an integral part of the auralization chain that describes the sound propagation from a sound source to a receiver inside of rooms. More details on acoustical simulation methods are given in Chap. 5.

2.1   Acoustical Point Sources

When a sound source radiates sound, energy of wave motion is propagated outward from the sound source's center, whereby the corresponding sound-carrying air particles move backward and forward, parallel to the wave motion's direction. This leads to an alternating increase and decrease of air pressure. The most important terms for sound wave propagation in air are the *sound pressure p*, which describes the position- and time-dependent fluctuation of the wave's air pressure, and the vectorial *sound particle velocity* $\vec{v}$, which is a term for the oscillation velocity of the medium's particles around their resting position. These two terms are associated with each other by the following equations,

$$-\text{grad } p = \rho_0 \frac{\partial \vec{v}}{\partial t} \qquad \text{and} \qquad -\text{div } \vec{v} = \frac{1}{\rho_0 c^2} \frac{\partial p}{\partial t}, \qquad (2.1)$$

where ρ_0 is the static density of air and c is the speed of sound in air. One can eliminate the sound particle velocity $\vec{v}$ by simply inserting the latter equation into the other, which results in the so-called *wave equation*:

$$\Delta p = \frac{1}{c^2}\frac{\partial^2 p}{\partial t^2}. \qquad (2.2)$$

In theory, any wave type can be theoretically derived from this equation, but in practice, most solutions have to be approximated due to the analytic complexity. However, a simple solution of the wave equation is a spherical wave due to its symmetry, with

$$p(r,t) = \frac{\rho_0}{4\pi r}\frac{\partial Q}{\partial t}\left(t - \frac{r}{c}\right), \qquad (2.3)$$

where r is the distance to the sound source and Q is the volume velocity, which is a function that describes the propagation of a pressure distortion evenly into all directions with the velocity c, starting from a *point source* S (r=0). Thus, the equation describes a spherical wave with a force proportional to r^{-1}.

A basic quantity for describing the mean energy flow of a sound wave through an reference area is called *sound intensity* $\vec{I}$, which describes the energy that is transported per second through an area A, with

$$\vec{I} = \overline{p \cdot \vec{\nu}} = \frac{1}{T}\cdot\int_0^T p \cdot \vec{\nu}\, dt. \qquad (2.4)$$

The sound power P then follows accordingly to $P = \int_A \vec{I}d\vec{A}$, which solves for spherical waves to

$$P = \frac{\rho_0\omega^2\hat{Q}^2}{8\pi c} \qquad \text{and} \qquad I = |\vec{I}| = \frac{P}{4\pi r^2}. \qquad (2.5)$$

A closer examination of the latter equation shows that I varies inversely with the square of distance r. In addition, the intensity I is attenuated by the propagation medium itself, resulting in an additional exponential term with $I(r) = I_0 e^{-mr}$. Here, the absorption constant m represents the air attenuation, which is caused by the air's viscosity, heat conduction and thermal relaxation of the oxygen and nitrogen molecules and starts to dominate the energy loss above 4 kHz. Whereas the first two processes lead to an increasing in the absorption constant m, the attenuation by relaxation depends on the sound frequency, temperature and air humidity in a quite complex way [Ber80]. Strictly speaking, all these equations are only valid for acoustical point sources which exist only in theory as they are defined with an infinitesimal small expansion. However, the simple description of point sources is still a very good approximation for the far sound field as long as the size of the sound source is small against the wavelength of the emitted sound. In addition, directional pattern, so-called directivities, can easily be applied to acoustical point sources by simply scaling the intensity with a directivity factor $\beta(\varphi, \Theta)$, with φ and Θ describing the azimuth angle and elevation angle, respectively, in a spherical coordinate system where the point source resides at the origin, $I_\beta(\varphi, \Theta) = \beta(\varphi, \Theta) \cdot I$, with $0 \leq \beta \leq 1$. More details on directivities of sound sources are given in Sect. 3.1.

2.2 Sound Absorption

If a plane sound wave hits[1] an infinitely large and smooth medium, it will be reflected on the surface according to Snell's law[2], which means that the wave's angle of incidence is equal with the reflection angle. A reflection is the abrupt direction change of the wave front at an interface between two dissimilar media, most likely with a change of both amplitude and phase. In the case of a specular reflection, the incident and the reflected wave front can be written as

$$
\begin{aligned}
\underline{p}_i(x,y,t) &= \hat{p}e^{j(\omega t - kx\cos(\Theta) - ky\sin(\Theta))} \quad \text{and} \\
\underline{p}_r(x,y,t) &= \hat{p}\underline{R}e^{j(\omega t + kx\cos(\Theta) - ky\sin(\Theta))},
\end{aligned}
\tag{2.6}
$$

where Θ is the angle of incidence and reflection, k is the wave number, and $\underline{R}$ is the reflection factor following

$$
\underline{R} = \frac{\underline{p}_r}{\underline{p}_i} = \frac{\underline{Z}\cos(\Theta) - Z_0}{\underline{Z}\cos(\Theta) + Z_0},
\tag{2.7}
$$

with $Z_0 = \rho_0 c$ denoting the characteristic air impedance and $\underline{Z}$ representing the surface impedance, which is the ratio between the total sound pressure and the surface normal component of the total sound particle velocity, both at the point of incident.

For a local reacting surface, which means that the surface impedance is independent of the angle of incidence, the remaining intensity I_r of the reflected wave relates to the incidence intensity I_r multiplied by the absolute value of the squared reflection factor, i.e., $|\underline{R}|^2$ of the surface. Hence, the absorbed energy relates to the factor $1 - |\underline{R}|^2$, called *absorption factor* α, which is defined as the ratio between the lost energy portion and the impacting sound energy, with

$$
\begin{aligned}
\alpha &= \frac{|p_i|^2 - |p_r|^2}{|p_i|^2} \\
&= 1 - |\underline{R}|^2 \\
&= \frac{4Re(\varsigma)\cos(\Theta)}{1 + 2Re(\varsigma)\cos(\Theta) + |\varsigma|^2\cos^2(\Theta)}, \quad \varsigma = \underline{Z}/Z_0.
\end{aligned}
\tag{2.8}
$$

By means of this absorption coefficient, the intensity of the reflected sound wave can be expressed by the simple equation $I_r = (1-\alpha)I_i$. However, the absorption factor depends on the angle Θ meaning that α has to be averaged over all possible angles of incidence. Since this would be quite impractical in general, absorption coefficients are usually measured in a reverberation chamber according to DIN EN ISO standard 354 [ISO03].

---

[1]The sound wave of an acoustical point sources can usually be assumed to be plane in the far-field.
[2]Willebrord Snellius, Dutch astronomer and mathematician, 1580 - 1626.

2.3   Sound Scattering

In most cases, a surface is not ideally smooth, as is assumed in the previous section. It rather contains regular and irregular dents, bumps and other textures that influence the reflection of the plane wave (see Fig. 2.1). If the wavelength is very large compared to the dimensions of the surface irregularities, the specular reflection will not be influenced, i.e., the surface can be treated as smooth and the wave front is reflected accordingly. In contrast, if the wavelength is very small compared to the surface texture, the incident wave is specularly reflected on the texture's faces and not on the surface's plane as in the previous case. However, within an intermediate range, where the height h and length a of the surface's corrugation profile are in the order of half of the wavelength λ, a scattered wave will occur in addition to the specular reflection, whereby a distinct portion of the sound energy is scattered in all directions resulting in so-called *diffuse* reflections. In other words, a reflection on a corrugation surface decomposes the wave front into both a specularly reflected and a diffusely reflected sound energy portion, $E_{r,specular}$ and $E_{r,diffuse}$,

$$E_{r,specular} = (1-s)(1-\alpha)E_i, \quad E_{r,diffuse} = (s)(1-\alpha)E_i, \quad \text{and} \quad E_r = (1-\alpha)E_i, \quad (2.9)$$

with E_r describing the total reflected energy, α denoting the absorption coefficient of the surface, and s giving the ratio of the non-specularly reflected sound energy to the totally reflected energy – the so-called *scattering coefficient* [Kut00, VM00, CDD$^+$06].

The scattering coefficient can be measured according to the ISO standard 17497 [ISO04a] (either under free-field or diffuse field conditions), but numerical solutions are also available for some types of corrugated surfaces. It should be mentioned that the term 'surface' relates here to a 3D texture that is not limited in size, meaning that the scattering coefficient can also be used to describe bigger structures such as furniture.

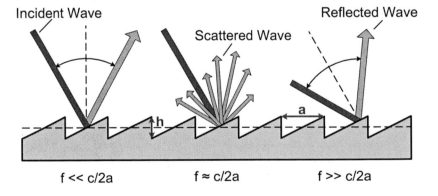

Figure 2.1: Frequency-dependent reflection patterns of a rough surface with structural elements of height h and length a. Here, f denotes the frequency of the incident wave and c the speed of sound.

2.4 Sound Transmission

If a sound wave hits a constructional element that separates two
rooms, for instance a wall, part of
the sound is transmitted through the
separating element into the adjacent
room, with a quiet and dull sound
characteristic since sound transmission
through solid structures isolates higher
frequencies more than lower ones (low-
pass characteristic). The acoustic performance of a constructional element
can be expressed by the *sound reduction index R*, which describes the ratio
of the incident sound intensity I_i on
this element in relation to the transmitted intensity I_t,

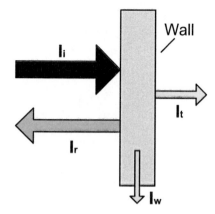

Figure 2.2: Sound transmission through a
constructional element.

$$R = -10 \log \tau = 10 \log \frac{I_i}{I_t}, \qquad (2.10)$$

with τ denoting the transmission coefficient, $\tau = I_r/I_t$, I_r the intensity of the reflected
sound and I_w the amount of sound intensity that is absorbed by the constructional
element (see Fig. 2.2). Under free-field conditions and only for plane waves and a
specific angle of incidence, R is identical to the sound level difference D (see below).
In room-to-room situations, however, the apparent sound levels not only depend on
the excitation of the sound source and the sound transmitting element, but also on the
reverberation in both rooms, especially in the receiving room. By assuming diffuse
sound fields in both rooms[3], the sound reduction index can be determined by

$$R = L_S - L_R + 10 \log \frac{S}{A_R} \qquad (2.11)$$

with L_S and L_R denoting the levels in the source and receiving room, S denoting
the partition area, and A_R giving the equivalent absorption area of the receiving
room. The latter term describes a compensation for the influence of reverberation
on the sound level difference in the receiving room. If the sound reduction index is
measured in a building, the influence of additional sound transmission over flanking
paths cannot be avoided; thus, it is dependent on the whole room-to-room situation.
In literature this type of sound reduction index is called *apparent sound reduction
index R'*, with

$$R' = -10 \log \tau' = -10 \log \left(\sum_{i=1}^{N} \sum_{j=1}^{M} \tau_{ij} \right) = -10 \log \left(\sum_{i=1}^{N} \sum_{j=1}^{M} 10^{-R_{ij}/10} \right), \qquad (2.12)$$

---

[3]The distance between the wall and the source and receiver, respectively, exceeds the critical
distance of the specific rooms.

where N and M relate to the number of transmission paths from the source room into the receiving room via flanking elements. As mentioned above, the *level difference* D is the second important quantity for classifying of the insulation characteristics of a structural element, which is independent of the area of the partition and includes the whole room-to-room situation. There are two versions of D which differ in the description of the sound field in the receiving room,

$$D_n = L_S - L_R - 10\log\frac{A}{10m^2} \quad \text{and} \quad D_{nT} = L_S - L_R + 10\log\frac{T}{0.5s}. \quad (2.13)$$

Here, the normalized level difference D_n refers to an equivalent absorption area of $10m^2$, whereas the standardized level difference D_{nT} refers to a reverberation time of $0.5s$ in the receiving room. Measuring specifications for both parameters, R and D, are given in the standard DIN EN ISO 140-3 [ISO04b].

2.5   Sound Diffraction

Diffraction is a wave phenomenon that is experienced in mostly any daily life situation. Just imagine a walk through a corridor of an office building where sound sources are located in each room. Here, the sound field does not change abruptly when an open door is passed. The transition is rather smooth which comes from sound energy that is bent around the door entrance's edges, i.e. sound diffraction. When a sound wave hits an obstacle, a frequency-dependent shadow zone occurs behind the object (related to the direction of sound propagation).

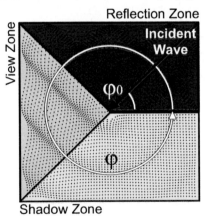

Figure 2.3: Sound propagation around a semi-finite rigid edge (according to Möser [Mös05]).

If the object is small in comparison to the wavelength, the incident wave remains unaffected. However, a shadow zone appears and grows clearer and sharper with decreasing wavelength and increasing frequency, respectively. This shadow zone results from a total cancellation of the incident wave by the diffracted wave, which is radiated from the edges or perimeter of the respective object. A good example that elucidates these physical processes analytically is sound diffraction at a semi-finite rigid edge (a complete derivation of the following equations is given in [Mös95]). Starting with the sound propagation of a plane wave in free-field conditions,

$$p_S(r) = \hat{p} \cdot e^{-jkr} \quad \text{with} \quad k = \frac{2 \cdot \pi}{\lambda} \quad (2.14)$$

the sound field for a semi-infinite rigid edge can be described by

$$p(r,\varphi) = p_S(0) \cdot \frac{1+j}{2} \cdot \left\{ e^{j \cdot k \cdot r \cdot cos(\varphi-\varphi_0)} \cdot \Phi_+ + e^{j \cdot k \cdot r \cdot cos(\varphi+\varphi_0)} \cdot \Phi_- \right\}$$

$$(2.15)$$

with

$$\Phi_+ = \frac{1-j}{2} + C\left(\sqrt{2 \cdot k \cdot r} \cdot cos\frac{\varphi-\varphi_0}{2}\right) - j \cdot S\left(\sqrt{2 \cdot k \cdot r} \cdot cos\frac{\varphi-\varphi_0}{2}\right)$$

$$\Phi_- = \frac{1-j}{2} + C\left(\sqrt{2 \cdot k \cdot r} \cdot cos\frac{\varphi+\varphi_0}{2}\right) - j \cdot S\left(\sqrt{2 \cdot k \cdot r} \cdot cos\frac{\varphi+\varphi_0}{2}\right)$$

where φ_0 is the angle between the edge and the origin of the wave, φ denotes the angle between the edge and the observation point, and $C(x)$ and $S(x)$ are called *Fresnel-Integrals*,

$$C(x) = \sqrt{\frac{2}{\pi}} \cdot \int_0^x cos(t^2)dt \quad \text{and} \quad S(x) = \sqrt{\frac{2}{\pi}} \cdot \int_0^x sin(t^2)dt. \quad (2.16)$$

Substituting now the arguments of the Fresnel integrals with $u = \sqrt{2 \cdot k \cdot r} \cdot cos\frac{\varphi-\varphi_0}{2}$ and $v = \sqrt{2 \cdot k \cdot r} \cdot cos\frac{\varphi+\varphi_0}{2}$, the Φ-functions can be approximated by

$$\Phi_+ \approx \frac{j \cdot e^{-j \cdot u^2}}{\sqrt{2 \cdot \pi} \cdot |u|} \qquad \Phi_- \approx \frac{j \cdot e^{-j \cdot v^2}}{\sqrt{2 \cdot \pi} \cdot |v|} \qquad \text{if u,v} < 0 \text{ and } |u,v| \gg 1$$

$$\Phi_+ \approx (1-j) \qquad \Phi_- \approx (1-j) \qquad \text{if u,v} > 0 \text{ and } |u,v| \gg 1.$$

Using these approximations, one can take a further look at the sound field divided into three important zones around the edge: the reflection zone, the view zone and the shadow zone (see Fig. 2.3). Actually the view zone also covers the reflection zone, but in this interpretation, the view zone describes only the area where the incident wave is not disturbed by the reflected wave.

Reflection zone, $\varphi < \pi - \varphi_0$:

$$p(r,\varphi) \approx p_S(0) \cdot \left\{ e^{j \cdot k \cdot r \cdot cos(\varphi-\varphi_0)} + e^{j \cdot k \cdot r \cdot cos(\varphi+\varphi_0)} \right\} \qquad (2.17)$$

Only specular reflections can occur in this zone. The approximation gives the *exact* solution for the sound field in front of an infinite rigid wall, whereby the first term and the second term describe the incident wave and the reflected wave, respectively. Thus, diffraction has only little influence on this zone.

View zone, $\pi - \varphi_0 < \varphi < \pi + \varphi_0$:

$$p(r,\varphi) \approx p_S(0) \cdot e^{j \cdot k \cdot r \cdot cos(\varphi-\varphi_0)} \qquad (2.18)$$

The approximation gives again the *exact* solution, here for a plane wave. Diffraction has only little influence on that zone, too.

Shadow Zone, $\varphi > \pi + \varphi_0$:

$$p(r, \varphi) \approx p_Q(0) \cdot \frac{j-1}{2 \cdot \sqrt{2 \cdot \pi}} \frac{e^{-j \cdot k \cdot r}}{\sqrt{2 \cdot k \cdot r}} \left\{ \frac{1}{\left\| cos \frac{(\varphi - \varphi_0)}{2} \right\| + \left\| cos \frac{(\varphi + \varphi_0)}{2} \right\|} \right\} \quad (2.19)$$

This equation describes the sound pressure at an arbitrary point within the shadow zone. As one can see from the equation, diffraction has a significant influence on that zone that cannot be neglected.

A plot of the sound pressure distribution using the equations given above is depicted in Fig. 2.3. It shows the typical behavior of a reflected and diffracted wave at an edge - here with a very smooth transition from the view zone into the shadow zone.

2.6 (Binaural) Room Impulse Response

Whenever a sound source radiates sound into an enclosed room, the propagating sound waves are reflected on the constructional elements of the room, diffracted on edges, scattered on surface textures, absorbed by surface materials, and attenuated by air, until they finally reach the receiver. Thus, a perceived hearing event not only consists of the excitation by the source but also of the response of the room, which comprises delayed and attenuated reflections. The human hearing then summarizes all these emerging reflections to an overall hearing impression. If the source signal is a single pulse that excites all frequencies of interest, and a monophonic receiver is applied, e.g., a microphone, this response is called Room Impulse Response (RIR), which can be seen as the 'acoustical fingerprint' of the room. It is a common practice to divide the RIR into three parts, which differ in their properties and also in the

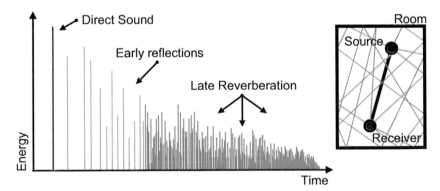

Figure 2.4: Subdivision of a room impulse response according to the perception and processing of the human hearing. Whereas the direct sound and the early reflections contain information on the position, level, and width of the sound source, the late reverberation relates to the individual response of the room.

perception and processing by the human hearing, called (1) the direct sound, (2) the
early reflections and (3) the late reverberation (see Fig. 2.4).

Direct Sound This first and strongest arriving impulse is evaluated by the human
hearing for localizing the sound source, also known as *precedence effect* [Bla96].
The direct sound is delayed by the distance d between source and receiver and
attenuated only by air.

Early Reflections The first reflections from the surrounding constructional elements or other obstacles in the room arrive at the listener. These (low-order)
reflections are added to the initial direct sound by the human hearing meaning
that they cannot be perceived separately, even if their level is up to 10 dB higher
(Haas effect [Bla96]). Information about the sound source such as position, distance, source width, and loudness, are mostly related to these first reflections
(direct sound and early reflections).

Late Reverberation Typically with a delay of 50-80 ms to the direct sound, the
number of reflections increases gradually and the human hearing cannot perceive them as single events anymore. This diffuse-like sound field forms a late reverberation which is nearly independent of the listener's position, as the human
hearing starts to perform a quite rough energetic integration over a certain time
slot and angle field [Bla96]. Reverberation is a very important and probably the
most conspicuous acoustical attribute of a room, since certain characteristics,
such as room volume and room shape, are directly associated with it, thereby
giving the room its very individual sound.

Most room acoustical parameters, such as reverberation time, clarity and gain, are
directly derivable from the RIR [Vor08]. Yet an auralization (see next section) would
lack a proper spatial representation of the sound source, since a very important piece
of information is missing in the response, i.e., the influence of the human head and
the torso, which reflect, diffract and retard the arriving sound waves significantly.

For instance, a sound wave propagating from a source located on one side of
the head travels a longer time to the contralateral ear than to the lateral ear, called
Interaural Time Difference (ITD), and the signals at both eardrums vary in their level,
called Interaural Level Difference (ILD). The Just Noticeable Differences (JNDs)[4] of
ILD and ITD depend on the direction of sound incidence and also on the characteristics of the presented signals; e.g., the source localization only works for signals
with frequency components above 200 Hz. The smallest JND-values are found in the
horizontal plane of the head-related coordinate system, where both, ILD and ITD
are very high. Here, the localization is accurate to 1° for frontal sources, whereas the
precision decreases to 10° for sources from the left or right side, and to about 5° for

---

[4]The JND is the smallest detectable difference between a starting and secondary level of a particular sensory stimulus (Weber's Law of Just Noticeable Difference).

backward sound incidence. For sound sources directly above or below the head, the localization is worst with an inaccuracy of about 20° [Bla96].

In general, the spatial hearing of the human auditory system is performed by analyzing both, monaural signals which are identical for both ears and binaural signals that differ for the two eardrums in terms of arrival time, phase and level. For a proper spatial representation of the sound source, these effects have to be taken into account either by measuring the RIR with an artificial dummy head (see Fig. 2.5) as binaural measurement microphone, or by using a set of angle-dependent filters that describe the linear sound distortion of the head and torso in acoustical simulations, called Head Related Impulse Responses (HRIRs) and Head Related

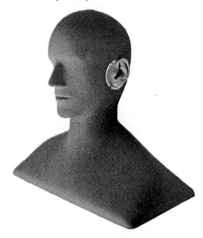

Figure 2.5: Artifical dummy head (ITA).

Transfer Functions (HRTFs) in the time domain and frequency domain, respectively. A Binaural Room Impulse Response (BRIR) is therefore a two-channel RIR where each channel additionally contains the head-related auditory cues for the corresponding ear. More information on spatial perception and evaluation by the human auditory cortex are given in [Bla96].

2.7 Principle of Auralization

Almost any medium, whether it is solid, liquid or gaseous, can transmit vibrations and thus sound waves. In most cases, a sound transmitting system of coupled media can be assumed to be linear and time-invariant, or in other words, it is assumed that the system is at rest during the time of inspection. By definition, the propagation of a signal through such an Linear Time-Invariant (LTI)- system is unambiguously describable by the corresponding *impulse response*. Thus, an LTI-system with known impulse response $h(t)$ and input signal $s(t)$ will yield an output signal $g(t)$ with

$$g(t) = \int_{-\infty}^{\infty} s(\tau)h(t-\tau)d\tau = s(t) * h(t) \qquad (2.20)$$

or in the frequency domain with

$$\underline{G}(f) = \underline{S}(f) \cdot \underline{H}(f), \qquad (2.21)$$

where $\underline{H}(f)$ is called the *transfer function*. Here, the description in the frequency domain is usually preferred, since it avoids the more complex convolution operator. Upon now considering a room with a sound source and a listener, as such a system in

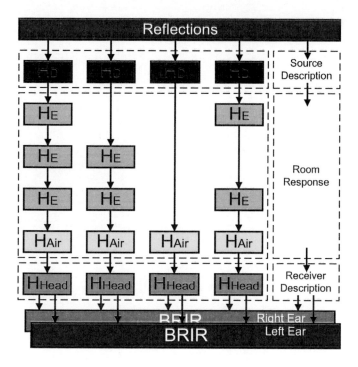

Figure 2.6: Chain of transfer functions that represent single sound reflections. Here, H_D describes the directional pattern of the sound source for the angle of emission; H_E denotes the transfer function of a hit constructional element such as a wall or an edge; H_{air} takes into account the air absorption for the complete path of propagation, and H_{Head} comprises the two HRTFs corresponding to the angle of sound impact. The sum of all these contributions can be interpreted as the two-channel BRIR.

the frequency domain, then $\underline{S}(f)$ relates to the frequency function of the dry source signal $s(t)$; $\underline{H}(f)$) describes the Binaural Room Transfer Function (BRTF), and $\underline{G}(f)$ refers to the modified source signal at the listener's eardrums. In this interpretation, the BRTF can be seen as the sum of transfer functions from LTI-subsystems, i.e., single sound reflections (see Fig. 2.6). Such a subsystem then comprises the transfer functions of the sound source's directional pattern H_D, all hit constructional elements H_E, the air attenuation H_{air}, and both ears H_{Head} including head and torso, with

$$H_{Reflection} = H_D \cdot H_{Air} \cdot H_{Head} \cdot \prod_{HitWalls} H_{E_i}. \qquad (2.22)$$

By now convolving the source signal with the BRIRs, the response of the room is added to the source signal. If the BRIRs are exact, the output signal $g(t)$ will sound identical to the real event including the spatial perception.

Chapter 3

Multimodal Representation of Airborne Sound Sources

'He is not seeing real people, of course. This is all a part of the moving illustration drawn by his computer according to specifications coming down the fiber-optic cable. The people are pieces of software called avatars. They are the audiovisual bodies that people use to communicate with each other in the Metaverse.'

(*Snow Crash*, Neal Stephenson, American writer)

In order to gain a certain user acceptance of virtual scenarios where natural airborne sound sources are involved, a realistic representation of these sources is required, since the user will always intuitively assign directional patterns and motions to objects producing sound, in compliance with individual everyday experiences. Therefore, the multimodal representation of virtual sound sources, called *avatars* in the following, not only demands a good visualization and high-quality input audio data, but also the inclusion of directional patterns of the source's sound radiation and the sound source's natural movements - at least in more complicated cases such as a human speaker or a musician. Just imagine avatars of a jazz band performing in a virtual concert hall (see Fig. 3.1). Rather than static people, one would expect a more lifelike situation where the musicians are performing with a certain passion leading to characteristic movements of the players and their instruments. Most likely, these movements would result in a change of the coloration and level of the produced sound depending on the user's position and orientation. Obviously, the lack of such authenticity diminishes the overall acceptance of the presented scenery which means that the user will stop behaving naturally at a certain point, even if other senses are stimulated adequately [Mor05, JNW06].

In connection with the representation of natural sound sources, numerous investigations have been carried out concerning either the determination of directional patterns of sound sources or the description and reproduction of corresponding animated avatars. However, they have rarely been conducted in a cross-disciplinary way. Consequently, there are only very few resources available that provide such

(a) Screenshot 1.

(b) Screenshot 2.

Figure 3.1: Exemplary virtual scenario: a jazz band, represented by avatars, is rehearsing in a concert hall.

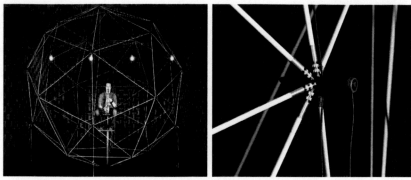

(a) Musician performing inside the measurement setup.   (b) Close up of a microphone housing building a corner of the pentakis dodecahedron.

Figure 3.2: Microphone array for measuring directional patterns of sound sources.

audiovisual data for creating avatars with a satisfying quality and content. These circumstances lead to a measurement series of performing musicians in order to generate such data. In this series, a sphere-like microphone array was installed in a hemi-anechoic room for recording input data and measuring directional patterns of the player. In a subsequent step, optical tracking devices were used for capturing the musician's movements while performing the recorded song for a second time in order to extract realistic motion patterns for the virtual counterpart. In the following, this measurement series will be briefly described and general issues will be discussed. A detailed description is given in [Reu08, SRA08].

3.1 Directional Pattern of Sound Sources

Even though basic directional patterns of musical instruments are widely known and described in literature, e.g., [Mey09], there are only some resources providing such data in a satisfying resolution. To mention here is the recent work by Zotter and Sontacci from the University of Music and Performing Arts Graz [ZS06], Giron from Ruhr Universität Bochum [Gir96], Lentz and Pollow from ITA [Sle04, Len07, PB09], Pätynen and Lokki from Alto University [PL10], and Otondo and Rindel from the Technical University of Denmark [OR04], all of whom have performed detailed investigations on directivities of musical instruments in real performance situations.

For measuring directional patterns of sound sources, a microphone array with 32 measurement points was constructed and built at ITA [Reu08, BPS08]. The setup features 32 microphones (Sennheiser KE4 capsules) that are mounted on the corners of a special frame with the shape of a pentakis dodecahedron (see Fig. 3.2). A pentakis dodecahedron is constructed from a regular dodecahedron where pentagonal pyramids are added to the 12 faces of the dodecahedron resulting in 32 corners, i.e.,

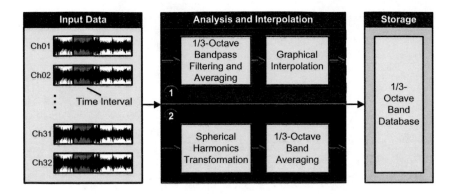

Figure 3.3: Extraction of the sound source's frequency-dependent directional patterns. A signal segment of the raw input data is usually analyzed and missing data points are computed by one of two different approaches: (1) Graphical interpolation and (2) Spherical harmonics decomposition.

measurement points all equidistant to the center. In ITA, the microphone array was installed in the hemi anechoic room equipped with sound-absorbing wedges on all four walls and the ceiling providing a hemi free-field characteristic down to frequencies of around 200 Hz. To gain an anechoic character for the directivity measurements, the floor was additionally covered with sound-absorbing wedges. The measurement setup was mounted on the ceiling of the anechoic room, where one microphone was located at the top ('north pole'), one at the bottom ('south pole') and six in the musician's median plane (azimuth angle of zero degree), whereby three microphones were positioned in front and three microphones behind the musician. A 33rd microphone (Brüel & Kjaer 4190) was placed in the main direction of sound radiation to record a dry master track, which is required as input data for auralization (see Sect. 2.7).

After the whole setup (microphone recording levels and positions) was calibrated, a musician was positioned at the center of the microphone array by using a stable chair that was adjustable in height and orientation (see Fig. 3.2(a)). Then the musician was asked to play both some songs and some octaves in chromatic scale, at random and at a maximum level. This had two reasons: first, the musician was given the opportunity to become familiar with the free-field characteristics of an anechoic room, and second, the input levels of the preamplifiers were adjusted accordingly in order to prevent an overload during the recordings. After this initial session, selected songs were played by the musician, and the songs were simultaneously recorded on all 33 channels and stored as raw data for later analysis. Here, the musician used an in-ear monitoring system for staying synchronized with the backing group.

Figure 3.3 illustrates a general scheme for the extraction of directional patterns from the recorded 32-channel raw data. At first, a signal segment is cut out, whereby the segment length should be oriented to the desired field of application. For an

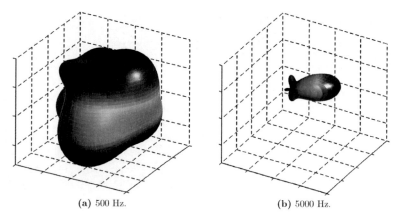

(a) 500 Hz.   (b) 5000 Hz.

Figure 3.4: Directional patterns of an alto-saxophone at 500 Hz and 5000 Hz, obtained by a spherical harmonics decomposition of fourth-order.

immersive simulation of the musician performing the recorded song, short signal segments should be chosen to also cover changes in the directivity over time, i.e., to
create a time-dependent directivity database that fits to the recorded song. The size
of the time segments can either be equal over the whole signal, or dynamic with larger
segments for situations where the musician does not move much, and vice versa. For
all other simulations, the analysis of long signal segments is more reasonable, since
it produces directional patterns where temporal changes are averaged out making
them applicable also for other audio input, e.g., more songs by the musician where
no directional data was recorded. This, however, is less authentic, but usually good
enough for a plausible representation.

Nonetheless, the difficulty of both approaches is to extract directional patterns
from the input data in order to generate directivity databases with a high spatial
resolution for auralization – keeping in mind that a database resolution of only 5
degrees (azimuth and elevation angle) results in more than 2500 data points that
have to be estimated from a set of only *some* measurement points. Thus, graphical interpolation methods [Kom07] are commonly applied which in most cases are
based on a Delaunay[1] triangulation[2]. These methods work fine and generate plausible results for sound sources with a simple directional pattern such as trumpets
or trombones. However, they lack a proper data representation near the poles and
the equator since the input data is usually represented by an internal grid-like data
structure. This means that data points are interpolated independently from the elevation angle leading to high resolutions near the poles and low resolutions near the
equator, i.e., the interpolation depends on the position of the poles. A graphical
interpolation is usually conducted for each frequency band with the corresponding

---

[1]Boris Nikolaevich Delaunay, Russian mathematician, 1890 - 1980.
[2]A mathematical method for constructing a triangle grid out of a set of points.

 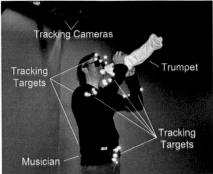

(a) Tracking targets for different applications: (b) Musician prepared for motion tracking. Here, Each target features four or more spherical tracking targets are attached to his body and the markers with a silver retro-reflective coating. instrument is wrapped in a non-reflective material.

Figure 3.5: Motion capturing of a trumpet player.

averaged spectral functions of the microphones' pressure amplitudes as input data (see Fig. 3.3(1)). In recent years, spherical harmonics decomposition [Wil99] came into focus for directivity modeling. Similar to the Fourier transformation, the signal is decomposed into spherical functions (instead of sine waves), which are weighted by their corresponding spherical harmonics coefficients. Once a set of coefficients is determined, all required data points in azimuth and elevation direction for a given frequency are directly given through this spatial function, making an additional interpolation obsolete. The contributions of each frequency at a certain data point are then averaged over the corresponding frequency band and stored in a database (see Fig. 3.3(2)). For more information on the extraction of directional patterns, please refer to the literature cited above.

Both approaches for extracting directional patterns from the recordings were applied generating databases with a spatial resolution of 5 degrees. Exemplary directivity balloon plots are shown in Fig. 3.4 using a fourth-order spherical harmonics decomposition. Then, auralizations with both databases were compared in a subsequent listening test, but no noticeable difference in the auralization could be perceived [Reu08] – probably due to the very dominant directional patterns of the recorded instruments. During the whole recording sessions, measurements were carried out with several performing musicians playing on various instruments such as cymbals, snare drums, conga drums, trombones, trumpets, and saxophones. In the meantime, Pollow et al. measured a huge series of directivities of natural sound sources in cooperation with the Audio Communication Group at the Technische Universität Berlin [PBS10], by using the same microphone array for their measurements. The measured directional patterns are freely available for download [Opeb], and are stored in the Open Directional Audio File Format (OpenDAFF) [Opea].

3.2   Motion Capturing of Sound Sources

Motion capturing is a technology for tracking movements of subjects or objects, usually in real-time. It is a common technique for making a system react to the tracked user's movement, or recording motion sequences, e.g., to animate an avatar or analyze the user's behavior and reactions in certain situations. For this purpose an actor is equipped with tracking targets, such as sensors and markers, that enable a tracking of their current positions and orientation. Different tracking technologies are available, such as electromechanical systems, inertial systems, fiber-optic systems, electromagnetic systems, acoustical systems and optical systems (more details are given in, e.g., [BC03]). In connection with the simulation of natural sound sources, a non-intrusive motion capturing procedure should be applied in order to avoid disturbances of the performing musician by the tracking devices. Here, optical tracking systems meet these demands, since they work with a small amount of tiny rigid-body tracking targets that are attached to the actor[3]. Within the given possibilities the optical tracking devices were used that are integrated in the CAVE-like environment at RWTH Aachen University. The system consists of six infrared cameras with a fixed update rate of 60 Hz and measures six degrees of freedom if tracking targets are used that feature four or more spherical markers with retro-reflective coating (see Fig. 3.5(a)).

For recording the motion of the performing musician, eight tracking targets were attached to the actual body: one to each forearm and upper arm, one to the back

---

[3]Some systems even work with no markers using image processing algorithms to determine the actor's position and orientation.

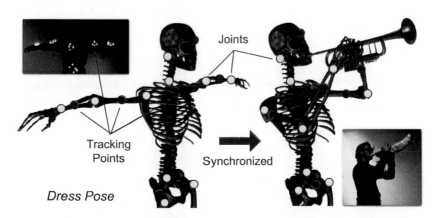

Figure 3.6: Dress pose calibration: the actor has to strike a dress pose, which is shown on the left-hand side. The global positions and orientations of the actor's tracking targets are then transformed and mapped to the joints of the local physical model of the avatar shown here as skeleton. After this reference calibration, the movements of the actor and the corresponding avatar are synchronized with each other.

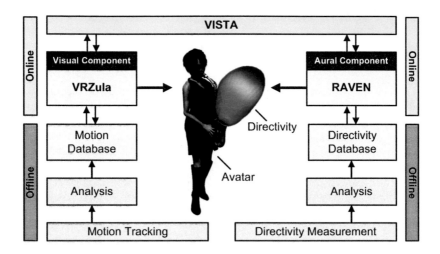

Figure 3.7: Concept for the audiovisual representation of natural sound sources. After extracting all relevant data from the measurements and storing them in fast-to-access databases, the visual component was generated by the software VRZula, which is a software toolkit for the simulation of virtual humanoids. For auralization, the real-time room acoustical simulation software RAVEN was used, which is described in all details within the scope of this thesis.

between the shoulders, two around the pelvis (with one target at the back and one at the front using a belt), and one between the eyes (see Fig. 3.5(b)). In addition, musical instruments with highly reflective surfaces were wrapped in non-light-reflecting material to keep them from reflecting the infrared light, which would seriously disturb the tracking results. A calibration of the tracking system was required before starting the actual motion recordings. Here, the actor was positioned in a so-called *dress pose*, which is a reference pose for matching the global positions and orientations of the tracking targets to the local coordinate system of the avatar (see Fig. 3.6). After these preparations, the motion capturing session was started, and the previously recorded audio tracks were reproduced by a loudspeaker system. The musicians were asked to move in accordance to their music and try to reproduce the corresponding movements. During each recording session, the tracking data were directly transformed according to the Humanoid Animation standard ISO/IEC-FCD 19774 [FCD], called H-Anim, and recorded on a hard drive using the Biovision Hierarchy file format. The H-Anim standard specifies a number of segments, such as upper arm, forearm and hand, which are connected to each other by joints, such as shoulder, elbow and wrist. It is the underlying model of almost any application for creating virtual humanoids, i.e., human-like avatars. However, errors caused by marker occlusion, interference, noise, and tracking target dropouts were an issue during the recording sessions leading to missing frames as well as to position and rotation errors of the corresponding body parts. Therefore, a post-processing of the data was applied in order to amend short occlusion errors and achieve smooth, synchronized and plausible movement patterns of the virtual musician.

3.3   Audiovisual Avatars

With the processed input data, synchronized audiovisual representations of natural sound sources were created and applied to immersive simulations to further improve their authenticity, whereby the overall concept is summarized in Fig. 3.7. The visual component of the avatars was generated by the software VRZula [Val07], which is part of the real-time software platform for VR-applications at RWTH Aachen University, called ViSTA [AK08]. VRZula is a software toolkit for the simulation of virtual humanoids and is based on a layer model according to the human anatomy. Using this toolkit, avatars were created and animated at runtime by directly applying the recorded motion data to the underlying avatar's physical model at interactive rates resulting in quite natural movements of the avatar. For the aural component, directional patterns of the sound sources that corresponded to the current time interval of the song were taken into account by simply importing the generated databases in RAVEN and adding the radiation characteristics to the point source description of the acoustical simulation (see Chap. 5).

Chapter 4

Modeling and Handling of Complex Environments

'There is something new: A globe about the size of a grapefruit, a perfectly detailed rendition of Planet Earth, hanging in space at arm's length in front of his eyes. Hiro has heard about this but never seen it. It is a piece of CIC software called, simply, Earth. It is the user interface that CIC uses to keep track of every bit of spatial information that it owns - all the maps, weather data, architectural plans, and satellite surveillance stuff.'

(*Snow Crash*, Neal Stephenson, American writer)

In contrast to trivial outdoor situations, the real-time auralization of especially indoor scenarios, which come along with a more reverberant sound field characteristic, requires for a physical-based room acoustical simulation in order to generate a natural sounding and adequate aural stimulus for the current situation (see Chap. 5). Regarding real-time constraints, an efficient concept of modeling and handling complex geometric environments is needed to overcome the complexity of such simulations and keep computation times at a low level. In this chapter, the transformation of real-world scene data into a computer simulation representation is described and model limitations are briefly discussed. This also includes the basics of spatial subdivision, which significantly speeds up the processing time of geometric operations. The most common space-partitioning strategies are introduced, whereby two of them, Binary Space Partitioning and Spatial Hashing, are discussed in detail, since they are applied in RAVEN. This chapter closes with introducing a concept for processing multiple dynamically-linked geometric subspaces, which will be the basis for the entire auralization concept of complex virtual environments (see Sect. 5.5).

4.1 Polygonal Scene Model

A suitable model that represents all necessary physical aspects of the real-world scene is required to simulate room acoustics with the computer. Not only does such a model comprise the dimensions and exact form of the scene objects, but also information on the sound absorption and sound-scattering characteristics of scene materials, temperature, humidity and air pressure (see Chap. 2). For the geometrical representation of the environment, polygonal models are most commonly used as they provide several advantages, such as the efficient storage in spatial data structures (see Sect. 4.2) to solve common simulation requirements, e.g., the fast determination of ray intersections with the scene (see Chap. 7).

A *polygon* is a planar geometric object composed of a finite number of *vertices*, which define a sequence of non-intersecting straight lines, called *edges* in the following, that enclose an area. This area represents the *surface* of the polygon. There are two types of polygons having either *convex* or *concave* shape (compare Fig. 4.1(a, b)). A polygon is convex if no edge extension cuts any other edge or vertex. While a convex polygon which is split by a line results in at most two new convex polygons, a split operation on concave polygons requires a non-trivial algorithm to automatically determine all resulting polygons. The use of convex polygons is therefore strongly recommended. It should be noted that this demand causes no restrictions on the scene modeling, because every concave polygon can be built out of a set of convex polygons (see Fig. 4.1(b)). Similarly, *a set of polygons* is convex if no polygon plane cuts any other polygon. With respect to real-time applications, additional constraints on the scene construction are required to enable the implementation of fast scene processing algorithms, such as point-in-polygon and intersection tests (see Chap. 7). Here, the most important rules are: a) the orientation of the polygon's normal vectors must be consistent; b) each polygon must be spanned in the same order (clockwise/counter-clockwise) and c) a polygon may be tangent to one or more other polygons, but never crosses any of them in order to avoid undefined subareas.

Figure 4.2 shows the conversion of the real-world ELMIA concert hall in Jönköping, Sweden, into an appropriate simplified acoustic model. The geometrical aspects of the concert hall are represented by a set of polygons, each with a defined surface material (see Fig. 4.2(b)). In general, acoustic models are much simpler than their respective counterpart in visualization as the required level of detail is frequency-dependent.

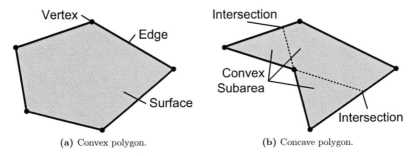

(a) Convex polygon.   (b) Concave polygon.

Figure 4.1: Possible polygon shapes.

 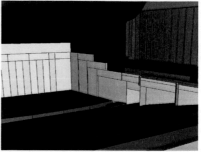

(a) View on ELMIA Hall's stage area. Picture by courtesy of Physikalisch-Technische Bundesanstalt (PTB) Braunschweig, Germany.

(b) Corresponding acoustic room model using polygon colors as material codes. The model is valid for middle-range frequencies.

Figure 4.2: ELMIA concert hall in Jönköping, Sweden.

In particular, the model is only valid for frequencies above $f \geq c/2a$, meaning that reflections on the geometrical objects are physically incorrect below that frequency (see Sect. 2.3). As an example, the minimum element size a for frequencies above 100 Hz relates to $a = c/2f = 344\frac{m}{s}/2 \cdot 100\,Hz = 1,72\,m$.

4.2 Spatial Data Structures

4.2.1 General

Spatial data structures aim at encoding a given geometric scene efficiently in order to significantly accelerate common operations such as intersection tests, collision detection and culling algorithms [FvDFH96, AMH02]. Most methods are based on a space subdivision that is encoded in tree-like or cell-like data structures following either an object-oriented or space-oriented partitioning strategy.

Bounding Volume Hierarchys (BVHs), Binary Space Partitioning (BSP)-trees and Octrees (in 2D space Quadtrees) belong to the group of hierarchical tree data structures. Here, BVHs wrap all geometric objects in bounding volumes, such as spheres and (axis-aligned) bounding boxes, that are then enclosed within larger bounding volumes in a recursive way until the whole geometry fits into exactly one bounding volume (see Fig.4.3(a,b)). Octrees subdivide a 3D space by means of planes as partitioners that recursively subdivide the space evenly along all three axes resulting in 8^n new subspaces for n iterations (see Fig.4.3(c,d)). BSP-trees, on the other hand, can be generated in three basic variants, either with an arbitrary, axis-aligned or a polygon-aligned space partitioning. A space partitioning with no constraints on the choice of the dividing planes apparently yields the best possible encoding of the geometry. The crucial part is to find partitioners that produce a balanced tree of minimum height which is the most efficient tree structure in terms of search operations. As there is an infinite number of possible partitioners, heuristic approaches are commonly used to optimize the space partioning. Computation times vary here in the range from minutes to hours, to weeks. In contrast, axis-aligned BSP-trees and Octrees can be computed much faster as they follow a given subdivision pattern. Axis-aligned BSP-trees are created similarly to Octrees but with only one instead of three partitioning planes (see 4.3(e,f)). Polygon-aligned BSP uses planes spanned by the geometry's polygons. It will be discussed in more detail in the next subsection as it is one integral part of RAVEN's real-time capability.

Another strategy of spatial subdivision is called voxelization which belongs to the group of cell data structures. Similar to the rasterization of a 2D scene, voxelization (non-)uniformily subdivides the 3D space into box-shaped subspaces that are organized in a 3D data grid where each grid cell contains the geometry that is enclosed within the respective subspace. As a matter of principle, search operations on this type of data structures can never compete with the performance of a balanced tree data structure. Instead, voxelization supports other important operations that are the fast insertion, manipulation and deletion of polygonal scene objects. It should be kept in mind that hierarchical tree data structures always require a recomputation when the geometry has changed while only a few subspaces have to be updated in a voxelized space. The most efficient method for addressing such a cell data structure is called Spatial Hashing (SH), which significantly reduces the complexity of a change in geometry. More details on Spatial Hashing are given later in this section, as this concept is used in RAVEN to handle scene modifications in real-time (see Chap. 6).

4.2.2   Binary Space Partitioning (BSP)

In 1969 Shumacker et al. first described the BSP-tree [SBGS69], which is a hierarchical binary tree structure that subdivides an (N)-dimensional space into (N)-dimensional subspaces by means of $(N-1)$-dimensional directed partitioners. The use of non-linear curved partitioners is possible but is not suitable due to analytical complexity. Therefore $(N-1)$-dimensional hyperplanes are widely used. A hyperplane in $I\!\!R^n$ is a linear, affine or projective subspace of codimension 1.

$$(\vec{n} \cdot \vec{x}) - (\vec{n} \cdot \vec{a}) = (\vec{n} \cdot \vec{x}) - d = u \quad , u \in \mathbb{R} \tag{4.1}$$

In the vectorial notation (Eq. 4.1) d describes the scalar product of the hyperplane's (N)-dimensional normal vector $\vec{n}$ with an in-plane point $\vec{a}$, $\vec{x}$ an arbitrary point in $I\!\!R^n$ and u a rational number. This simple equation, called *Hessian*[1] *normal form*, is quite powerful as it enables one to determine the position of $\vec{x}$ in relation to the hyperplane or to define the hyperplane itself. There are three cases depending on u's value:

$$(\vec{n} \cdot \vec{x}) - d = 0 \quad \Rightarrow \vec{x} \text{ is on the hyperplane,} \tag{4.2}$$

$$(\vec{n} \cdot \vec{x}) - d > 0 \quad \Rightarrow \vec{x} \text{ is in front of the hyperplane,} \tag{4.3}$$

$$(\vec{n} \cdot \vec{x}) - d < 0 \quad \Rightarrow \vec{x} \text{ is behind the hyperplane.} \tag{4.4}$$

---

[1]Ludwig Otto Hesse, German Mathematician, 1811 - 1874.

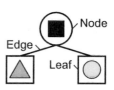

(a) The scene consists of a cube that encloses two other objects, a sphere and a cone.

(b) Corresponding BVH. The biggest volume is chosen as root node, where the outgoing edges point to the other two objects that are enclosed by the cube.

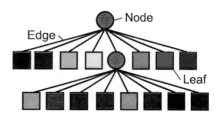

(c) Octrees subdivide the space into 8 smaller subspaces.

(d) Corresponding Octree. Leaf nodes represent a subspace, while outgoing edges (eight per node) point to smaller subspaces.

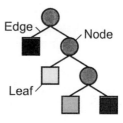

(e) BSP-trees subdivide the space into 2 smaller subspaces.

(f) Corresponding BSP-tree. Leaf nodes represent a subspace, while outgoing edges (two per node) point to smaller subspaces.

Figure 4.3: This figure illustrates the space partitioning mechanisms of three approaches: BVH (a,b), Octrees (b,c) and BSP-trees (e,f).

The classification depends on the direction of the hyperplanes's normal vector. A point $\vec{x}$ lies in front of the hyperplane, which means that it is on the same side as the normal vector $\vec{n}$ points to, if u is greater than zero (Eq. 4.3). The opposite case, i.e. the point $\vec{x}$ lies behind the hyperplane, leads to Equation 4.4. A hyperplane itself is represented by a set of all points $\vec{x}$ that fulfill Equation 4.2, which also can be used to test if a point $\vec{x}$ lies on the hyperplane.

In the case of $I\!\!R^3$, the hyperplane's equation $(\vec{n} \cdot \vec{x}) - d = 0$ defines a two-dimensional plane. An arbitrary plane could be chosen as partitioner, but, as mentioned before, it would unreasonably decelerate the BSP-tree creation. Therefore, it is suitable to use planes spanned by the scene polygons as partitioners, since it makes the BSP-tree creation faster and more transparent. Each *tree node* contains one partitioner that divides the current subspace into two smaller subspaces (see 4.3(e,f)). The point in question can have three possible relative locations: 1) on, 2) in-front-of and 3) behind the partitioner. In the first case, the query can be stopped. To pursue the latter two cases, the test is continued by branching to the respective son of the node, left for 'behind', right for 'in-front'. The tree's root node therefore refers to the whole space, while a leaf node refers to a subspace which cannot be further subdivided reasonably, i.e., the remaining partition is a convex set of polygons (see Sect.4.1).

Contrary to the naive approach to test the position of a point against all planes, the tree structure allows one to determine this position by testing only a subset of planes, which significantly speeds up operations such as intersection tests. This subset is defined by the path in the tree. By using a balanced tree, i.e., a tree of minimum height, the number of tests can also be minimized, which drops the search complexity from $\mathcal{O}(N)$ to $\mathcal{O}(logN)$, where N is the number of polygons. Here, the crucial part is to choose an appropriate partitioner from the polygon set where two factors are important: the resulting sets of polygons for the two subspaces should be nearly equal in size to obtain a balanced tree. On the other hand, polygons which cross the partitioner need to be split and the resulting polygons must be assigned to the respective sets. Since this operation increases the overall polygon count, these cuts should be kept to a minimum. A criterion which reflects these two aspects has been proposed in [RE01]. It measures the ratio $r(p)$, $0 \leq r(p) \leq 1$, between a set of polygons P on both sides of a possible partitioner $p \in P$ and the number of polygons $s(p)$ that must be split when choosing p as a partitioner.

$$r(p) \quad := \quad \min_{p \in P} \left\{ \frac{\sum_{p' \neq p} \delta_{\text{in front}}(p', p)}{\sum_{p' \neq p} \delta_{\text{behind}}(p', p)}, \frac{\sum_{p' \neq p} \delta_{\text{behind}}(p', p)}{\sum_{p' \neq p} \delta_{\text{in front}}(p', p)} \right\} \qquad (4.5)$$

$$s(p) \quad := \quad \sum_{p' \neq p} \delta_{\text{crosses}}(p', p) \qquad (4.6)$$

Here, δ counts the number of occurrences for polygonal spatial relationships and p'

iterates over all other polygons in P.

$$\delta_{\text{in front}}(p',p) \;=\; \begin{cases} 1 & \text{if } p' \text{ is in front of p} \\ 0 & \text{otherwise} \end{cases} \tag{4.7}$$

$$\delta_{\text{behind}}(p',p) \;=\; \begin{cases} 1 & \text{if } p' \text{ is behind p} \\ 0 & \text{otherwise} \end{cases} \tag{4.8}$$

$$\delta_{\text{crosses}}(p',p) \;=\; \begin{cases} 1 & \text{if } p' \text{ crosses p} \\ 0 & \text{otherwise} \end{cases} \tag{4.9}$$

The plane of polygon p is chosen as partitioner if it has an 'acceptable' ratio and results in the lowest number of splits $s(p)$. The definition of 'acceptable' is specified by a threshold t: $r(p)$ is acceptable if $r(p) > t$. If t is small, a small number of polygon splits is preferred which, however, causes the BSP-tree to be unbalanced. A high value of t results in a more balanced tree, but also many polygon splits. Therefore, the best choice of t is scene-dependent.

Figure 4.4 illustrates the computation of a BSP-tree for a simple geometry. At the beginning, the BSP-tree only consists of an empty node called the tree's *root* which refers to the whole geometry. Now, a partitioning plane that conforms with the above-mentioned criteria has to be determined. For the initial partitioning process, the planes spanned by polygon 4 and 6 fit best as partitioner, as they provide both the best ratio $r(p)$ and the smallest number of splits (Tab. 4.1, step 1). In this example, the latter plane is chosen as partitioner, which causes a split of polygon 1 into two new polygons (1a and 1b, see Fig. 4.4(a)). The partitioning plane subdivides the

Step	Polygon	$\sum \delta_{\text{crosses}}(p',p)$	$\sum \delta_{\text{in front}}(p',p)$	$\sum \delta_{\text{behind}}(p',p)$	$r(p)$
	0,1,2,3,7	0	0	7	0.0
1	4,6	1	5	3	0.6
	5	2	6	3	0.5
	1b,2,3	0	0	4	0.0
2	4	1	2	3	0.7
	5	1	3	2	0.7

Table 4.1: Determination of the best partitioners: whereas in step one polygon 4 and 6 provide the best ratio, polygon 4 and 5 fits best during step two.

room geometry into two new sets of polygons and is stored in the BSP-tree's node. The BSP-tree's branches are designated with a plus, meaning the partition lies 'in front of' the dividing plane, or a minus, representing the 'behind' subset. Convex subsets are stored in *leaf nodes* of the BSP-trees (denoted through squares), whereas non-convex subsets have to be further subdivided until only convex sets remain. In this example, the 'behind' branch leads to leaf L1 which contains a convex set of polygons that cannot be further subdivided reasonably. The set of polygons lying on the positive side of the partitioner is not convex, so the respective BSP-tree branch points to the hexagon H1 representing the remaining subset (see Fig. 4.4(a)). As the negative branch already points to a leaf node, only a new partitioner has to be

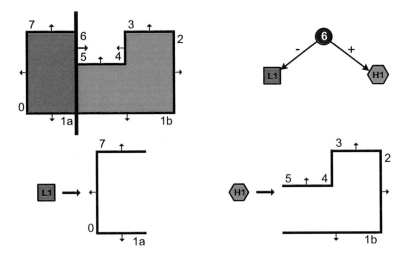

(a) The room is divided into two subspaces using polygon 6 as partitioner, where the root node stores the partitioner and connects two new elements via edges. Whereas L1 stores a convex polygon set, H1 stores a concave polygon set which has to be further subdivided.

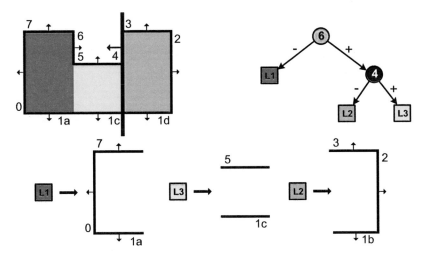

(b) The subspace lying in front of partitioning plane 6 is further subdivided by using polygon 4 as new partitioner. The leaf nodes L2 and L3 are attached to a new node, which stores the chosen partitioner. L2 and L3 now store convex polygon subsets and the spatial subdivision terminates.

Figure 4.4: BSP-tree generation for a simple example.

specified for the residual non-convex polygon set. Polygons that are coplanar to the current partitioning plane do not have to be considered in subsequent steps, because they do not provide any additional information for the partitioning process. In this example, the planes spanned by polygon 4 or polygon 5 would fit as next partitioner as both provide the same ratio (Tab. 4.1, Step 2). In Fig. 4.4(b) the plane of polygon 4 was chosen, resulting in a split of polygon 1b into the polygons 1c and 1d, whereas the partitioner is stored in the newly created node. Both novel subsets are convex now and the node's outgoing branches point to the new leaf nodes L2 and L3 which store the sets of polygons lying on the positive (leaf L3) or on the negative (leaf L2) side of the partitioner. The termination condition for BSP-tree creation is reached at this point, because the whole room geometry is subdivided into convex subspaces now, i.e., there is no further reasonable subdivision.

4.2.3 Spatial Hashing

Spatial Hashing originates from CG and has lately been applied to speed up applications such as the real-time collision detection of huge deformable objects [THM+03]. The concept of SH is based on the idea of subdividing the space by primitive volumes called *voxels* and map the infinite voxelized space to a finite set of one-dimensional hash indices, i.e., a *hash table*, which are en/decoded by a hash function. Using a hash function for spatial subdivision is a very efficient strategy. Each voxel contains the respective encapsulated scene polygons and is addressed by the corresponding hash index. These indices can be computed as follows: by considering an axis-aligned cubical voxel with edge length a as the subdividing volume, the coordinates (x, y, z) of an arbitrary point are quantized to the voxel coordinates (u, v, w), in particular, the coordinates are subdivided by the voxel's edge length a and floored to the next integer with

$$u = \left\lfloor \frac{x}{a} \right\rfloor, v = \left\lfloor \frac{y}{a} \right\rfloor, w = \left\lfloor \frac{z}{a} \right\rfloor. \tag{4.10}$$

Then the voxel coordinates (u, v, w) are mapped to a hash index i using a special hash function. In this work two different hash functions h_1 and h_2 are considered, which are defined to

$$i = \begin{cases} h_1(u, v, w) & = (u \cdot p_1 \oplus v \cdot p_2 \oplus w \cdot p_3) \bmod n \\ h_2(u, v, w) & = (u \cdot p_1 + v \cdot p_2 + w \cdot p_3) \bmod n \end{cases}, \tag{4.11}$$

where i is the hash index, p_1, p_2, p_3 are large prime numbers, $\oplus$ denotes the logical XOR-operator and n stores the size of the hash table. As one can see, the modulo operation reduces the infinite 3D space to a finite 1D set, which unfortunately could result in the mapping of two or more voxels to the same hash index, so-called *hash collisions*. Hash collisions do not necessarily result in a simulation error, as they can easily be intercepted, though this causes an additional computational effort and should be kept minimal – at least in real-time applications. To reduce the number of hash collisions, three factors are important: 1) the hash function should distribute the hashes uniformly over the output space to avoid multiple mapping to the same

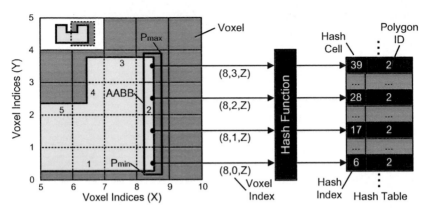

Figure 4.5: Example of hashing geometrical objects in a voxelized space. Every voxel in space is mapped to an entry (hash index) in the hash table. The intersection of an object with these voxels is stored in the hash table.

index; 2) the hash table size should be kept at a moderate level in terms of memory management, and 3) the voxel's edge length in relation to the scene's dimensions should be optimized, since it strongly influences the overall performance of search operations. All these factors will be thoroughly discussed in Sect. 11.

Figure 4.5 illustrates the voxelization of the same simple geometry that was used in the previous subsection. The concept of SH will be demonstrated for polygon 2 using the second hash function h_2 that was described above. In this example, the hash function's prime numbers are indiscriminately set to $p_1 = 7, p_2 = 11, p_3 = 13$, the hash table is $n = 50$ in size, and the voxel's edge length is assumed to be $a = 2$. At first the Axis-Aligned Bounding Box (AABB) of polygon 2 is computed, but only the AABB's minimum and maximum coordinate values are actually of interest, denoted as $P_{min} = (17, 0.5, 0)$ and $P_{max} = (17, 6.5, 3)$ in Fig. 4.5. These two points are then mapped to the corresponding voxel coordinates V_{min} and V_{max}, with

$$V_{min} = (\left\lfloor \frac{P_{min,x}}{a} \right\rfloor, \left\lfloor \frac{P_{min,y}}{a} \right\rfloor, \left\lfloor \frac{P_{min,z}}{a} \right\rfloor) = (8, 0, 0) \qquad (4.12)$$

$$V_{max} = (\left\lfloor \frac{P_{max,x}}{a} \right\rfloor, \left\lfloor \frac{P_{max,y}}{a} \right\rfloor, \left\lfloor \frac{P_{max,z}}{a} \right\rfloor) = (8, 3, 1). \qquad (4.13)$$

All possible voxels between the discretized minimum V_{min} and the discretized maximum V_{max} of the AABB have to be traversed, but only the lowest voxel row $(min(z) = 0.5)$ is further regarded, i.e., $V_1 = (8, 0, 0)$, $V_2 = (8, 1, 0)$, $V_3 = (8, 2, 0)$ and $V_4 = (8, 3, 0)$, as the hashing procedure always follows the same pattern. Here, the corresponding hash indices of the four voxels are:

$$
\begin{aligned}
i_1 &= (8 \cdot 7 + 0 \cdot 11 + 0 \cdot 13) \; mod \; 50 = 6 \\
i_2 &= (8 \cdot 7 + 1 \cdot 11 + 0 \cdot 13) \; mod \; 50 = 17 \\
i_3 &= (8 \cdot 7 + 2 \cdot 11 + 0 \cdot 13) \; mod \; 50 = 28 \\
i_4 &= (8 \cdot 7 + 3 \cdot 11 + 0 \cdot 13) \; mod \; 50 = 39
\end{aligned}
\tag{4.14}
$$

After computation of the voxels' hash indices, polygon 2 is sorted into the respective cells of the hash table and the next scene polygon is proceeded in the same way. The advantage of SH over other spatial data structures such as BSP-trees is that the insertion/deletion of m points into/from the hash table takes only $\mathcal{O}(m)$ time. Thus, this method is perfectly qualified to efficiently handle modifications of a polygonal scenery in order to enable a real-time auralization of a dynamically-changing environment (see Chap. 6).

4.3   Dynamic Coupling of Rooms

In contrast to simple one-room situations, the real-time auralization of complex environments requires a very fast data handling and convenient interaction management. Imagine an office floor where sound emitting sources are located in each room. Sound propagation and transmission paths have to be computed from any source to the receiver. To overcome the complexity of such huge geometric models, a logical and spatial subdivision is required that enables a dynamic scene decomposition into acoustically separated volumes. Rooms inside a building are such volumes, but also the building's outer surroundings, resembling a more free-field-like situation with less reflections. In the following the term *room* is used for both volume types. Rooms are interconnected by *portals*, which are logical and physical room separators, e.g., walls, doors and windows. Portals can have individual *states*, for instance, a door can have the state *closed* or *opened*, while a solid wall has to be understood as a permanently closed portal. Rooms that are interconnected by open portals are handled as one integral acoustic space, called *room groups*. The advantage of this type of scene decomposition is that it allows a very controlled and efficient simulation of sound propagation and sound transmission which will be thoroughly described in Sect. 5.5.

The topological structure of the scene can be represented by a *graph*, which is a general data structure for the logical concatenation of entities, called *nodes*. In the following, this graph will be referred to as Acoustic Scene Graph (ASG). Here, each node stores the spatial representation of a single room, including the polygonal model (encoded with BSP and SH), material data, temperature, humidity and air pressure. The ASG's *edges* represent polyhedral portals which connect adjacent rooms, i.e., nodes. As sound waves will pass the portals from both sides, these edges are undirected. The connectivity between two nodes is steered by the state of the respective portal. The state *closed* dissociates two rooms from each other, while state *opened* pools two adjacent rooms in the same room group. Figure 4.6 further

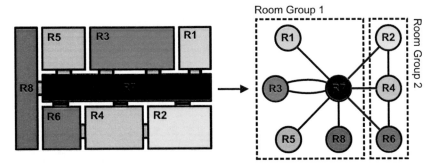

Figure 4.6: Logical and spatial subdivision of a complex scene by the example of a typical office floor plan. The scene consists of eight rooms that are interconnected by doors. Here, gray doors are opened, while red doors are closed. The corresponding ASG describes the topological structure of the acoustical scene. Portals are represented by the graph's edges, whereby gray and red edges relate to the state opened and closed, respectively. With the given portal configuration, the rooms can be pooled in two room groups representing two separated acoustic spaces.

illustrates the concept of ASG by the example of an office floor. The floor plan is given on the left-hand side. The scene contains eight rooms that are interconnected by ten doors, which are defined as portals. All this information is encoded in the ASG, which perfectly matches the auralization concept of coupled rooms that is further described in Sect. 5.5. An example is shown in Fig. 4.6, where – according to the given portal configuration – the scene is divided into two room groups representing the currently coupled acoustic spaces.

Chapter 5

Room Acoustics Simulation

'In the silence of dead monitors, the hardcopy hums into trays, signal after signal from the chaos, the various voices are collected, and after the final signal, one can listen and wait for the encoded call of the void.'

(Frank Drake, American astrophysicist)

Today, artificial methods, such as reverberation generators, are applied in many VR-systems for auralizing virtual indoor environments, since they are easy and fast to implement and provide reasonable results at the first listening. However, while this might be sufficient in gaming or other applications where no accurate representation of the virtual scene is necessary, these methods are absolutely inappropriate for an immersive representation of real-word scenarios, as they are totally unable to cover the whole complexity of room acoustics. Thus, a physical-based simulation of sound propagation is obligatory in order to gain an auditory representation of the scene with a certain realistic behavior. This chapter describes – after a brief overview on room acoustics simulation in general – all physical simulation models that are implemented in RAVEN. A hybrid simulation model is introduced that combines both room acoustics and building acoustics and that generates BRIR with a quality that can truly compete with commercial state-of-the-art off-line solutions[1], while maintaining a highly flexible handling for the real-time application (the latter is described in more detail in the next chapter).

5.1 General

The era of computer-based room acoustics simulation began in the 1960's, where scientists started to realize the big advantages that came with the development of computers, as they offered a much faster calculation of numerical problems than ever before[2]. Then, in 1968, Asbjørn Krokstad, Svein Strøm and Svein Sørsdal at the Norges Teknisk-Naturvitenskapelige Universitet (NTNU) in Trondheim, Norway,

---

[1]Demonstration videos and sound files are available for download under www.ravenaudio.de.

[2]And one should not forget that computers at that time had a memory capacity of a few kilobyte and a processing power of a today's off-the-shelf washing machine.

published the first paper about the computer-based calculation of an acoustical room response by means of a Ray Tracing (RT)-technique [KSS68], inspired by a visionary presentation by Manfred Schroeder at the International Congress on Acoustics in 1962 [SAB62]. With increasing processing power of successive computer generations, extensive effort was put into the development of improved and more complex simulation methods, but still, after 40 years of development, none of the existing approaches holds as the *ultimate* method, even though state-of-the-art implementations can compete with the established and reliable scale models [Vor08]. As mentioned earlier, sound propagation in a certain medium is described by the *wave equation*, which is a second-order linear partial differential equation of waves. This equation has to be solved in order to determine the RIR (see Sect. 2.6), but usually no analytic solutions exist apart from simple case studies. Thus, they must be approximated, which is usually done by means of basically two different approaches: wave-based methods and methods of GA (or combinations of both).

Numerical wave-based methods, for instance the Finite Element Method (FEM) and the Boundary Element Method (BEM), provide most accurate simulations of acoustical wave propagation in air, fluids and solids by discretizing the room into a finite number of subspaces and solving the corresponding partial and constrained differential wave equations [Zie00, vE00, Mec02]. The great disadvantages of these numerical approaches are their computational costs, where computation times range from minutes to hours, days, and weeks. Whereas the propagation of low frequency sound waves in small room geometries can be calculated rather fast [KDS93, Pie88], the computation time explodes for room acoustical simulation involving the whole frequency band and for room geometries of higher complexity. Therefore, wave-based methods are usually applied for simulating low-frequency RIRs that represent the room's modal structure up to Schroeder frequency. Above that frequency, room modes are statistically overlapping and the faster methods of GA can be applied. In GA, the sound field description is reduced to the dispersion of incoherent sound particles with a dictated frequency and amount of energy, similar to the wave-particle dualism in physics[3]. Each sound particle represents a spherical wave with infinitely small opening angle and decreasing intensity according to the basic $1/r^2$ distance law. Considering the division of the RIR into three parts – the direct sound, the early reflections, and the late reverberation – it was shown that each part has its individual requirements, mostly dependent on the human's perception of room acoustics (see Sect. 2.6). In summary, the direct sound and the early reflections have to be as precise as possible in aspects of timing and spectral information, because small deviations directly affect the localization of sound sources. By contrast, the late part of the RIR is evaluated by the hearing with a much lower temporal resolution, where the total reverberant energy is integrated over certain time slots and angle fields. Late reverberation is usually dominated by scattered reflections and can be interpreted as a diffuse sound

---

[3]In this interpretation, delay line models and radiosity methods are considered to be basically geometric as well, since wave propagation is reduced to the time-domain approach of energy transition from wall to wall.

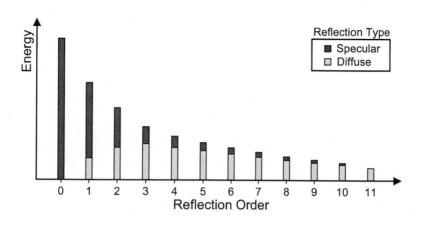

Figure 5.1: Conversion of specularly into diffusely reflected sound energy, illustrated by an example (according to Heinrich Kuttruff [Kut95]).

field. Therefore, it is not necessary to model the overlapping reflections as accurately as possible, but the overall intensity by specular and scattered reflections in a certain time slot has to be energetically correct.

Today, all deterministic simulation models of GA are based on the physical model of Image Sources (ISs) (this model is completely described in Sect. 5.2) and only differ in the way how ISs are identified by using either forward (ray) tracing or reverse construction. Variants of this type of algorithm are, for instance, hybrid ray tracing, beam tracing, pyramid tracing, frustum tracing, and so forth [Vor89, Far95, Ste96, FTC+04, LCM07]. ISs are a good approximation for perfectly reflecting or low-absorbing surfaces in large rooms with large distances between the sound source, wall, and receiver [SN99]. In addition, RIRs from image-like models are easy to construct and consist of simple filtered Dirac delta functions, which are arranged accordingly to their delay and amplitude, and sampled with a certain temporal resolution (see Sec 5.2.2). Round robin tests of room acoustics simulation programs [Vor95, Bor00] revealed the drawback of the IS-method, though, which is the incapability of simulating surface and obstacle scattering. In the temporal development of the RIR, however, scattering is a dominant effect already from reflections of order two or three that cannot be neglected, even in rooms with rather smooth surfaces [Kut95]. From this it follows that pure image source modeling is perfectly qualified for determining the direct sound and the early reflections, but it does not yield satisfactory results for the late part of the RIR (see Fig. 5.1).

Better results are achieved by combining ISs with stochastic models for the simulation of the room's reverberant sound field, usually referred to as *hybrid* methods of GA. Solutions for the problem of surface scattering are given by either stochastic RT or radiosity methods [Wal80, VvM86, Vor89, Hei93, Nay93, Lew93, Ste96, Dal96,

Lam96, CR05]. The fast radiosity methods are based on the irradiation and reradiation of sound energy among surface elements in order to calculate the total energy density at a receiving point via direct and reverberant paths [Kut00]. Here, ideal diffuse reflections are assumed meaning that the directional pattern of arriving sound is equally distributed over all directions and the energy decreases exponentially with time. This assumption is, however, too rough if the room geometry is extremely long or flat and if it contains objects such as columns or privacy screens. Room acoustical effects such as (flutter) echoes or curved decays could therefore stay undetected [Rin04]. In addition, and with regard to auralization, the level, direction of arrival, and temporal distribution of late arriving reflections have a strong influence on the listener's spatial impression and should therefore not be randomized [BS95]. Fortunately, all these limitations do not apply for stochastic RT, which is a Monte Carlo method for computing the quantized energy envelope of the RIR. This envelope comes in a time- and frequency-dependent energy histogram, where the size of both time slots and frequency bands is orientated to the human hearing, i.e., time slots are used with the size of a few milliseconds, and the overall frequency range is separated in (1/3-) octave bands (a complete description is given in Sect. 5.3).

As a matter of principle, basic methods of GA do not cover the important wave phenomenon of sound diffraction (see Sect. 2.5), and fail to correctly simulate sound propagation from hidden sound sources to a receiver where the direct line of sight is blocked by other objects. However, there are several approaches for incorporating diffraction into deterministic and stochastic GA simulation methods. A very simple solution has been described by Maekawa [Mae68]. Additionally to the length c of the direct sound path from a sound source to a receiver, the effective path length around the obstacles $a + b$ is calculated. The detour $d = a + b - c$ is then used as input parameter for calculating a wavelength-dependent sound insulation. Unfortunately, this simple approach is too much of an approximation for auralization, but it is accurate enough in cases where rough estimations do suffice, e.g., during the planning stage of a noise barrier. Another approach is to model edge diffraction following the principle of Huygens[4]-Fresnel[5], which states that any point on a primary wavefront can be thought of as secondary sources that produce a new wavefront in the direction of propagation and that interfere with each other. The space between the source and the receiver is subdivided into concentric ellipsoids, so-called Fresnel ellipsoids [BW99]. Here, diffraction is modeled as a loss of sound energy where the energy of each Fresnel zone is summed up and scaled by a visibility factor to determine the amount of energy at the receiver position [KJM05]. An alternative approach, which is based on the Geometrical Theory of Diffraction [Kel62], is the Uniform Theory of Diffraction (UTD) [KP74]. The UTD is a high-frequency approximation and models an infinite edge as a secondary source of diffracted waves that can be reflected and diffracted again on their way to the receiver. For a given source and receiver position, the energy attenuation caused by edge diffraction is described by complex valued

---

[4]Christiaan Huygens, Dutch mathematician and physicist, 1629 - 1695.
[5]Augustin-Jean Fresnel, French physicist, 1788 - 1827.

diffraction coefficients that are computed by means of geometrical information about the shortest paths through the respective edge sequences to the receiver (following Fermat's[6] principle). A very accurate approach which makes no assumption about the frequency and (w)edge shape is the formulation for finite edges of the Biot-Tolstoy-Medwin Expression (BTME) for diffraction [BT57, Med81], which uses the concept of secondary sources. It gives an exact solution for diffraction from a rigid wedge. However, this method is inappropriate for the use in real-time applications due to its computational complexity. Fortunately, Svensson et al. derived a fast and quite exact method for the computation of edge diffraction impulse responses [SFV99] from this formulation. Here, directivity functions for these secondary sources are computed directly from geometrical information such as the wedge's open angle, edge length, and the source- and receiver position. Another diffraction model was developed by Stephenson where energy particles are bent around an obstacle following a deflection angle probability density function which is derived from Heisenberg's uncertainty principle[7] [Ste04]. This diffraction model fits perfectly to algorithms that model sound propagation as the dispersion of energy particles, such as stochastic RT. Comparisons between Svensson's and Stephenson's model have shown that both methods provide similar results [SS07], although they are based on totally different assumptions.

In multi-room situations, another aspect of sound propagation has to be taken into account: the wave phenomenon of sound transmission (see Sect. 2.4). Prediction models are well established such as the Statistical Energy Analysis (SEA) and the method applied in the European Standard EN 12354. In SEA, sound transmission in a stationary building is described by the power flow between subsystems which represent resonant systems with high modal density [LM62, CP69, CP70]. Each subsystem describes one part of the whole building structure and oscillates rather independently of other parts in the building, whereby different wave types, such as bending, longitudinal and transverse waves, are handled separately. Now, upon feeding power into one of these subsystems, part of the energy dissipates, while the remaining energy is further distributed to adjacent subsystems. A good allegory for SEA is the comparison with water containers that are interconnected via a tube system. The energy of sound sources can be seen as water that is pumped into one or many water containers and then further distributed among other connected containers. While losses from damping and radiation can be interpreted here as water leaks of the respective containers, coupling refers to the cross-section and capacity of the connecting tube [Vor08]. Although never explicitly referred to SEA, the prediction model which is used in the European Standard EN 12354 [EN97] is actually equivalent to first-order SEA, i.e., direct paths and flanking paths via one junction are taken into account for sound transmission calculations. It is mainly based on the work by Gerretsen, who developed a fundamental equation system for describing sound insulation in buildings [Ger79, Ger86] by means of fitting transmission coefficients (more details are given in Sect. 5.5).

---

[6]Pierre de Fermat, French lawyer and mathematician, 1601 - 1665.
[7]Werner Heisenberg, German physicist, 1901 - 1976.

In summary, state-of-the-art of room acoustics simulation methods are wave-based methods for frequencies below the Schroeder frequency, and hybrid methods of GA for simulations above that frequency. Hybrid methods account for both specular and diffuse reflections, and also for the wave phenomenon of sound diffraction if adequate model extensions are used. For calculating the sound transmission between coupled rooms, reliable SEA prediction models are available. Samuel Siltanen et al. recently introduced an interesting concept that aims at generalizing all these simulation methods in one integral room acoustic rendering equation [SLKS07]. So far, an acoustic radiance transfer method of GA is derived from this equation that handles specular and diffuse reflections, but a model upgrading to sound diffraction and sound transmission is planned for the future.

In real-time applications, however, a separate handling of the specular and diffuse part of the BRIR is advantageous to gain filter update rates that correspond to human perception (more details are given in the next chapter). In the following, RAVEN's fundamental prediction models for room acoustics simulation will be further discussed. In detail, they are:

- A hybrid simulation method of GA combining ISs with stochastic RT, where both methods can handle sound diffraction adapting the prediction models by Svensson and Stephenson (see Sect. 5.2 and 5.3).

- A secondary source model for sound transmission that utilizes room acoustical simulations and filter functions from interpolated spectra of transmission coefficients for rendering auralization filter networks (see Sect. 5.5).

5.2   Deterministic Image Source Method

5.2.1   General

The IS-method by Allen and Berkley [AB79] (and in its extended version by Borish [Bor84]) is a procedure for constructing specular reflections between two points, e.g., a point-like Primary Source (PS) S and a point receiver R, located inside an arbitrary polyhedral compound, e.g., a room (see Sect. 4.1). The deterministic method became very popular not only in acoustics but also in radiowave physics and in CG, because it is relatively simple. It is based upon the determination of virtual secondary sources, i.e., ISs, that can be considered to cause specular reflections (see Fig. 5.2(a)). These ISs are generated by mirroring primary/secondary point sources on the room's faces, which is a basic and simple geometrical operation and further illustrated in Fig. 5.2(b). Here, $\vec{S}$ represents the point source that is supposed to be mirrored on the plane, $\vec{n}$ the normalized plane's normal vector, $\vec{P}$ a point that lies on the plane, $\vec{r}$ the connection vector between $\vec{S}$ and $\vec{P}$, and α the angle between $\vec{n}$ and $\vec{r}$. A directed vector, which is perpendicular to the plane and ends at the point source $\vec{S}$, is required to determine the mirrored secondary point source $\vec{I}$. Obviously, this vector is the product of $\vec{n}$ with the source's distance to the plane, i.e., $\vec{n} \cdot |\vec{r}|cos(\alpha)$. The mirrored source $\vec{I}$ is

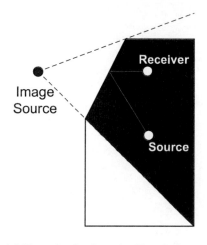

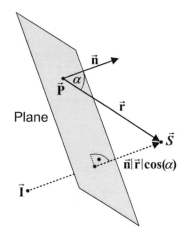

(a) Example of a first-oder IS and the respective specular reflection for the given source/receiver position. Valid reflections can only occur in the marked area.

(b) Geometrical relations for mirroring a point S on a plane.

Figure 5.2: Basic principle of constructing ISs.

subsequently computed by subtracting this directed vector two times from the origin source's position, which leads to the following equation:

$$\vec{I} = \vec{S} - 2 \cdot \vec{n} \cdot |\vec{r}| \cdot \cos(\alpha). \qquad (5.1)$$

Using this procedure, the IS methods starts by mirroring the primary source S on all room walls. Every so generated secondary source I, i.e., IS, is proceeded the same way until a predefined IS order is reached, which declares the maximum number of wall reflections. Thus, the method takes all possible plane sequence permutations into account, whereby the number of generated ISs rises exponentially with reflection order. Below, the following notation for ISs is used where the indices n and i represent the respective wall ID and the IS order, respectively, as each IS can be understood as the last element of a source chain, with

$$S \to I_{n_1} \to I_{n_1 n_2} \to I_{n_1 n_2 n_3} \to \dots \to I_{n_1 n_2 n_3 \dots n_i} \ .$$

However, only a small percentage of generated ISs are audible for a point receiver, since most of the determined specular reflections are invalid: either the wall intersections lie outside the respective wall boundaries or the sound path is blocked by other walls. Therefore, an audibility test is required which checks whether a valid specular sound path for the tested image source exists by stepping backwards from the source chain and testing if the directed connection line $\overline{I_{n_{k-i}} I_{m_{k-i-1}}}$ (at first $\overline{R I_{n_k}}$) hits a wall, i.e., a polygon that lies on the plane on which $I_{m_{k-i-1}}$ (at first I_{n_k}) was mirrored on, before it hits any other wall.

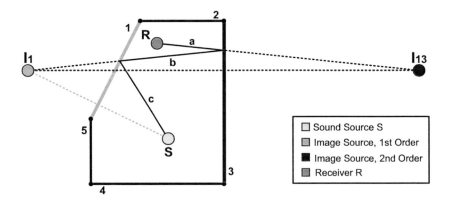

Figure 5.3: Example of an audibility test: the second-order IS I_{13} is tested by stepping back from the source chain, starting from the receiver position. The corresponding ISs are constructed by mirroring the primary source on wall element 1 (first-oder IS I_1, orange color), which is then mirrored on wall element 3 (second-order IS I_{13}, red color).

Figure 5.3 shows a simple example that serves to elucidate this procedure in more detail by testing the second-order IS I_{13} on audibility. At first, a connection line from the receiver R to the last element of the source chain, i.e., IS I_{13}, is drawn and tested if it intersects with the proper wall element on which the image source was mirrored. Here, the connection line intersects the right wall element, i.e., wall 3, where only the line segment that is enclosed by the geometry is declared as valid (see Fig. 5.3, line segment a). The audibility test proceeds with checking the next source chain's element. One step back from the source chain of IS I_{13}, a new connection line between I_1, i.e., the IS that generated I_{13}, and the last intersection point is drawn (see Fig. 5.3, line segment b). The remaining element of the source chain is the primary source S itself, as it can be interpreted as an IS of zeroth-order. The connection line $\overline{I_1 S}$ must not hit any wall element, otherwise I_{13} is not audible. In the given example this path is unblocked, which means that a specular reflected path from the primary source to the receiver exists that reflects two times on the wall element 1 and 3, respectively (see Fig. 5.3, line segment a, b, c). Hence, the IS I_{13} is audible, but only for the current source/receiver position. While a receiver movement only requires all ISs for retesting, a change of the primary source's position additionally requires a regeneration of the respective ISs.

5.2.2   Construction of the Room Impulse Response (IS)

Constructing a RIR from audible ISs is rather simple. Each reflection initially shows up as a Dirac delta function, which is delayed by the travel time and attenuated by both the wall absorption on each reflection and the absorption by air according to the travel distance (see Fig. 5.4). Additionally, if the sender or the receiver features

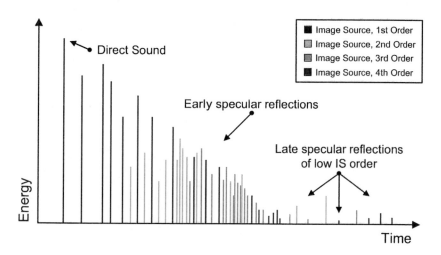

Figure 5.4: Example of a RIR constructed from a set of ISs up to fourth-order.

a non-negligible directional pattern, this information has to be added to the RIR leading to the following equation (according to [Dal95]):

$$\underline{H}_j = \frac{e^{-j\omega t_j}}{ct_j} \cdot H_{air}(ct_j) \cdot \underline{H}_{Source}(\theta, \phi) \cdot \underline{H}_{Receiver}(\vartheta, \varphi) \cdot \prod_{i=1}^{n_j} \underline{R}_i. \qquad (5.2)$$

Here, $\underline{H}_j$ denotes the spectrum of the jth reflection path, i.e., audible IS, t_j the path's delay with resulting phase shift $j\omega t_j$, $1/(ct_j)$ the distance law for spherical waves, $\underline{H}_{Source}$ the directional pattern of the PS, $\underline{H}_{Receiver}$ the directional pattern of the receiver, H_{air} the air attenuation and $\underline{R}_i$ the reflection factors of the walls that were hit by the reflection. To construct a BRIR, a pair of HRTFs that relates to the respective impact angle of the reflection is used for $\underline{H}_{Receiver}$ resulting in two impulse responses $\underline{H}_{j,L}$ and $\underline{H}_{j,R}$, one for each channel.

5.2.3 Diffraction

As a matter of principle, the traditional IS approach neglects energy that is actually bent into shadow zones caused by obstacles (see Fig.5.5) as only specular reflections on surfaces are taken into account by this method. Therefore, the IS method has to be extended for handling diffraction by introducing another type of secondary source, called Diffraction Source (DS) in the following. These DSs are located on top of each edge (see Fig.5.6, D_A and D_B) and set active if the direct path between a source (PS or IS) and a receiver is blocked in order to avoid discontinuities of the perceived sound field. This is motivated by the idea that the contribution of the diffracted waves in the view zone is small compared to the primary wave and, therefore, can be neglected in order to reduce the complexity of this diffraction model (see Sect. 2.5).

Similar to the generation of ISs for a PS, each edge along with its respective DS is mirrored on the room's surfaces up to a predefined reflection order which allows the additional computation of specular sound reflections in between the diffraction paths. In the following, these mirrored edges are called Diffraction Image Sources (DISs) (see Fig.5.6, D_{A2}, and D_{B2}).

For a fast computation of specular sound paths between PSs, ISs, DSs, DISs and the receiver, visibility information for each source can be computed and stored in tree-like data structures which allow a fast access and update at runtime (this is further described in Sect. 9.1). By means of these 'visibility trees' a path search algorithm quickly computes construction plans for impulse responses that describe the respective sound paths where the maximum reflection order is set by the user. The search algorithm

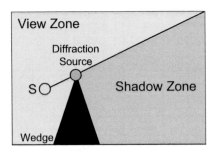

Figure 5.5: Room subdivision into view zone (yellow) and shadow zone (orange) of the PS S introducing a diffraction source that radiates into the shadow zone that is caused by a wedge.

returns a data container that carries logical and geometrical information of each audible sound path (see Fig. 5.7). Here, the sound propagation paths are decomposed into three different types of subpaths denoted by the following logical descriptors: *S2D*: Source (PS or IS) to edge (DS), *D2D*: Edge (DS or DIS) to edge (DS), and *D2R*: Edge (DS or DIS) to receiver. Using this decomposition scheme, the transfer function of each sound path can efficiently be computed in the frequency domain by multiplying the transfer function of the PS's directional pattern H_{PS} with the transfer functions

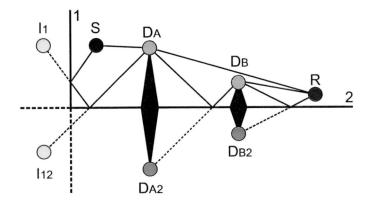

Figure 5.6: Sound paths between the PS S and the receiver R. ISs and DSs are denoted by I and D, respectively. Some sound paths are omitted for the sake of a clear arrangement.

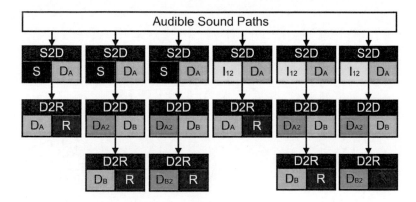

Figure 5.7: Construction plan for impulse responses extracted from edge visibility information. Each container denotes one sound path and the respective sound subpaths are described by their type (S2D, D2R and D2D), their respective sender (S, D, I) and receiver (D, R).

of each sound subpath H_n and the receiver H_R following the equation

$$H_{AudibleSoundPath_i} = H_{PS} \cdot H_R \cdot \prod_n H_n. \tag{5.3}$$

The total impulse response h_{sum} is then obtained by summing up the respective impulse responses $h_{AudibleSoundPath_i}$ in the time domain with

$$h_{sum}(t) = \sum_i h_{AudibleSoundPath_i}(t). \tag{5.4}$$

While the computation of impulse responses for subpaths of type S2R is straight forward (see above), more complex computations are required for sound paths where DSs/DISs are involved. These edge diffraction impulse responses can be derived from the BTME, which states that any point on the edge can be thought of as a secondary point source. Thus, not only the shortest path over the edge has to be taken into account, but also paths with a longer detour (see Fig.5.8(a), L_0 describes the shortest path over the edge from a source to the receiver, L_1-L_4 describe the outermost detours for both sides of the edge). The total time-discrete and decaying impulse response is determined by summing up the respective Dirac delta functions of each path via the edge. As the edge is supposed to be finite, attention has to be paid at time τ_{min} and τ_{max} which describe the delay from the source to the receiver over the edge's starting point and end point with

$$\tau_{min} = \frac{L_1 + L_2}{c} \quad \text{and} \quad \tau_{max} = \frac{L_3 + L_4}{c}. \tag{5.5}$$

The energy is reduced by half at time τ_{min} as no further pairs of secondary sources exist with the same delay, while from τ_{max} on the energy is set to zero since no

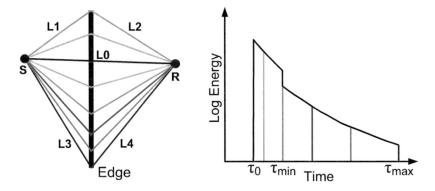

(a) Sound paths from S to R via an edge. While L_0 describes the shortest path over the edge, L_1-L_4 describe the maximum detours over the edge.

(b) Energetic edge diffraction impulse response. τ_o is the delay of the path L_0, τ_{min} and τ_{max} describe the delay from S to R over the edge's starting point and end point.

Figure 5.8: Determination of the edge diffraction impulse response.

valid secondary sources exist anymore (compare Fig.5.8(a) and Fig.5.8(b)). From this discrete formulation, an explicit expression can be derived where the impulse response at time τ is given by

$$h_{n,diff}(\tau) = \frac{-c\nu}{2 \cdot \pi} \cdot \frac{\beta(\tau)}{r_S \cdot r_R \cdot sinh(\eta(\tau))} \cdot H(\tau - \tau_0) \qquad (5.6)$$

with

$$\beta(\tau) = \beta_{++}(\tau) + \beta_{+-}(\tau) + \beta_{-+}(\tau) + \beta_{--}(\tau),$$
$$\beta_{\pm\pm}(\tau) = \frac{sin[\nu \cdot (\pi \pm \theta_S \pm \theta_R)]}{cosh[\nu \cdot \eta(\tau)] - cos[\nu \cdot (\pi \pm \theta_S \pm \theta_R)]},$$
$$\eta(\tau) = cosh^{-1}\frac{c^2 \cdot \tau^2 - (r_S^2 + r_R^2 + z_R^2)}{2 \cdot r_S \cdot r_R},$$
$$\nu = \frac{\pi}{\theta_W} \quad \text{and} \quad \tau_0 = \frac{L_0}{c},$$

where r_S, θ_S and z_S are the cylindrical coordinates of the source, r_R, θ_R and z_R are the cylindrical coordinates of the receiver, θ_w is the open angle of the edge, c is the speed of sound, ν describes the edge index , $H(\tau - \tau_0)$ is Heaviside's unit step function and the β-expressions account for sound scattering on the edge (a complete derivation of this formula is given in [Med81, SFV99]). Here, the z-components of the cylindrical coordinates are always related to the edge axis. These impulse responses are then transformed into the frequency domain to enable a fast filter computation also for sub paths where multiple diffraction edges are included (compare Equ. 5.3). Consequently, the sound path from the primary source S to the receiver R via k edges[8] is described

---

[8]The respective edges' intersection points are called apexes and are determined by spanning an elastic band from source to receiver via the edges.

by k impulse responses of type $h_{n,diff}$, where each impulse response represents one segment of the complete sound path.

In order to conveniently describe these sub-paths, the connection lines between apexes are further subdivided by additional receivers which are located in the middle of each path between two apexes. An example is given in Fig. 5.9. Here, the transfer function H_n from S to R via two edges (this relates to the logical sub path descriptors S2D, D2D and D2R) is determined by multiplying two edge diffraction transfer functions (computed as described above), whereby $H_{1,diff}$ describes the path from S via the first edge to an additional receiver M, and $H_{2,diff}$ describes the path from M via the second edge to R. It should be pointed out here that this is certainly an approximation. Second-order diffraction would be implemented correctly by summing up all little contributions from every edge element on Edge 1 via all edge elements on Edge 2

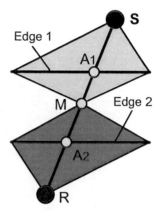

Figure 5.9: Edge-to-edge situation. The additional receiver and the edges' apexes are denoted by M, A_1, and A_2.

into one second-order diffraction expression, but this would increase the computational complexity extremely.

5.3 Stochastic Ray Tracing

5.3.1 General

Stochastic RT emulates the propagation of a sound impulse from a sound source by means of energy particles which travel on discrete rays, become reflected on geometric objects, and are detected by receivers in order to compute the respective energy envelope of the RIR (see Fig. 5.10(a)). The simulation starts by emitting a finite number of particles that are evenly distributed on the source's surface and travel with the speed of sound (derived from the room's temperature, humidity and air pressure [Cra93]). Each particle carries a certain amount of energy that depends on the source's directional pattern (see Sect. 3.1). While propagating, each particle loses energy due to air absorption and occurring reflections, i.e., material-dependent absorption and scattering of sound.

These reflections are either *specular*, that is, the angle of incidence is equal to the angle of reflection, or *diffuse*, that is, in random direction. This is decided by comparing a random number between $\{0,1\}$ with the scattering coefficient s of the hit object. The scattered energy is usually assumed to be distributed according to Lambert's[9] cosine law, i.e., the intensity of a reflected particle on an ideal diffuse

---

[9]Lambert, J. H., Swiss mathematician, physicist and astronomer, 1728 - 1777

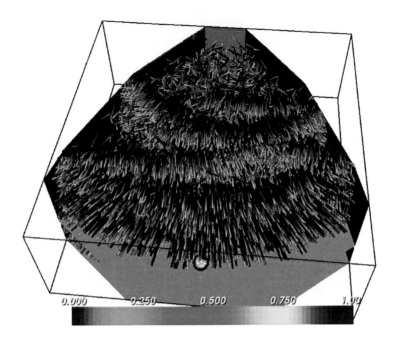

(a) Visualization of propagating energy particles within a room.

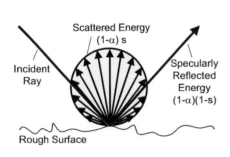

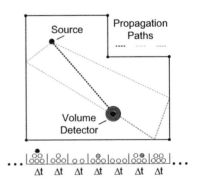

(b) Illustration of the separation of reflected energy into scattered and specular components (according to Vorländer and Mommertz [VM00]).

(c) Simple example: three energy particles propagate inside a room and are detected by a receiver. The particle energy is sorted into the detector histogram according to the particle's travel time and frequency.

Figure 5.10: Basic principle of Ray Tracing.

scattering wall is independent of the angle of incidence but proportional to the cosine of the angle of reflection [Kut00]. However, angle-dependent energy distributions are also applicable and should be used to describe special types of geometries that scatter in a preferred direction [CDD+06]. As it follows from the definition of the scattering coefficient (see Sect. 2.3), the factor s has to be taken into account for the energy attenuation of each particle in addition to the absorption coefficient α (see Sect. 2.2). Therefore, the particle's energy is weighted with s if the reflection was diffuse and with $(1-s)$ if the reflection was specular (see Fig. 5.10(b)). Each particle is traced until a predefined termination condition is fulfilled, e.g., exceeded simulation length or under-run of a minimum particle's energy threshold.

In contrast to the IS method, receivers are represented by detectors that have either a volume or a surface, as the probability for hitting a point-like receiver in a 3D space with a finite number of particles is equal to zero. Whenever a particle hits a detector, the current particle's energy, angle of incidence, and running time is logged and stored in the respective entry of the detector's *particle histogram* (see Fig. 5.10(c)). The histogram is organized as a clustered container of time slots Δt, where the size of Δt should be orientated to the time resolution of human hearing and the desired relative energy variance. Hence, Δt should be selected in the range of a few milliseconds, whereby the detection resolution can be reduced over time allowing greater Δt for the late part of the impulse response and vice versa. Since material data (absorption- and scattering coefficients), directional patterns of emitting sources, and the energy attenuation by air are strongly frequency-dependent, RT can only be performed for a certain frequency. Thus, a complete RT comprises not only one but several cycles where the center frequencies of either octave bands or one-third octave band are usually chosen as simulation frequencies resulting in 10 and 31 cycles, respectively, for the audible frequency range. From this one receives a three dimensional histogram from the ray tracing simulation, with k time slots of length Δt on the abscissa, the n frequency bands on the ordinate and the time- and frequency-dependent energies $E(k, n)$ on the applicate. These values can either be seen as temporal energy distribution $E_n(k)$ for a certain frequency band or as short-time spectral energy density $E_k(n)$ for a time slot Δt. In the following, the term *histogram* will refer to this type of data structure and can be regarded as the temporal envelope of the energetic spatial impulse response.

5.3.2 Diffuse Rain

In Monte Carlo methods, such as RT, stochastic fluctuations occur in the simulation results, which are mostly dependent on the number of energy particles, the mean reflection rate of the room, and the detector size (more details are given in [Vor08]). Diffuse rain now offers a concept to lower the number of necessary particles without increasing these errors [Hei94, SDV07, PSV11]. Similar to radiosity, each diffuse reflection causes a secondary radiation starting from the respective particle's point of intersection in direction to the detector. The additional energy obtained by the detector depends on the wall's absorption- and scattering coefficients, the distribution of scattered energy, e.g., following a Lambert distribution (see Fig. 5.11), and the detector's hit probability P_{Hit}.

This hit probability is influenced by the detector's size, distance to the particle's point of intersection, and overall position. The total hit probability is determined by integrating the respective probability density function $w(\theta)$ over the solid angle $\Omega = A/r^2$, which is formed by the contour A of the receiver projected onto a sphere with radius r around the intersection point, with

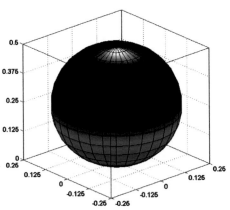

$$P_{\text{Hit}} = a \cdot \iint_\Omega w(\theta)d\Omega. \qquad (5.7)$$

Here, the total hit probability P_{Hit} of the complete half space (that re-

Figure 5.11: Lambert distribution, $cos(\theta)$.

lates to a solid angle of 2π) must be exactly *one*. Before taking a look at a Lambert distribution, a uniform distribution of the density function is assumed first $(w(\theta) = 1)$ to determine the required compensation factor a for the solid angle. In a mathematical notation, the integral over the complete half space in spherical coordinates can be expressed by:

$$P_{\text{Hit},equal} = a \cdot \iint_\Omega w(\theta)d\Omega = a \cdot \int_0^{2\pi} \int_0^{\pi/2} 1 \cdot sin(\theta)d\theta d\varphi \qquad (5.8)$$

$$= a \cdot \int_0^{2\pi} -cos(\theta)|_0^{\pi/2} \, d\varphi = a \cdot \int_0^{2\pi} 1 \cdot d\varphi \qquad (5.9)$$

$$= a \cdot 2\pi \overset{!}{=} 1 \rightarrow a = \frac{1}{2\pi}. \qquad (5.10)$$

In case of a Lambert distribution with $w(\theta) = b \cdot cos(\theta)$, where b denotes a second compensation factor, the integral then follows to

$$P_{\text{Hit}} = a \cdot \iint_\Omega b \cdot cos(\theta)d\Omega = a \cdot \int_0^{2\pi} \int_0^{\pi/2} b \cdot cos(\theta) \cdot sin(\theta)d\theta d\varphi \quad (5.11)$$

$$= a \cdot b \cdot \int_0^{2\pi} -\frac{1}{2} \cdot cos^2(\theta)\Big|_0^{\pi/2} \, d\varphi = a \cdot b \cdot \int_0^{2\pi} \frac{1}{2}d\varphi \qquad (5.12)$$

$$= a \cdot 2\pi \cdot b \cdot \frac{1}{2} \overset{!}{=} 1 \rightarrow b = 2. \qquad (5.13)$$

Now the crucial part is to find an appropriate approximation for this equation for arbitrary solid angles since an analytic computation is too complex, especially when keeping in mind that this has to be computed for millions of diffuse-reflected energy particles at runtime. The angle-dependent Lambert distribution is therefore replaced by a constant term in order to reduce the complexity of the respective integral equation. A good approximation is to evaluate this distribution only for a fixed angle

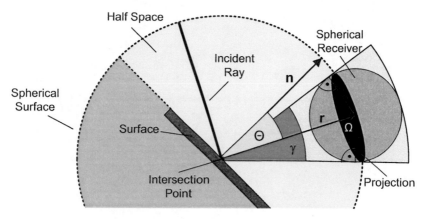

Figure 5.12: Diffuse rain on a spherical receiver.

Θ, which is the angle between the surface normal and the connection vector $\vec{r}$ between the intersection point and the receiver's centroid, where the hit probability P_{Hit} follows to

$$P_{\text{Hit}} = P_{\text{Hit},equal} \cdot P_{Lambert}(\Theta). \tag{5.14}$$

Here, the produced error decreases with larger distances between the intersection point and the receiver, since the seen angle range $\sphericalangle\ \theta$ becomes increasingly smaller over distance. Furthermore, good approximations for the solid angle are required, which will be discussed in the following for three types of receivers: spherical, cylindrical and plane detectors.

Spherical Detectors

Finding a good approximation for spherical detectors is relatively simple, because a sphere has always the same visible surface from any point of view and, as mentioned above, the solid angle depends only on the detector's size and distance to the particle's point of intersection (see Fig 5.12). Assuming the scattered energy is equally distributed in the half space, the hit probability for a certain solid angle can be calculated as follows:

$$P_{\text{Hit},equal} = a \cdot \frac{A_{Intersection}}{r^2} = \frac{1}{2\pi} \cdot \frac{A_{Intersection}}{r^2}, \tag{5.15}$$

with $A_{Intersection}$ representing the intersection area with a half sphere around the particle's intersection point with radius r, which is the distance between the intersection point and the center of the spherical detector. Including Lambert's probability distribution, the total hit probability of a spherical detector then is

$$P_{\text{Hit}} = P_{\text{Hit},equal} \cdot P_{Lambert}(\Theta) = a \cdot \frac{A_{Intersection}}{r^2} \cdot b \cdot cos(\Theta), \tag{5.16}$$

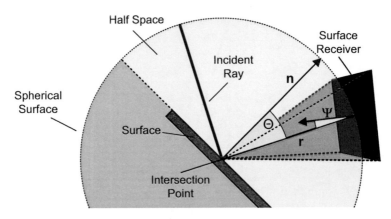

Figure 5.13: Diffuse Rain on a surface receiver.

which directly leads to an equation for the detected scattered energy E_s with

$$E_s = E_P \cdot (1 - \alpha) \cdot s \cdot P_{\text{Hit}} \cdot e^{-m \cdot r} \tag{5.17}$$

$$= E_P \cdot (1 - \alpha) \cdot s \cdot a \cdot \frac{A_{Intersection}}{r^2} \cdot b \cdot cos(\Theta) \cdot e^{-m \cdot r} \tag{5.18}$$

$$= E_P \cdot (1 - \alpha) \cdot s \cdot \frac{1}{2\pi} \cdot \frac{2\pi \cdot r^2(1 - cos\frac{\gamma}{2})}{r^2} \cdot 2 \cdot cos(\Theta) \cdot e^{-m \cdot r} \tag{5.19}$$

$$= E_P \cdot (1 - \alpha) \cdot s \cdot (1 - cos\frac{\gamma}{2}) \cdot 2 \cdot cos(\Theta) \cdot e^{-m \cdot r}, \tag{5.20}$$

where E_P denotes the energy of the particle short before it hits the wall, α and s denote the absorption and scattering coefficients of the wall, γ the opening angle, r the distance from the particle's intersection point to the center of the spherical detector, Θ denotes the angle between the wall's normal and $\vec{r}$, and $e^{-m \cdot r}$ the respective energy attenuation by air over a distance r. Since geometrical relations are analytically exact, the only approximation in the case of spherical receivers is the assumed fixed Lambert distribution, which, however, is a good approximation in the far field (see above).

Surface Detectors

In the case of two dimensional plane detectors (portals are used as surface detectors, see Sect. 5.5), the computation of an exact solid angle is infeasible under real-time constraints, since that would require the complex determination of projections of arbitrary-shaped polygons on a spherical surface. Instead, the hit probability of the detector surface can be approximated well by using the volume of a pyramid built by the detector surface and the intersection point $V_{Pyramid}$ in relation to the volume of the half sphere around the intersection point $V_{HalfSphere}$ (see Fig. 5.13)[10]. The total

---

[10]The comparison of volumes instead of areas minimizes the overall estimation error.

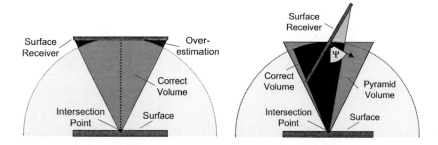

(a) The pyramid volume slightly overesti- **(b)** Change of the irradiated detector area ac-
mates the correct volume (red area). cording to the surface orientation.

Figure 5.14: Estimation of the systematic error due to the pyramid volume approximation.

hit probability of a surface receiver then is:

$$P_{\text{Hit}} = P_{\text{Hit,equal}} \cdot P_{Lambert}(\Theta) = \frac{V_{Pyramid}}{V_{HalfSphere}} \cdot cos(\Psi) \cdot 2 \cdot cos(\Theta), \qquad (5.21)$$

where the second cosine term $cos(\Psi)$ scales the hit probability of the detector area
according to the surface orientation. This is required as the volume of the pyramid
and, thus, the hit probability is independent of the orientation of the detector area,
but the irradiated (or seen) area changes over the orientation angle of the detector
surface (see Fig. 5.14). Here, the pyramid volume slightly overestimates the correct
volume, but this can be neglected for large distances between the intersection point
and the receiver, which is assumed anyway for the Lambert distribution. From this
it follows that the detected scattered energy E_s can be described by

$$
\begin{aligned}
E_s &= E_P \cdot (1 - \alpha) \cdot s \cdot P_{\text{Hit}} \cdot e^{-m \cdot r} && (5.22) \\
&= E_P \cdot (1 - \alpha) \cdot s \cdot \frac{V_{Pyramid}}{V_{HalfSphere}} \cdot cos(\Psi) \cdot 2 \cdot cos(\Theta) \cdot e^{-m \cdot r} && (5.23) \\
&= E_P \cdot (1 - \alpha) \cdot s \cdot \frac{A}{2\pi \cdot r^2} \cdot cos(\Psi) \cdot cos(\Theta) \cdot e^{-m \cdot r} && (5.24)
\end{aligned}
$$

with E_P denoting the particle's impacting energy on the wall, α and s the respective
absorption and scattering coefficients of the surface material, A the detector area, r
the distance between the intersection point and the portal centroid, Θ and Ψ the angle
between $\vec{r}$ and the surface's and detector's normal vector, respectively, and $e^{-m \cdot r}$
the energy attenuation by air on a distance r.

Cylindrical Detectors

Assuming again an equal distribution of scattered energy on a conceived half sphere
around the intersection point, the total hit probability of a cylindrical detector can
be described similar to that of surface detectors (cylindrical detectors are used for

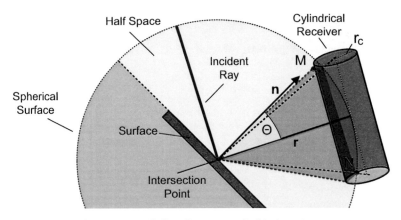

Figure 5.15: Diffuse Rain on a cylindrical receiver.

the simulation of edge diffraction, see next subsection), with

$$P_{Hit} = P_{\text{Hit},equal} \cdot P_{Lambert}(\Theta) = \frac{V_{Pyramid}}{V_{HalfSphere}} \cdot P_{Lambert}(\Theta). \qquad (5.25)$$

Here, the cylinders's hit probability $P_{\text{Hit},equal}$ is approximated by the ratio between the volume of the half sphere around the intersection point and the volume of a pyramid with

$$V_{Pyramid} = \frac{1}{3} \cdot A \cdot r = \frac{1}{3} \cdot 2 \cdot r_c \cdot |N - M| \cdot r, \qquad (5.26)$$

where N and M are the intersection points on a sphere with the connection lines between the particle's intersection point I and the cylinder's starting point and end point, respectively (see Fig 5.15). From this it follows that the detected energy of the secondary particle, which was shot in direction of the visible cylindrical detector, can be assumed to be:

$$E_s = E_P \cdot (1 - \alpha) \cdot s \cdot \frac{r_c \cdot |N - M|}{\pi \cdot r^2} \cdot 2 \cdot cos(\Theta) \cdot e^{-m \cdot r}, \qquad (5.27)$$

with E_P denoting the impacting energy on the wall, α the wall absorption coefficient, and s the wall scattering coefficient. It can be shown that the inherent systemic error in this approximation is also negligible in the case of cylindrical receivers (more details are given in [Poh08], pp. 80).

5.3.3   Diffracted Rain

To extend the stochastic RT method for edge diffraction additional finite cylindrical detectors, called deflection cylinder (DC), are used in the following. Whereas the cylinder's axis is always identical with the respective edge, the cylinder's radius depends on the current frequency with $r = 7\lambda$ (see Fig.5.16(a)). If a DC is hit by an

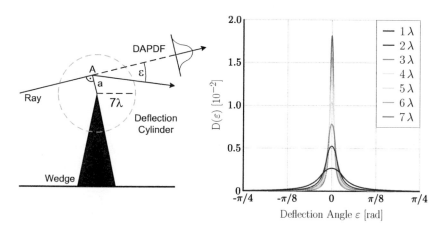

(a) The edge's influence on the particle is described by the DAPDF.

(b) Deflection angle probability density function as function of v.

Figure 5.16: Determination of the edge diffraction impulse response.

energy particle, the edge's influence on the particle, in terms of diffraction strength in relation to the shortest fly-by distance of the particle, can be described by a 2D-Deflection Angle Probability Density Function (DAPDF), proposed by Stephenson in [Ste04, SS07]. The DAPDF (see Fig.5.16(b)) is derived from the Fraunhofer expression for diffraction at a slit and is defined as

$$D(v) = D_0 \cdot \left\{ \begin{array}{ll} 1 - v^2 & \text{if } |v| \le v_0 \\ \frac{1/2}{\sqrt{2} - 1 + v^2} & \text{if } |v| > v_0, \end{array} \right\} \tag{5.28}$$

with

$$v_0 = \sqrt{1 - \frac{1}{\sqrt{2}}} \approx 0.5412 \quad \text{and} \quad v = 2 \cdot b \cdot \epsilon$$

where b is the apparent slit width, ϵ is the deflection angle and D_0 is a normalization factor such that the integral over all deflection angles is 1. It can be shown that $b = 6a$ turns out to be a good approximation for a particle that passes only one edge instead of a slit, where a describes the shortest distance between the edge and the particle's propagation path (see Fig.5.16(a)). With $v_{low} = 2 \cdot b \cdot \epsilon_{low}$ and $v_{high} = 2 \cdot b \cdot \epsilon_{high}$, $D(v)$ can be integrated piecewise:

$v_{low} < -v_0$ and $v_{high} < -v_0$

$$D_0 \cdot \left[\frac{1}{3} \cdot \left(v_{low}^3 - v_{high}^3 \right) + \left(v_{high} - v_{low} \right) \right] \tag{5.29}$$

$v_{low} < -v_0$ and $|v_{high}| \leq v_0$

$$D_0 \cdot \left[\frac{1}{3} \cdot \left(v_0^3 + v_{low}^3 \right) - (v_0 + v_{low}) + \frac{1}{2 \cdot \sqrt{2} \cdot v_0} \left(\arctan \frac{v_{high}}{\sqrt{2} \cdot v_0} + \arctan \frac{1}{\sqrt{2}} \right) \right]$$

$$(5.30)$$

$v_{low} < -v_0$ and $v_{high} > v_0$

$$D_0 \cdot \left[\frac{1}{3} \cdot \left(2 \cdot v_0^3 + v_{low}^3 - v_{high}^3 \right) - (2 \cdot v_0 + v_{low} - v_{high}) + \frac{1}{\sqrt{2} \cdot v_0} \arctan \frac{1}{\sqrt{2}} \right]$$

$$(5.31)$$

$|v_{low}| \leq v_0$ and $|v_{high}| \leq v_0$

$$D_0 \cdot \left[\arctan \frac{v_{high}}{\sqrt{2} \cdot v_0} - \arctan \frac{v_{low}}{\sqrt{2} \cdot v_0} \right] \tag{5.32}$$

$|v_{low}| \leq v_0$ and $v_{high} > v_0$

$$D_0 \cdot \left[\frac{1}{3} \left(v_0^3 - v_{high}^3 \right) - (v_0 - v_{high}) \right] + \left[\frac{1}{2 \cdot \sqrt{2} \cdot v_0} \left(\arctan \frac{1}{\sqrt{2}} - \arctan \frac{v_{low}}{\sqrt{2} \cdot v_0} \right) \right]$$

$$(5.33)$$

$v_{low} > v_0$ and $v_{high} > v_0$

$$D_0 \left[\frac{1}{3} \left(v_{low}^3 - v_{high}^3 \right) + (v_{high} - v_{low}) \right] \tag{5.34}$$

In the traditional interpretation, each impacting particle energy has to be logged and further distributed among a large number of outgoing secondary energy particles to keep occurring stochastic fluctuations to a minimum. To overcome the complexity of this time-exploding approach, a selective transfer of sound energy to other Deflection Cylinders (DCs) and detection spheres is used, called *diffracted rain* in the following (see Fig.5.17). Here, the energy portion of a certain angle field $\Delta \epsilon$ can be calculated by integrating $D(\epsilon, b)$ over the respective angle range. Thus, the outgoing energy is dispersed on a plane which is described by the normal vector $\vec{n}$, with

$$\vec{n} = \vec{D}_{Ray} \times \vec{N}_{Edge} \tag{5.35}$$

and a point A which lies on that plane. In Equ. 5.35, $\vec{N}_{Edge}$ describes the bisecting line of the wedge, located on top of the edge and pointing into the room, and $\vec{D}_{Ray}$ the particles's direction vector. Any visible object (DC or R) that intersects with this plane in direction of sound propagation detects an energy portion according to

$$E_{out} = E_{in} \cdot e^{-m \cdot h} \cdot \int_{\epsilon_{min}}^{\epsilon_{max}} D(\epsilon, b) d\epsilon \tag{5.36}$$

with

$$\epsilon_{min} = \phi - \epsilon_1 \quad \text{and} \quad \epsilon_{max} = \phi + \epsilon_2 \quad . \tag{5.37}$$

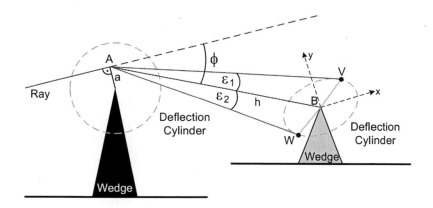

Figure 5.17: Diffracted rain for an edge-to-edge situation using the 2D-DAPDF. The outgoing energy is dispersed on a plane which intersects with a second DC.

If a detection sphere is hit, the intersection between the plane and the sphere is always a circle. The angles ϵ_1 and ϵ_2 are identical and easily calculated by:

$$\epsilon_1 = \epsilon_2 = arcsin(\frac{r_{sphere}}{h}), \tag{5.38}$$

where r_{sphere} is the sphere's radius, and h is the distance between A and the center of the intersection B. In the case of a deflection cylinder the intersection between the plane and the cylinder is always elliptical which leads to:

$$\epsilon_1 = arccos\left(\frac{(V - A) \circ (B - A)}{|V - A| \cdot |B - A|}\right) \tag{5.39}$$

$$\epsilon_2 = arccos\left(\frac{(W - A) \circ (B - A)}{|W - A| \cdot |B - A|}\right) \tag{5.40}$$

where V and W describe the osculation points of the tangent lines to the respective intersection (compare Fig.5.17). This selective transfer of energy, i.e., the diffracted rain, can be performed recursively until a user-defined depth is reached, meaning that any DC can forward the received energy to other visible detectors (detection spheres, portals and DCs) that intersect with the plane in sound propagation direction. The diffuse rain method (see Sect. 5.3.2) is proceeded in the same way where subsequently each DC which is hit by a secondary particle further distributes the impacted scattered energy as described above. In a subsequent step, the detected energy particle is 'bent' around the edge according to the respective distance a and travels further until it hits a surface or other detectors, whereby direct hits of detectors that were already covered by the diffracted rain are skipped.

5.3.4   Construction of the Room Impulse Response (RT)

As mentioned above, a detector's energy histogram represents only the energy envelope of the RIR. While many room acoustical parameters, e.g., reverberation time
and clarity, can be easily calculated from such histograms, they cannot be applied
directly to auralization due to the lack of an appropriate temporal resolution. However, the RIR's temporal fine structure can be synthesized well by means of a Poisson[11]-distributed noise process [Hei94]. By assuming a sound reflection as event, the
probability $w_n(\Delta t)$ of the occurrence of n events in a time interval Δt is given by

$$w_n(\Delta t) = \frac{(\mu \Delta t)^n}{n!} e^{-\mu \Delta t} \qquad n = 0, 1, 2, ..., \ \mu > 0, \ \Delta t \geq 0, \tag{5.41}$$

where μ denotes the mean event occurrence. On the other hand, a time interval $\Delta_A t$
of two consecutive events of a temporal Poisson process is exponentially distributed
and the associated density distribution $w(\Delta t_A)$ follows [Ros70]

$$w(\Delta t_A) d\Delta t_A = \mu e^{-\mu \Delta t_A} d\Delta t_A. \tag{5.42}$$

Using this equation, the interval size Δt_A can be derived as a function of a uniformly
distributed random number z, leading to

$$\Delta t_A(z) = \frac{1}{\mu} ln\left(\frac{1}{z}\right) \qquad 0 < z \leq 1, \tag{5.43}$$

where the mean event occurrence μ relates to the mean reflection density of the room
with

$$\mu = \frac{4\pi c^3 t^2}{V}. \tag{5.44}$$

Based on this equation, the noise process can be synthesized by using Dirac delta
functions with constant magnitude as random events. Starting at a time

$$t_0 = \sqrt[3]{\frac{2V \ln 2}{4\pi c^3}} \approx 0,0014 \sqrt[3]{V}, \tag{5.45}$$

which describes the minimum time between $t + \Delta t_A$, the sequence of Dirac deltas is
consecutively generated using Equ. 5.43 until a maximum length is reached [Dro06,
Pel07]. In order to adapt to the sampling frequency of the RIR, the Dirac deltas are
optionally signed counting Dirac deltas positive and negative in the temporal first
and second half of a sample, respectively, and restricting the number of Dirac deltas
per sample to one (see Fig. 5.18(a)). Furthermore, μ can be kept at a maximum
of $\mu = 10,000 \ s^{-1}$ without generating acoustical artifacts such as rattling [Hei94].
In the following, these sequences of Dirac deltas are the basis for constructing both
monaural and binaural RIRs.

Monaural Room Impulse Response

With regard to real-time auralization, the monaural RIR can efficiently be constructed
by preprocessing bandpass-filtered Dirac delta sequences that are weighted online with

---

[11]Poisson, S.-D., French mathematician, geometer, and physicist, 1781-1840

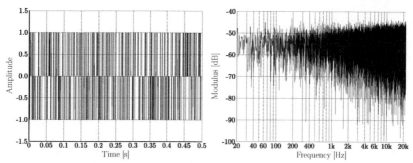

(a) Generated Poisson-distributed sequence of Dirac deltas in time domain.

(b) Transfer function of the Poisson-distributed sequence of Dirac deltas.

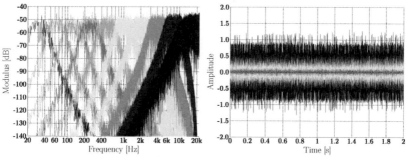

(c) Octave-filtering of the sequence in frequency domain.

(d) Octave-filtered sequence in time domain.

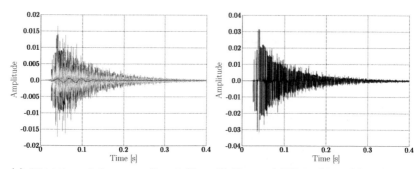

(e) Weighting of the octave-filtered Dirac delta sequence by the energy envelope of the RIR.

(f) The total RIR is obtained by summing up the weighted octave-filtered Dirac Delta sequence.

Figure 5.18: Construction of a monaural RIR (exemplary with octave-band filtering).

the simulated energy envelope of the RIR. Consequently, the Dirac delta sequence h_d (see Fig. 5.18(a)) is transformed to frequency domain (see Fig. 5.18(b)) and filtered by an asymmetrical high/low-pass-combination with differing slope and shape of a Raised Cosine Filter $RCF(n)$ with

$$RCF(n) = \begin{cases} 0 & \text{if } f \ < f_{low} \\ \frac{1}{2}\left(1 + \cos\left(\frac{2\pi f}{f_n}\right)\right) & \text{if } f_{low} \leq f < f_n \\ \frac{1}{2}\left(1 - \cos\left(\frac{2\pi f}{f_{n+1}}\right)\right) & \text{if } f_n \ \leq f < f_{high} \\ 0 & \text{if } f \ \geq f_{high}, \end{cases} \tag{5.46}$$

where f_n denotes the center frequency of the nth frequency band, and f_{low} and f_{high} describe the lower and upper limit of the frequency band, respectively (see Fig. 5.18(c)). Then the filtered spectrum is transformed back to the time domain resulting in n bandpass-filtered Dirac delta sequences $h_d(n)$ (see Fig. 5.18(d)). As long as the volume of the room does not change drastically, these sequences have to be computed only once, which can be accomplished during a preprocessing step of the simulation. The monaural RIR $s(i)$ can then be quickly constructed online by weighting $h_d(n)$ sample-wise with

$$s_i = v_i \cdot \sqrt{\frac{E_n(k)}{\sum_{i=g(k-1)+1}^{g(k)} v_i^2}} \cdot \sqrt{\frac{BW}{f_s/2}} \tag{5.47}$$

$$\text{with} \quad g(k) = \lfloor k \cdot f_s \cdot \Delta t \rfloor,$$

where Δt denotes the length of the histogram's time slot, v_i the value of the ith sample of $h_d(n)$, f_s the sampling frequency, BW the width of the regarded frequency band n, and $E_n(k)$ the energy of the histogram's k^{th} time slot that relates to the ith sample (see Fig. 5.18(e)). In a final step, summing up all weighted noise sequences in the time domain leads to the overall monaural RIR(see Fig. 5.18(f)).

Binaural Room Impulse Response

Constructing a BRIR from a detector's energy histogram is somewhat more complex compared to the monaural case. For a human receiver, HRIRs that relate to the directions of incoming sound reflections have to be additionally taken into account. Instead of assuming an ideal diffuse sound field where the direction of arriving sound reflections is totally randomized, *binaural detectors* can be used in order to gather temporal and spectral information on impacting energy particles in a more realistic way. RAVEN's binaural detector is modeled as a sphere with head-related coordinate system, where the sphere's surface is subdivided into m discrete Directivity Groups (DGs) with a certain resolution in azimuth- and elevation direction. Energy particles are assigned to these groups depending on their angle of impact and resulting in m energy histograms, one for each directivity group (see Fig. 5.19(1)).

From this data, a hit probability for each DG can be calculated by averaging and comparing slot-wise the respective histograms' short time spectra $E_k(n)$, whereby high energy leads to high probability and vice versa (see Fig. 5.19(2)). During the

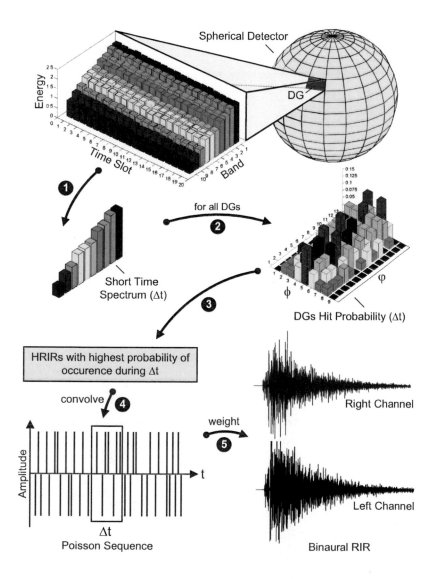

Figure 5.19: Construction of a BRIR using a binaural detector.

generation of the noise process (see above), a uniformly distributed random number z between $\{0,1\}$ is additionally drawn for each Dirac delta in order to select HRIRs according to the time-dependent DGs hit probability. This ensures that also HRIRs are taken into account with a lower probability of occurrence leading to an improved diffuseness of the late part of the BRIR. The pairs of Dirac deltas and HRIRs are then convolved with each other; this is a simple operation since the neutral Dirac delta just causes a delay d of the HRIRs that can be expressed by

$$HRIR_{s,r}(i) = \delta(i - d) * HRIR_r(i) \tag{5.48}$$

$$HRIR_{s,l}(i) = \delta(i - d) * HRIR_l(i), \tag{5.49}$$

with $HRIR_{s,r}(i)$ and $HRIR_{s,l}(i)$ denoting the time-shifted HRIRs, $\delta(i - d)$ the displaced Dirac delta, and $HRIR_r(i)$ and $HRIR_l(i)$ the HRIRs of the right and left channel (see Fig. 5.19(3,4)). Summing up the respective time-shifted HRIRs results in two noise sequences, $s_{Noise,r}(t)$ and $s_{Noise,l}(t)$, that now include spatial information of impacting sound reflections.

In a final step, the two noise sequences are weighted in order to obtain the overall BRIR. Thus, fragments of the noise sequences are subsequently cut out using a Hanning window with an overlap of fifty percent of the window length[12]. Each noise fragment is transformed into the frequency domain and then multiplied by the corresponding spectral magnitude of the detector's total histogram, which is built from the sum of all DG histograms. Here, the spectral energy density relates to the spectral amplitude density as follows:

$$E(f) \sim |S(f)|^2 \;\; , \;\; \mathscr{F}\{s(t)\} = |S(f)| \, e^{j\phi(f)}, \tag{5.50}$$

with $|S(f)|$ denoting the spectral magnitude with the associated phase $\phi(f)$. Thus, the square root of these values serves as the time slot's spectral magnitude. As the ray tracer determines only the mean statistical energy for discrete frequency bands, these values are linearly interpolated[13] according to the sampling rate and size of the time interval. In a final step, the weighted noise fragments are transformed back to the time domain where they are inserted into the resulting BRIR with an overlap of fifty percent due to the applied windowing (see Fig. 5.19(5)).

5.4   Hybrid Room Acoustics Simulation

As mentioned earlier, a hybrid room acoustics simulation is a symbiotic combination of simulation models in order to improve the overall simulation. When combining deterministic ISs with the stochastic energy particle model of the RT, attention has to be paid to two things: first, reflections must not be detected twice which means that specular reflections that come from the IS model must be excluded from the RT

---

[12]The window length is usually orientated to the size of a time slot Δt.

[13]With regard to real-time applications, a cubic-spline interpolation was omitted due to the higher computational complexity.

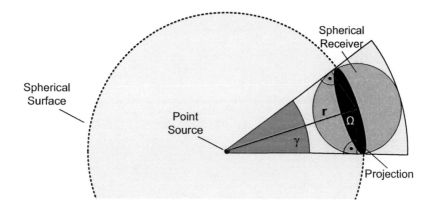

Figure 5.20: Sound source and spherical receiver under free-field conditions.

in order to preserve a correct energy balance. This also means that, in addition to pure diffuse reflections, the ray tracer only has to detect particles which have been specularly reflected with a diffuse history as long as pure specular reflections are covered by the IS model. However, no further restrictions apply for the RT above the maximum IS reflection order by taking into account all possible permutations of reflection types (e.g., diffuse, specular, diffuse, diffuse, etc.). Second, the underlying energy models have to match each other, thereby providing correct relative levels for both simulation types. This level calibration between IS and RT is easily performed by considering the detection of direct sound by a receiver with distance r to a sound source in free-field conditions, where the detected energy E_{IS} and E_{RT} needs to be equal for both models, with

$$E_{\mathrm{IS}} \;=\; E_{source} \cdot \frac{1}{r^2} \cdot e^{-mr} \tag{5.51}$$

for the IS-method and

$$E_{\mathrm{RT}} \;=\; E_p \cdot N \cdot \frac{1}{4\pi} \cdot \frac{A_{Intersection}}{r^2} \cdot e^{-mr} \tag{5.52}$$

$$=\; E_p \cdot N \cdot \frac{1}{2} \cdot \left(1 - cos\frac{\gamma}{2}\right) \cdot e^{-mr} \tag{5.53}$$

for RT with E_{source} denoting the initial energy of the IS of zeroth-order, r the distance between sound source and receiver, e^{-mr} the attenuation by air absorption, E_p the energy of one energy particle, N the number of launched energy particles and γ the open angle to the spherical detector (see Fig. 5.20). Here, $\frac{1}{2}(1 - cos\frac{\gamma}{2})$ indicates the receiver's hit probability by assuming a uniform distribution of energy particles in space (see Sect. 5.3.2). From this it follows that – under the prerequisite of $E_{\mathrm{IS}} = E_{\mathrm{RT}}$ – the energy of each launched particle has to be scaled by:

$$E_p = \frac{2 \cdot E_{source}}{N \cdot r^2 \cdot \left(1 - cos\frac{\gamma}{2}\right)}. \tag{5.54}$$

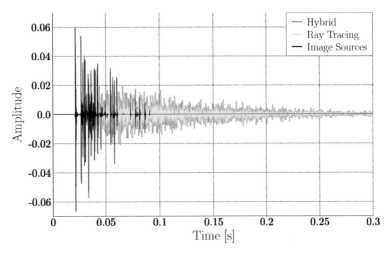

Figure 5.21: Superposition of RIR parts that come from a hybrid room acoustic simulation, using the IS method for modeling pure specular reflections and stochastic RT for the diffuse part of the response.

It should be noted that a specular reflection that comes from the image source model contains energy information for each frequency band at the same time, where E_{source} denotes the energy *per band*. With n being the number of frequency bands, the total energy of IS is $E_{IS} = n \cdot E_{source}$. In the ray tracing model, however, every launched particle belongs to one individual frequency band resulting in $N_{RT} = n \cdot N$ for all frequency bands. Two separate RIRs are computed by the hybrid simulation approach, where $h_{IS}(t)$ represents the direct sound and specular reflections up to the applied IS reflection order, and $h_{RT}(t)$ includes all reflections with a diffuse history[14]. Since methods of GA apply the superposition of sound pressure signals of single reflections at the receiver, the resulting RIR $h_{hybrid}(t)$ is simply the sum of both RIRs, i.e., $h_{hybrid}(t) = h_{IS}(t) + h_{RT}(t)$. An example is given in Fig.5.21.

5.5 Simulation of Sound Propagation between Rooms

5.5.1 Sound Transmission Model

Considering a walk through a complex of buildings, the user will typically be faced with a multitude of sounds originating from sound sources inside the user's room, but also from sound sources located in adjacent rooms. When a source emits sound inside a room, airborne sound impacts on the room's structural elements and becomes

---

[14]This certainly includes also purely specular reflections that are not covered by the IS method.

transformed into waves (in particular, bending waves). These waves are transmitted throughout the building structure by propagating from one element to another, whereby sound energy particularly flows through elements of low sound insulation such as doors. In turn, each element reacts to its excitation by airborne sound waves that propagate to a receiver and excite other structural elements, respectively. To elucidate, there are several types of sound transmission paths in a room-to-room situation that are depicted in Fig. 5.22 (the notation uses capital and lowercase letters for sound paths in the sender room and and the receiver room, respectively). While the dominant part of the sound energy is transmitted on *direct paths* (index Dd and Fd) through directly separating structural elements, e.g., walls, doors and windows, a smaller amount of sound energy is also transmitted via several *flanking paths* (index Df and Ff). By using this path separation scheme, the total portion of the sound power can be described as the sum of all transmission coefficients τ_u of occurring path combinations [Ger79], leading to

$$\tau' = \sum_u \tau_u = \sum_o \tau_{direct,o} + \sum_p \tau_{flank,p} \tag{5.55}$$

with

$$\tau_{direct} = \sum_q \tau_{Dd,q} + \sum_r \tau_{F_d,r} \quad \text{and} \quad \tau_{flank} = \sum_s \tau_{Df,s} + \sum_t \tau_{Ff,t} \; .$$

By now assuming a linear and time invariant system, the total transfer function H_{trans} between the sound source and the receiver via structural elements can be described by

$$H_{trans} = \sum_{x=0}^{X} \sum_{y=0}^{Y} H_{S,x} \cdot H_{x,y} \cdot H_{y,R} \; , \tag{5.56}$$

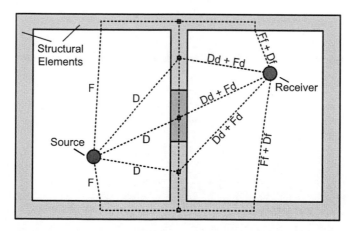

Figure 5.22: Sound transmission paths in two adjacent rooms including direct (D/d) and flanking paths (F/f) up to first-order junctions. Capital and lowercase letters denote sound paths in the sender room and and the receiver room, respectively.

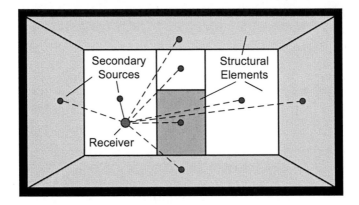

Figure 5.23: Secondary source model: The source room is acoustically substituted for seven secondary point sources located in the receiver's room, i.e., direct and first-order junctions are taken into account.

where $H_{S,x}$ denotes one of X room transfer functions between the sound source and the source room's structural element x, $H_{y,R}$ describes one of Y room transfer functions between the transmitting element y of the receiver room and the receiver itself, and $H_{x,y}$ expresses the transfer function of the transmission path between the structural elements x and y. While $H_{S,x}$ and $H_{y,R}$ can easily be obtained by either measurements or room acoustics simulations [VT00, SV07], $H_{x,y}$ describes a standardized filter function that is built from the interpolated transmission coefficients of the respective structural elements. Here, the transmission coefficient $\tau_{x,y}$ relates to the corresponding flanking sound reduction index $R_{x,y}$ [15] with

$$\tau_{x,y} = 10^{-R_{x,y}/10}. \tag{5.57}$$

Vorländer and Thaden introduced an efficient approach to auralize this type of sound propagation [VT00, Tha05] by introducing Secondary Sources (SSs) SS_y that represent the radiating structural elements y in the receiver room, which were excited by a sound source S in the source room via the corresponding transmission paths, with

$$SS_y = S \cdot \sum_{x=0}^{X} H_{S,x} \cdot H_{x,y}. \tag{5.58}$$

Although a partition element actually behaves like a surface source that radiates structure-borne sound into a room, listening tests showed that due to the low-pass characteristic of the transmitting elements, it was sufficient to use secondary point sources that were located at the center of each structural element in the receiver room

---

[15] As mentioned in Sect. 2.4 and Sect. 5.1, the single sound reduction indices can be measured accordingt to DIN EN ISO 140 [ISO04b], whereas their overall performance in the building structure, including direct and flanking transmission, can be computed according to standardized simulation models, e.g., the European Standard EN 12354 [EN97].

[Hol02]. An example is given in Fig. 5.23, where direct and first-order junctions of the sound transmission paths are represented by their corresponding secondary point sources.

5.5.2 Rendering Filter Networks

A complete simulation of *all* transmitting parts between coupled rooms is apparently infeasible under real-time constraints. Therefore, the simulation has to be restricted to a small number of directly coupling joints with a low sound level difference which dominate the overall level of transmitted sound. Referring back to the example of an office floor given in Fig. 4.6, these joints perfectly correspond to the ASG's portals. Thus, the transmission model described above can easily be integrated into the overall simulation management by extending the portal model from a simple logical and physical separator of the ASG to a coupling element with integrated sender, receiver and corresponding transfer function. The portal's sender is always modeled as a point source, i.e., a SS that is located at the center of the portal's surface (see above), while the hybrid implementation requires two different types of receivers: a point receiver[16] in the case of the IS method, and a surface receiver in the case of stochastic RT, where the portal's surface is used as detector area.

Considering this extended model, four different types of sound propagation paths can occur: (1) PS2R: PS to receiver, (2) PS2P: PS to portal, (3) SS2P: SS to portal, and (4) SS2R: SS to receiver. Cases 1 and 4 state the sound propagation to a binaural[17] receiver within the corresponding room group, where the sound is emitted from a PS and a SS, respectively. Since sources can be spatially localized in the receiver room group, binaural simulations of the respective sound paths are required for a good spatial impression. By contrast, case 2 and 3 resemble the sound propagation from a PS and a SS, respectively, to a portal that belongs to another room group. These sources reside outside the receiver room group, i.e., they are located behind closed portals, which makes a spatial localization of the source rather impossible for the receiver. Hence, monaural simulations are sufficient for both path types. With a given scene configuration, the first simulation step is to determine of all relevant sound propagation paths from a PS to a receiver. This can be performed by unrolling the ASG in a depth-first manner and encoding information on audible sound propagation paths for each PS/receiver-pair in a directed acyclic graph called Propagation Path Graph (PPG) (this is explained in all detail in Chap. 8). However, the PPG can be seen as a construction plan for a filtering network that simulates the total sound propagation (see Fig. 5.24). Starting with the graph's source node S, the PPG is traversed in direction to the receiver node via portal nodes which represent the respective transfer functions H_{Portal}. All nodes are connected by edges, where each edge states the propagation path's type inside the corresponding room group and is substituted with a simulated Room Transfer Function (RTF) and BRTF $\underline{H}_{RoomGroup}$,

---

[16]The point receiver is also located at the center of the portal's surface.

[17]Receivers are always modeled binaurally since they represent the real-world user.

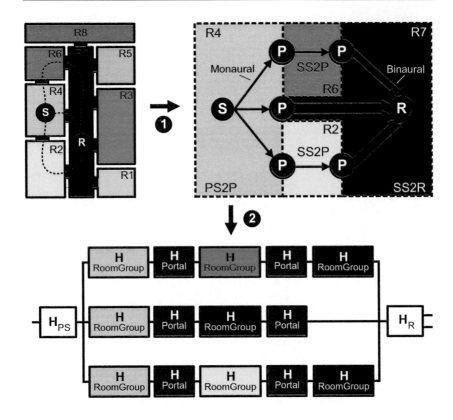

Figure 5.24: Example of tracking sound propagation paths throughout an office floor and constructing a corresponding filter network. The floor consists of eight rooms, where all doors, i.e., portals, are closed resulting in eight room groups (the office floor is shown on the top right-hand side of the figure). A PS S is located in room $R4$, while the receiver R is located in room $R7$. At first, all relevant propagation paths are determined and encoded in a graph structure, called PPG (shown on the top left-hand side of the figure). In a subsequent step, this graph serves as a construction plan for constructing the respective filter network (shown at the bottom of the figure) that represents the overall sound propagation from the PS to the receiver. Here, portal nodes are replaced by portal filter functions and the edges of the graph are substituted by their respective RIR and BRIR that come from room acoustical simulations.

accordingly. The resulting transfer function $\underline{H}_{PP}$ of one sound propagation path is then created by multiplying all involved room transfer functions $\underline{H}_{RoomGroup}$ with all involved portal transfer functions $\underline{H}_{Portal}$, and the respective directivity transfer functions of the PS $\underline{H}_{PS}$ and the receiver $\underline{H}_{R}$, which leads to

$$\underline{H}_{PP}|_{\text{left,right}} = \underline{H}_{PS} \cdot \prod_{p=0}^{P} H_{Portal}(p) \cdot \prod_{r=0}^{R} \underline{H}_{RoomGroup}(r) \cdot \underline{H}_{R}|_{\text{left,right}} . \qquad (5.59)$$

The scene's total transmission characteristics for a PS/receiver-pair is then easily determined by summing up the contributions of each propagation path that can be conducted either in the time domain or in the frequency domain. The simulation of sound propagation between rooms obviously requires a large number of simulation steps that cannot be handled on a single machine anymore, since each involved room group calls for a hybrid room acoustical simulation. Especially with regard to real-time auralization of *dynamically* changing scenes, a computing cluster of distributed systems should be employed in order to handle this significant rise in computational effort. This is further explained in the next chapter.

5.6   Limits of Geometrical Acoustics

Although state-of-the-art methods of GA usually provide good simulation results in practice, one should not forget that this approach of sound wave decomposition inherently has some important limitations, meaning that methods of GA can only approximate real-world sound propagation with a particular uncertainty.

Large rooms The most important constraint of GA is the restriction to large rooms. The IS-model as well as stochastic RT deal with geometric reflections of sound waves which postulates small wavelengths compared to the room geometry. Acoustic phase effects such as room modes, which significantly influence the low-frequency range, are not modeled by geometrical approaches.

Broadband source signals Broadband signals are required for auralization, as they conceal phase effects which would occur with single tone source signals.

CAD room models Important for good simulation results are appropriate room models. In this context, an appropriate model does not necessarily refer to a high level of detail, but to an accurate reproduction of the reflection characteristics of objects and room boundaries using adequate absorption and scattering coefficients as surface descriptors.

Low absorption coefficients The IS-model is only exact for reflection coefficients of $R = 1$ and $R = -1$, respectively, with $|R| = \sqrt{1 - \alpha}$, but it is still a good approximation for low absorption coefficients. However, the assumed plane wave field for the moment of reflection is well suited only if a spherical wave is considered with a large distance between the wall and the sound source and the receiver, and a constant angle of incidence, where the latter is only a valid approximation for angles of up to 60° between the impacting reflection and the surface normal.

Chapter 6

Dynamically Changing Virtual Environments

'Experience is not what happens to you. It is what you do with what happens to you.'

(*The Highest State of Consciousness*, Aldous Huxley, English writer)

A prerequisite for any immersive simulation is the creation of a dynamic representation of the virtual scene, because real-world scenarios are usually not static. While the real-time visualization of dynamic scenes is a rather fast operation in CG, a small change in the scene configuration affects the whole auralization chain - this includes rather simple operations such as the motion of sound source and user, i.e., the listener, but also the more complex modification of scene geometry, either of geometrical scene objects or of scene portals. By recalling the scene graph representation of the virtual scene (see Sect. 4.3 and Sect. 5.5), the number of sound paths that have to be taken into account for the simulation increases drastically with the number of nodes and portals. Unfortunately, room acoustical simulations are the most complex operation among all other system tasks that must respond to user interactions at interactive rates. To overcome the simulation complexity, several approximations are necessary; they will be described in this chapter. Upper limits for the computation time of simulation events are identified that yield a smooth and plausible auralization with best possible simulation quality within the given time constraints. Furthermore, filter update strategies are introduced that aim at keeping computation costs low by updating only relevant parts of the BRIR using a very fast data handling and convenient interaction management. Finally, a concept for parallel computing is described. Here, simulation processes are distributed on a computing cluster of multi-core shared-memory machines in order to handle the simulation workload at interactive rates even in complex scenarios.

6.1 Real-time Constraints

By considering the situation in a virtual environment, the complex calculation of BRIRs (see previous chapter) is just one small fragment in the input-output auralization chain. Other system components such as motion tracking, audio hardware, signal convolution, and audio reproduction already produce latency which limits the maximum permissible computation time for room acoustics simulations. This means that the overall quality of auralization is scaled by the available computation power, whereby the system's minimum quality must not under-run the constraints given by human perception. For the total delay between the user's action and the system's reaction, a lag of about 50 ms can be regarded as generally acceptable and the continuous audio stream should be updated with 60 Hz [Vor08]. Obviously, this is practically impossible, since hardware itself already causes a lag of more than 50% of the total processing time (50 ms) – at least today. Fortunately, when taking a closer look at the situation in a virtual environment, one will see that these rules do not necessarily apply for all elements of the auralization chain. It was shown in psycho-acoustical experiments that the visual and auditory sensory perceptions are allowed to be slightly shifted to each other, whereby a good perceived coincidence of the visual and aural stimuli was still found for an additional delay up to 35 ms [KvdPvEJ06, vdPK00]. This is important for the synchronization of audiovisual stimuli such as avatars (see Chap. 3). Furthermore, Brungart et al. found that a lag of 70 ms between the tracking event and the system's auditory response remains unnoticed by the user [BSM+04]. Besides psycho-acoustical studies, behavior patterns of users in specific simulation situations[1] are also relevant for assessing simulation constraints, but theoretical and empirical investigations on typical movements of users operating in virtual environments are still a subject of research (e.g., [AB95, WO95, CHV02, LJ03]). In general, user movements in CAVE-like environments can be classified into three categories:

Inspection The user is inspecting a static object by moving up and down and from one side to the other in order to gather more detailed information. User interaction such as the creation, manipulation and destruction of objects can be seen as part of that category, too.

Observation The user is standing at a fixed spot and uses both head and body rotations to watch at different display surfaces of the CAVE-like environment.

Exploration The user is exploring the virtual environment by simultaneously walking[2] and looking at the scenery.

Consequently, Lentz et al. carried out user studies to gather more detailed information on typical behavior patterns for each classification type by tracking head movements of users who were interactively inspecting, observing and exploring an architectural scenario of a virtual concert hall [Len07]. In all cases, head rotations were identified

---

[1]Here, user task and simulation environment have to be regarded in particular.
[2]Mostly indirect via the control interface.

as fastest and most abrupt movements with peak values of about 45° per second, while translational position changes were rather smooth, mostly in the range of 30-50 cm/s. Rotational head movements thus require very fast updates, since this type of behavior results in a drastic change of the auditory event. Here, processing times should not exceed the tracking constraint of 70 ms (see above) to maintain a synchronized audiovisual simulation. In the current configuration of RWTH's VR-system, about 35 ms lag is produced by other system components, which means that only 35 ms remain for the complete auralization event. As long as the positions of both sound sources and user are rather fixed, most simulation data stays unchanged and only changing directional patterns of sound sources and user have to be updated[3]. In contrast, translational movements of sound sources and user require at least a partial resimulation of the BRIRs as sound propagation paths (may) have changed. Investigations by Witew et al. showed that the overall sound impression in a room does not change dramatically in the immediate vicinity of the listener [Wit04, WD07]. This means that low update rates of the room acoustics simulation can be seen as sufficient for translational movements. By assuming 25 cm[4] and 1 m as thresholds for triggering the recalculation of the specular and diffuse part of the BRIR, respectively, and taking into account the results from the user studies, maximum permissible computation times for the room acoustics simulation can be identified [Len07]:

- To catch 70% of the translational movements greater than 25 cm, a recalculation has to be performed approximately every 750 ms.

- Correct early specular reflections in about 90% of translational movements greater than 25 cm require an update every 550 ms.

From this it follows that computation times for ISs (specular part of the BRIR) should not exceed 550 ms, while 2 s[5] is set as maximum computation time for processing the computationally demanding ray tracing, since the late reverberant sound field will hardly change within one meter. Thus, BRIRs are updated gradually according to the position changes of sound sources and user.

A more demanding interaction event is user modification of the scene geometry either by creating, manipulating or destroying geometrical objects. In such situations, the sound field might change drastically, e.g., by inserting a reflector panel to the virtual scene (see Fig. 6.1). Most likely the user will *inspect* and *observe* the dynamic object in a very concentrated way, where rotational and translational head movements occur at a high and low level, respectively, while less information is extracted from the aural stimuli due to the change of concentration focus. A first update of the whole BRIR within 35 ms[6] after the modification event would be ideal, but a complete room acoustical simulation of a geometrically changed environment including both specular and diffuse part of the BRIR comprises too many algorithmic operations to

---

[3]This is a very fast operation with processing times far below 35 ms.

[4]25 cm relate to the half width of a common concert hall seat.

[5]This relates to a maximum velocity of sound sources and receiver of 0.5 m/s.

[6]70 ms - 35 ms system lag = 35 ms, see above.

run within these constraints (more details are given in the next section). Thus, update times should be kept at a minimum to maintain a plausible auralization aiming at processing times in the same order of magnitude as for translational movements of sound sources and receivers, i.e., 550 ms and 2 s for the specular and diffuse part of the BRIR, respectively.

Another interaction event where geometry is modified by the user is portal interaction, for instance, when the user opens a door to an adjacent room. During such operations, the sound field will significantly change if the closed door is just slightly opened. However, no huge differences result if a half-opened door is completely opened. It is a basic requirement that the simulation is able to handle this sound field change with a smooth crossover, since this event is best known from everyday experiences. However, room acoustics simulations that take into account all (or at least some) angular

Figure 6.1: Interaction event: a user is adjusting a reflector panel in order to optimize the stage acoustics of the virtual concert hall.

steps of the opening process are infeasible within such a short time interval, as doors are usually opened quite fast. A good compromise yields the caching of BRIRs, whereby whenever the user is approaching a portal, a second BRIR of the scene with an inversed state of the corresponding portal is simulated in parallel and cached until the user disappears again. In the case the user decides to change the portal state, a cross-fading to the cached BRIRs is accomplished, whereby the transition follows a function that maps the relative aperture angle of the portal onto a cross-fading factor (more details are given in the next section). A direct switch from one BRIR to another would sound too unnatural in most cases, as the change of the sound field might be drastic (e.g., from a dry to a wet room acoustics). In summary, Tab. 6.1 gives an overview of all interaction events that are relevant for auralization together with their suggested update intervals of the specular and diffuse part of the respective BRIRs, i.e., the maximum computation times for the IS method and RT.

6.2   Process Analysis of Interaction Events

To keep computation times of the room acoustical simulation low, a strict separation of the overall simulation process into logical subprocesses is vital since in many situations, interaction events do not necessarily require a total recomputation of the entire simulation data. Therefore, essential simulation steps have to be identified and encapsulated in appropriate function calls in order to skip redundant computations

Interaction Event	Update interval	Filter Update
Source rotation	35 ms	BRIR, Specular Part Directivity
Head rotation	35 ms	BRIR, Specular Part HRTFs
Source/User translation >0.25 m translation >1.00 m	550 ms 2 s	BRIR, Specular Part BRIR, Diffuse Part
Geometry Modification	550 ms 2 s	BRIR, Specular Part BRIR, Diffuse Part
Portal Interaction	Cross fading of cached BRIRs	BRIR, Specular Part BRIR, Diffuse Part

Table 6.1: Update intervals on typical VR interaction events.

at runtime and, thus, save valuable processing time. In this section, detailed processing schemes for both the IS method and RT are described for the most important interaction events; i.e., the rotational and translational movements of sound sources and the user, the modification of geometry by creating, manipulating, or destroying geometrical objects, and the interaction with portals. All the described methods will relate to the room acoustical simulation of *one* room group, i.e., the room group where the interaction event is happening. All RIRs from other room groups that were calculated in a previous simulation step will stay unchanged for this specific event and, thus, do not require a resimulation (compare Sect. 5.5).

6.2.1 Rotational and Translational Movements of Sound Sources and the User

The identification of major simulation processes for this type of interaction event is relatively easy and has already been discussed in the previous section from a perceptional point of view. Here, four major events were identified: 1) head rotation, 2) source rotation, 3) head translation, and 4) source translation, and it was shown that rotational movements require much faster updates than translational ones. In the following, these considerations are taken into account for separating the hybrid room acoustics simulation into single simulation steps that satisfy the dictated real-time constraints by assuming a fixed geometry. More details on geometry modification are given in the next subsection.

Image Source Method

Before starting the online simulation of the virtual environment, all ISs of primary and secondary sound sources are preprocessed up to a specific reflection order and stored in data containers that are associated with the respective sound sources or edges (implementation details are given in Chap. 9). Since ISs are related to the room's geometry, the overall cloud of ISs does not change as long as the respective sound source is not moved and – as assumed – no geometrical modifications of the room are carried out. To handle the identified four major interaction events efficiently, it is reasonable to separate the IS method into three fundamental simulation steps:

IS Translation If the primary sound source is moved (all secondary sound sources are static for a fixed geometry), the corresponding position update also involves the associated ISs. To obtain the new positions of the ISs, displacement vectors are simply added to the current positions of the ISs. These vectors have to be computed individually for each IS and are the product of the displacement vector of the sound source multiplied by an IS-dependent translation matrix (more details are given in Chap. 9).

IS Audibility Test As described before, this test identifies all audible ISs for primary and secondary sources, and their properties with regard to sound source and user (angles of emission and impact, length of sound propagation path and the user's position) using several acceleration techniques which are described in detail in Chap. 7 and 9. These audible ISs are then stored in a separate data container that is associated with the respective (primary oder secondary) sound source.

IS Filter Construction For each audible IS, the filter construction consists of a multiplication of surface/edge-specific transfer functions, the sound source's directivity, and the HRTFs in the frequency domain. The resulting transfer function is transformed back into the time domain and shifted by the computed delay of the respective IS. The BRIR is then obtained by simply summing up the contributions of all ISs (see Sect. 5.2).

By using this separation scheme, three entry points into the IS simulation can be identified that handle the major four interaction events efficiently (see Fig. 6.2). The spin of both sound source and user's head is the most frequently occurring interaction event during a simulation and, fortunately, also the least time-consuming simulation step (entry point 3). Rotational movements only require a reconstruction of the binaural filter, since the set of currently audible ISs stays unchanged. During this reconstruction, HRTFs and/or the directivity of the sound source are simply exchanged by transfer functions that match the changed orientation resulting in a recomputed BRIR which adapts the new situation. More simulation steps are required for translational head movements (entry point 2). Here, the audibility of ISs may have changed, as for the new position some specular reflections may become blocked by geometrical objects while others are replaced by secondary diffraction image sources (and vice versa). This has to be be verified by executing additional IS audibility tests for primary source and secondary sources.

In the case of secondary diffraction IS, only the line of sight between the last elements of the edge chains and the head has to be retested before constructing the new BRIR, since all specular reflection paths among the edges stay unchanged for a fixed geometry (see Sect. 5.2.3). The most time-consuming interaction event in this category is the translational movement of sound sources, where not only the primary sound source is moved to a new position, but also all associated ISs (entry point 1). Obviously, this results in an additional computational effort, since the number of ISs is usually quite large. Then, all shifted ISs have to be retested for audibility, while audible ISs of secondary sources will most-likely stay audible and therefore do not require a complete retest. The only thing to check here are the direct lines of sight between the primary sound source and the first elements of the respective edge chains, because secondary sources of portals and their associated ISs are completely unaffected by translational movements of the primary source. The

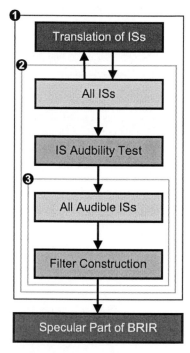

Figure 6.2: Different entry points (IS) depending on interaction events.

subsequent filter construction is proceeded in the same way as described for entry point 2.

Ray Tracing

Due to the underlying energy particle model of sound propagation, no meaningful separation exists unfortunately for stochastic ray tracing, as the construction of BRIRs for all four interaction events requires the results of a full ray tracing, i.e., the frequency-dependent energy histograms that are stored in the directivity groups of the binaural detector (see Sect. 5.3). However, there is still the possibility to skip time-consuming ray tracing for rotational interaction events, as sound propagation paths of energy particles will stay unchanged as long as no translational movement of the sound source occurs. As mentioned earlier, only a recomputation of the BRIR is required for rotational movements of the head. Here, the local spherical coordinate system of the binaural energy detector[7] is simply rotated for the same angle range, while the detection sphere itself containing the energy histograms for each directivity group stays fixed in space, or from the viewpoint of a fixed user, the detected energy is rotated around the head. Then the hit probability of each directivity group in relation to the rotated local coordinate system is recomputed, and the BRIR is constructed as described in Sect. 5.3.4.

This approach can also be applied for the rotation of sound sources by simply caching all reflection paths that have hit the detection sphere (energy on emission, energy and time on detection, associated directivity group), whereby the energy portion of each path is re-weighted according to the rotated directional pattern of the sound source, thereby resulting in a new time-dependent energy distribution on the detector surface, i.e., new energy histograms. Thus, both rotational interaction events require only a recomputation of the BRIR, which makes these movements less time-consuming (see Fig. 6.3, entry point 2). Theoretically, the caching of *all* reflection paths would allow one to skip the execution of a ray tracing process in case the user is performing translational movements. However,

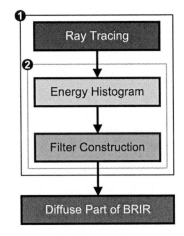

Figure 6.3: Different entry points (RT) depending on interaction events.

this approach is infeasible under real-time contraints. Apart from a corresponding huge amount of created data and keeping in mind that this would include the storage of millions of time-dependent reflection subpaths from one room element to another, the identification of an impacting energy particle from a set of time-dependent subpaths is more or less equal to the computation time of a complete ray tracing. A more promising idea is the voxelization of the room, where each voxel stores the incoming and outgoing energy particles together with their time and direction of arrival using binaural detectors with the radius of half of the voxel's edge length and located at the voxel's center. Thus, *one* ray tracing event produces *all* energy histograms for the voxelized space. At runtime, only the voxel that contains the user has to be determined and the associated histogram is assigned to the user's energy histogram. Although the energy detection with so many receivers slows down the overall ray tracing process, extensive memory is consumed (especially when one regards voxel sizes with an edge length of 1 m and below) and the energy histograms are not valid for the *exact* user's position[8], it is certainly the better alternative than performing a

---

[7]The local coordinate system of the detector is assigned to the orientation of the user's head.

[8]Nonetheless, one should keep in mind that the diffuse sound field does not change much in the immediate vicinity of user (see above).

complete ray tracing for each translational movement of the user. Thus, this interaction event is also assigned to entry point 2 in Fig. 6.3. For translational movements of sound sources, however, a complete ray tracing has to be performed, since the propagation paths of energy particle have changed, thereby making this event the most time-consuming (entry point 1).

6.2.2 Creation, Modification and Destruction of Dynamic Geometry

The most demanding interaction event is the modification of geometry at runtime, since this intervention massively influences the room acoustics simulation and necessitates a complete recomputation of the BRIR. Problems arise especially for the IS-method due to the real-time constraints for early reflections (see above). If geometrical objects are added to the scene, modified or destroyed, corresponding ISs have to be generated, translated, or removed accordingly, followed by an audibility test of ISs that are associated with the respective room group, since existing sound paths may have changed. Although these operations can be computed within the given time constraints (see Chap. 11), major problems arise from the update of the geometry-related data itself.

At runtime, RAVEN uses very fast BSP-accelerated simulation algorithms that enable a simulation of BRIRs in real-time for a static geometry (more algorithmic details are given in Chap. 7). As explained in Sect. 4.2, BSP belongs to the type of hierarchical spatial data structures that all have in common that they lack an efficient update of their encoded geometry data. Thus, the recomputation of BSP-trees yields a lag that might become critical for the update of specular reflections, i.e., ISs, in combination with all other required simulation tasks. In order to solve this problem, geometry modifications should be handled separately by using other types of spatial data structures for accelerating the simulation, such as SH, where geometry updates come almost for free[9]. Regarding the diffuse part of the BRIR, i.e., the ray

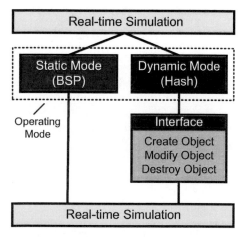

Figure 6.4: RAVEN features two operating modes for ISs: a *static* and *dynamic* mode.

---

[9]It is true that hierarchical data structures can be updated quite fast by only partially re-encoding the geometry, but a lag for this operation will always remain. In contrast, SH offers the modification of geometry data with a complexity of only $\mathcal{O}(1)$; thus, this type of interaction is independent of the complexity of the geometry.

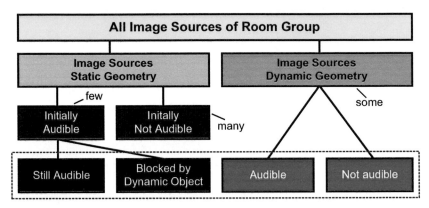

Figure 6.5: Logical differentation of ISs that enables an efficient handling of geometry-related modification events. Here, ISs that are associated with the initial *static* geometry and with *dynamic* objects are handled individually.

tracing simulations, it is sufficient to update the BSP-tree first and then perform a ray tracing, because BSP-accelerated intersection tests will always outperform SH (see Chap. 11). Here, the lag produced by the update of the hierarchical tree structure will be compensated multiple times, because ray tracing requires millions of inter-section tests more than the IS-method. Therefore, only the special handling of ISs during modification events will be further described, since ray tracing is always han-dled just straight forward. During a preprocessing step, a *static* geometrical scene is selected from a database, necessary parameters for the IS-method are defined and the respective ISs are generated. For a convenient handling of ISs during all interaction events, RAVEN uses hierarchical tree data structures, where all possible IS reflection permutations are encoded in that tree (more details are given in Chap. 9). Then, in order to handle the different types of user interaction at runtime, the simulation can be switched into two operating modes, either in *static* or *dynamic* mode (see Fig. 6.4). In the default *static* mode, RAVEN uses fast BSP-accelerated simulation meth-ods that handle all interaction events with a fixed geometry (see previous section). As soon as a geometry-related modification event happens, RAVEN is switched into *dynamic* mode, where all dynamic geometrical objects are handled separately from the *static* scene. Using the concepts of SH for a fast re-encoding of spatial data, six basic operations on dynamic objects are considered in this operating mode: creation, destruction, and manipulation, which includes the translation, the rotation, and the scaling of the object as well as the change of surface materials. It is reasonable to differentiate between ISs, which were generated in *static* and *dynamic* mode, as some interaction events allow an a priori exclusion of ISs (see Fig. 6.5, orange and light green box). While translational movements of sound sources or user always require an audibility test on all ISs of the room group, i.e., *static* and *dynamic* ISs, a categoriza-tion of ISs into four logical groups yields various advantages if the positions of sound source and user are fixed. This is not so unlikely during a user-driven scene modification, where one will most probably focus on the object and therefore not move much besides head rotations – which has no impact on the audibility of ISs. With these assumptions, the following consideration can be made: initially static inaudible ISs, i.e., ISs that belong to the *static* scene, will never become audible again, no matter how many dynamic objects are inserted, modified or destroyed, implying that only a few audible *static* image sources have to be checked in further considerations (see Fig. 6.5, light red boxes). Thus, if a new dynamic object is created, either imported from a database or sketched on-the-fly [RA08], the audibility test can be reduced to test only the newly created ISs, audible static ISs and audible dynamic ISs of previously inserted dynamic objects. Here, audible static ISs that became inaudible due to the object insertion are moved to the container of inaudible static ISs, while ISs that are associated to the newly created object are moved to the respective data containers for dynamic ISs (see Fig. 6.5, dark red and dark green boxes). In contrast, if a dynamic object is destroyed, only the existing inaudible ISs, both *static* and *dynamic*, have to be further checked, as already audible ISs stay audible in any case. In the case of object manipulation, such as translation, rotation and scaling operations, no ISs can be excluded from the audibility test (but the large number of initially inaudible ISs), which makes these operations the most time-consuming event in terms of retesting ISs. As mentioned above, algorithms based on SH cannot compete with the overall performance of BSP-trees (see Chap. 11). For this reason, RAVEN switches back to *static* mode as soon as all geometric modifications are carried out, whereby BSP-trees of modified rooms are recomputed accordingly.

6.2.3 Interaction with Portals

As pointed out before, a change of the portal state requires a smooth and non-linear transition between the current BRIR and the cached BRIR that was calculated in

Figure 6.6: Opening sequence of a door to a concert hall. As long as the door is not completely opened, the filter concatenation on the left hand side is used for auralization, where h_{Portal} is weighted according to the respective sound reduction and the opening angle of the door, increasingly gaining an all-pass characteristic. As soon as the door is completely opened, the simulation switches to the cached BRIR h_{PS2R} of the merged room group.

parallel for the inversed portal state while the user was approaching the portal. It was also shown in Sect. 5.5 that the sound propagation from a primary sound source to a receiver, i.e., the user, via a portal can be expressed by a convolution of the RIR h_{PS2P} of the source room with the portal filter h_{Portal} and the BRIR h_{SS2R} of the receiver room. By contrast, if the portal is opened, the sound propagation from the primary sound sound source to the receiver is described by the BRIR h_{PS2R} of the merged room groups only. The crucial part now is to crossfade from one BRIR to another that matches the opening and closing sequence in a natural way, especially in cases that are best known from real-world experiences, such as the opening and closing of a door or a window. Plausible results can be achieved by using n-th root functions, i.e., $y(x) = \sqrt[n]{x}$ with $x \in [0, 1]$, for weighting the portal's sound reduction indices according to the relative aperture angle of the portal. By using this function, the portal's sound reduction is continuously lowered during an opening sequence until h_{Portal} has gained an all-pass filter characteristic (portal completely opened). However in the opposite case, the sound reduction indices are increased again until they have reached their original values (portal completely closed). Figure 6.6 further illustrates this approach by the example of an opening sequence of a door. Here, as long as the door is not completely opened, the overall BRIR is described by the concatenation of three filters, h_{PS2P}, h_{Portal}, and h_{SS2R}, where h_{Portal} is modified as described above (see Fig. 6.6, (1) and (2)). Then, as soon as h_{Portal} has gained the all-pass characteristic, the auralization will sound very similar to the direct convolution with h_{S2R} of the merged room group (see Fig. 6.6, (3)) allowing a hard switch to the cached BRIR without any adverse effects [Pel07]. Demonstration videos are available for download under www.ravenaudio.de.

6.3   Parallel Computing

The real-time room acoustical simulation of a dynamic virtual environment that contains various rooms and sound sources by far exceeds the computational power of one CPU-Core. Thus, a parallel computation of single simulation processes has to be carried out in order to meet real-time constraints also for complex situations. Concepts for parallel computing are typically divided in two main categories according to their underlying memory architecture, i.e., either *shared* or *distributed* memory. One of the main solutions for parallel computing on distributed memory, such as computing clusters, is the Message Passing Interface (MPI) which is a platform-independent communication protocol for the data transfer between single processes by passing explicit messages, e.g., via a high-speed ethernet connection, from one or many computers to other computers [MPI08]. The respective counterpart for shared memory machines, e.g., multi-core PCs, is called Open Multi-Processing (OpenMP). OpenMP allows master threads to open parallel sub-threads following a fork-join strategy for the parallel execution of computation tasks in order to speed up the processing time of the overall operation [Ope08]. The idea itself suggests combining both approaches by using a computing cluster with multi-core worker clients that are connected via

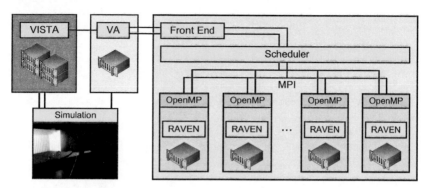

Figure 6.7: For distributed computing, one instance of RAVEN is run on each multi-core worker connected via high-speed ethernet and controlled by a scheduler. The scheduler can be seen as an interface between the front end of the main application, in this case VA, which receives scene updates from ViSTA, and the back end that has access to the physical computing cluster. The communication is set up by passing messages from one computer to another via the network. In this figure, black lines denote scene updates and simulation tasks, while red lines refer to simulation results.

ethernet – so-called hybrid solutions [Rab03]. The main task in such systems is to efficiently distribute the data processing on the worker clients without producing any bottlenecks in the data flow. Here, so-called *schedulers* are applied for a smooth routing of jobs to the worker clients usually following a master/slave-concept. This means that one scheduler (master) is used to control the processing on the worker clients (slaves), whereby the scheduler communicates with the main application via a front end for receiving jobs and returning results and uses the MPI protocol on a back end to send jobs to the worker clients and receive the respective results.

The VR-system at RWTH Aachen University also features such a hybrid solution for high-performance computing, whereby the framework Viracocha is applied for conveniently communicating with the computing cluster by using TCP/IP communication via high-speed ethernet [GHW+04]. During real-time auralization, Viracocha enables a communication layer between a front end that is integrated in Virtual Acoustics (VA) and a back end for accessing the computing cluster, where one instance of RAVEN is run on each worker. The scheduler on the back end processes all incoming messages that are sent via the front end and separates them into control commands, scene updates and simulation jobs. This data is then evaluated by the scheduler and the workload is further distributed among the workers according to job priority, job complexity and the number of idle workers in which decisions are influenced by the current scene configuration. After finishing the assigned jobs, each worker sends back the simulation results to the scheduler, where they get reassembled and subsequently forwarded to the front end (see Fig. 6.7, black and red connectors denote tasks and results, respectively).

In contrast to the scheduler which is permanently sending and receiving messages, a worker only executes simulation processes on demand. If a message is received from the scheduler, the worker updates the RAVEN instance according to scene changes that were encoded in that message, i.e., movements/rotations of sound sources and receiver and geometry modifications, and then starts to execute the desired simulation job for a dedicated room group using OpenMP for fast parallel computing.

Thus, the rendering of the filter network that describes the overall sound propagation from a sound source to a user in a multi-room situation (see Sect. 5.5.2) is distributed among the workers according to 'room group' and 'simulation method'. Here, simulation jobs are either finding audible ISs or executing a RT if the scene situation has changed in one or more room groups. If no changes took place in a room group, a filter reconstruction is apparently unnecessary and simulations for this specific group can be skipped. Before simulation results, i.e., a list of ISs or energy histograms, can be sent back to the front end, the respective data must be serialized for network transportation (see Fig. 6.8). Then, VA, i.e., the front end, deserializes the incoming results, generates new corresponding filters from the received data, re-renders the filter network

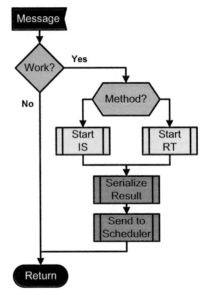

Figure 6.8: Flowchart for calling a worker instance.

and adds the new BRIR to the real-time convolution and reproduction process [WS09]. Unfortunately, a detailed description of the parallel processing would vastly go beyond the scope of this thesis. However, more details are given in [Sch09a].

Part III

Real-time Implementation

Chapter 7

Acceleration of Geometric Operations

"The first ten million years were the worst, said Marvin, and the second ten million years, they were the worst, too. The third ten million years I didn't enjoy at all. After that I went into a bit of a decline."

(*The Hitchhiker's Guide to the Galaxy*, Douglas Adams, British writer)

A prerequisite for real-time implementations is the profiling of function calls at runtime in order to identify bottlenecks in the overall simulation process. In methods of GA, these bottlenecks are usually two basic functions that are called extremely often during a room-acoustics simulation: 1) point-in-polygon test and 2) intersection tests of rays with scene objects, i.e., polygons and detectors. In the following, both function types will be elucidated and concepts for the implementation will be given, while their overall performance is thoroughly discussed in Chap. 11.

7.1 Point-In-Polygon Test

Even though there is a wide variety of approaches for an efficient point-in-polygon-test, no approach is the best in all application areas. Whereas some strategies are very fast, yet only work with a certain type of polygon, others can handle different kinds of polygons but operate poorly in terms of computing time. In addition, some approaches use preprocessing information to speed up the algorithms, but use more memory. Others, however, exclusively perform the test during runtime. The most commonly known and for general polygons speediest point-in-polygon test is the so-called crossing test [Shi62] which is based on *Jordan's Curve Theorem*[1]. Here, all polygon's vertices and the test point P are projected onto one of the xy-, xz-, or yz-planes (see Fig. 7.1(a)), where it is suitable to choose the plane which maximizes the area of the projected polygon to avoid numerical issues [Gla89]. Then, a ray is shot from the test point's projection P' into an arbitrary direction and the number of intersections with the projected polygon edges is counted, whereby, as stated by

---

[1]Marie Ennemond Camille Jordan, French mathematician, 1838 - 1922.

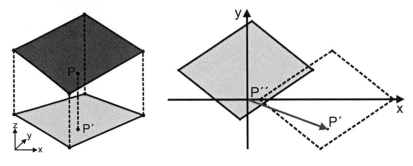

(a) The polygon and the point in question are projected into the x/y-plane.

(b) Crossing Test: The projected polygon is translated by vector $-\vec{P}'$.

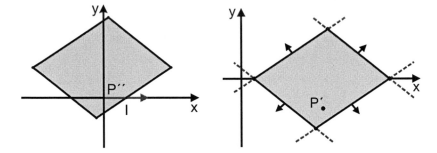

(c) Crossing Test: The number of intersections of the polygon with the positive x-axis is counted.

(d) Hesse Test: The normal vectors of the projected edges have to point outside.

Figure 7.1: Point-in-polygon test strategies.

the curve theorem, an odd number of crossings signifies that the point is inside the polygon. Instead of having to shoot a ray into random direction, this test can be simplified by translating P' and the polygon's vertices by a displacement vector $-\vec{P}'$ and test the edges against the positive x-axis[2] (see Fig. 7.1(b,c)). The advantage of this approach is that the number of intersection tests is reduced, as edges with the same sign of the y-coordinate are skipped, thereby accelerating the test (respectively the y- or z-coordinate, depending on the projection plane and axis that has been chosen for the crossing test). Problems occur in both variants if the ray intersects a vertex, because then the number of crossings is even. This can be solved by interpreting the vertex infinitesimally above the ray.

Although the simplified crossing test is very fast, a faster and more robust solution for real-time point-in-polygon-tests is applied in RAVEN. It takes advantages of the

---

[2]If the polygon is projected into the yz-plane, either the y- or the z-axis is chosen.

properties of convex polygons, whereby the projected edges are transformed into the *Hesse normal form* having outward-pointing normal vectors (see Fig. 7.1(d)). Here, the test whether the point P' lies inside the polygon is reduced to the classification of the relative position of P' in relation to the edges. If P' lies behind all edges, it is located inside the polygon, but if it lies in front of only one of the edges, the test can be stopped, since the point is definitely outside for a convex polygon. Thus, this test has an additional break condition in comparison to the crossing test, which further reduces the complexity of this simple operation.

7.2 Ray-Polygon Intersection Search

As mentioned above, the intersection test between rays, i.e., line segments, and polygons is the second fundamental atomic operation in room acoustics simulation algorithms due to GA's reduced sound field description of energy particles that travel on discrete rays through space. Here, the computation time of one single intersection test depends on the polygonal complexity of the room model and should be kept to a minimum with regard to real-time constraints of the room acoustical simulation (see Chap. 6). By considering that *one* single room acoustical simulation requires *millions* of intersection tests in more complex room models, simple Brute Force (BF) intersection tests cannot meet this claim. In a BF test, all scene polygons are tested against the ray, and resulting intersection distances are compared to each other in a subsequent step in order to determine the minimum path length that relates to the one valid intersection point. However, such a simple implementation is only an option if the number of polygons is very small, e.g., a shoe box-shaped room. Contrary to this naive approach, the intersection test can be significantly accelerated by using spatial data structures that were introduced in Sect. 4.2. In the following, search strategies of RAVEN's implemented intersection tests are further described using either BSP or SH.

7.2.1 Binary Space Partitioning

A BSP-tree based search of intersections between a ray and the BSP-tree's objects, i.e., polygons, is a very fast and efficient strategy. It rests upon a position classification of the ray's starting- and end point in reference to the BSP-tree's partitioners, similar to the classification of polygons during BSP-tree creation (see 4.2). The determination of a point's location relative to a scene by querying the BSP-tree is also recursively applicable with a ray connecting two points, i.e., starting- and end point.

Concerning the partitioner that is stored in one tree node, the ray might cross the partitioning plane. This can be easily tested by checking the positions of the two points relative to this plane, where four possible cases exist:

Both points lie on the same side If both points are located on the same side, the ray obviously does not cross the partitioning plane. Therefore, only the subspace containing both points has to be investigated further for the full (sub)ray.

Points lie on different sides As the points lie on different sides, the ray's intersection with the partitioning plane has to be determined. If this point is located inside one of the polygon that lie on that plane, the ray has collided with the respective polygon and the query terminates. Otherwise, the ray is split up and the subspace in search direction to the end point is further investigated. If a leaf node is reached during the query, the remaining set of convex polygons has to be checked completely following a BF approach.

One point lies on the partitioner In this case, the ray is moved into the direction of the point that does not lie on the partitioner.

Both points lie on the partitioner If the ray's starting- and end point lie on the partitioner, the ray is moved per definition onto the partitioning plane's positive side. Here, the negative side would work as well – it only has to be conducted consistently during the test.

The following example serves to elucidate this mechanism by finding the possible intersection point of a ray that propagates from a starting point S to an end point E

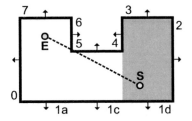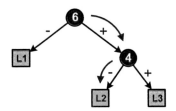

(a) The intersection search starts by identifying the subspace of the starting point which is leaf node L2 in this example.

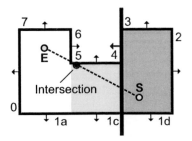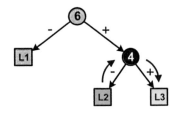

(b) The BSP-tree is traversed in the direction of the end point, whereby adjacent subspaces are tested one after another.

Figure 7.2: Intersection search using a BSP-tree.

within a very simple room model (see Fig. 7.2). It is the same room model that was used in Sect. 4.2 to explain the generation of the corresponding BSP-tree. Starting with the root of the BSP-tree, S is classified to be in front of the node-stored partitioner (plane of polygon 6). Since no leaf node is reached, the tree traversal continues by testing the point's location against the partitioner of the subtree (plane of polygon 4) , followed by a subsequent traversal to the leaf node L2. The starting node in the BSP-tree is now identified, and the intersection test starts by testing the ray against all polygons that belong to this subspace (see Fig. 7.2(a)). As no intersection occurs, the next subspace in direction to the ray's end point has to be checked. Therefore, the positions of S and E are tested against the partitioner that created that subspace (plane of polygon 4), where they are classified to lie on different sides. As explained above, the intersection of the ray with the partitioning plane is computed, and all polygons that lie on that plane are tested if they enclose the intersection point. In this example, the respective point-in-polygon test is negative, and the ray is further split up until the leaf of the adjacent subspace is reached, i.e., leaf node L3. The convex set of polygons is tested for intersection with the remaining sub-ray, and an intersection point is found for polygon 5 (see Fig. 7.2(b)). Since a strict order was used during the query process, intersection points are always identified in ascending order regarding their distance from the start point, which means that the intersection search can be terminated after the first valid intersection point is found.

7.2.2 Spatial Hashing

As a matter of principle, intersection tests based on SH cannot compete with the search complexity of hierarchical spatial data structures, nonetheless they are still faster than BF methods and provide an extremely fast recomputation of the underlying hash table if the scene geometry is modified. In the following, two intersection tests – one simple and one advanced approach – are described that are implemented in RAVEN.

Voxel Tracing

The first method, called Voxel Tracing (VT) in the following, checks only voxels that are explicitly hit by the ray segment. Beginning at the starting point S of the ray segment, the first voxel's hash index is computed. All polygons of the respective entry of the hash table are tested whether they intersect the ray segment. If no intersection occurred, the adjacent voxel in the direction to the ray segment's end point E is considered as the next intersection candidate. If more than one intersection points are computed for the voxel's set of polygons, the closest point in relation to the starting point is chosen. In order to catch hash collisions, each computed possible intersection point has to be tested if it is really enclosed by the currently examined voxel. Each polygon that has been tested on intersection with the given ray segment is marked with a *collision stamp* and will not be taken into further consideration for the current intersection search. The algorithm terminates if an intersection point is

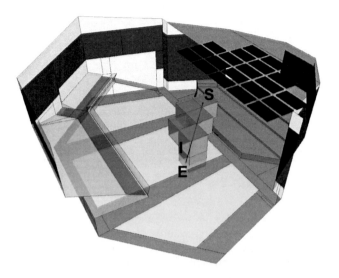

(a) Visualization of the Voxel Tracing (VT) algorithm for a single ray segment.

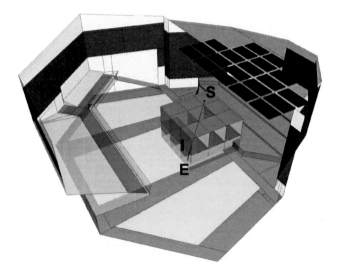

(b) Visualization of the Voxel Candidates (VC) algorithm for a single ray segment.

Figure 7.3: Intersection search using SH.

found or the end point of the ray segment is reached. The concept is illustrated in Fig. 7.3(a).

Voxel Candidates

The second applied method, the so-called Voxel Candidates (VC), uses no smart traversal of single voxels. Instead, all voxels that are enclosed by or intersect with the ray segment's AABB are regarded as possible intersection candidates. In a next step, an intersection test with all candidates, i.e., polygons that are stored in the respective voxels, is carried out and returns the intersection point with the closest distance to the ray segment's starting point (see Fig. 7.3(b)). Similar to VT, each tested polygon acquires a collision stamp to avoid multiple testing of the same candidate. A polygon is usually stored in more than one voxel, whereby the total number depends on the voxel size. The advantage of this approach is that hash collisions can be neglected. It is sufficient to check in a final test if the identified intersection point is enclosed by the ray segment's AABB, which is a fast and simple operation. On the other hand, the identification of intersection candidates is quite rough and probably leads to a higher number of intersection tests.

7.3   Collision Tests

For further considerations, it should be noted that in the current implementation the detailed geometry of spherical and cylindrical detectors is not added to the geometrical scene but is handled separately for three reasons:

Virtual Objects Logically, the shape of volume detectors does not belong to the physical scene, since they refer only to points (receiver positions) or line segments (edges).

Accuracy Intersection tests on detectors with curved surfaces would be too rough, since their geometrical scene representation must be heavily approximated to avoid an explosion of the overall polygon count.

Re-computations A separate handling avoids re-computations of the rooms' underlying spatial data structures each time a detector is moved.

This also means that intersection tests between rays and the scene geometry that are executed at any case during the RT simulation, do not return whether one or more detectors were hit. Thus, this has to be investigated in an additional step. Fortunately, only a qualitative intersection test is required in many algorithmic situations that relate to detectors, whereby it is sufficient to determine whether the ray collides with the detector without the need of detailed knowledge about the intersection points' positions (e.g., to decide whether the diffuse rain has to be triggered for a detector). In addition, these tests can be efficiently reduced by adding information about essential detector points, such as corner points and centroids, to the underlying spatial data structures and, thus, checking only detectors that lie within the subspaces between the ray's starting and end point[3]. In the following, only quick collision tests for spherical and cylindrical detectors will be further described, since this information comes directly from the ray intersection test with the geometrical scene for plane detectors, i.e., portals. More information regarding efficiently computing relations between geometrical objects can be found in series such as Andrew Glassner's *Graphics Gems* series [Gla93, Arv91, Kir92, Hec94, Pae95].

Spherical Detectors

The test whether a ray collides with a spherical detector can be reduced to a 2D problem by spanning a plane that is defined through the direction vector $\vec{b}$ of the ray and the connection vector $\vec{a}$ between the ray's starting point S and the sphere's centroid C. The intersection area of a sphere with a plane that goes through the centroid is always a circle with the same radius r as the sphere, which is depicted in Fig. 7.4(a). The closest point P on the ray segment between the starting point S and the end point E to the centroid C is along a perpendicular $\vec{d}$ from C to the ray's direction vector $\vec{b}$, which can be described by

$$P = \vec{S} + u \cdot \vec{b} \qquad \text{with} \qquad \vec{b} \circ \vec{d} = 0, \ \vec{b} = E - S \ \text{and} \ \vec{d} = C - P. \qquad (7.1)$$

The shifting factor u is easy to compute by substituting one equation into the other, which results in

$$u = \frac{\vec{a} \circ \vec{b}}{\vec{b} \circ \vec{b}}, \qquad (7.2)$$

where $\vec{a}$ is the connection vector between C and S. The last step of this test is to compare the length d of $\vec{d}$ against the radius of the sphere: if r is smaller than d, a collision of the ray with the sphere is impossible. An additional testing if the point P lies in between S and E ($0 \leq u \leq 1$) can be omitted, since rays travel from surface to surface and detectors will always be located in between.

Cylindrical Detectors

In the case of cylindrical detectors, the collision test can also be expressed by very simple geometrical operations. In the following, the same vector notation is used as in the previous test with S_E, whereby $\vec{s_E}$ and $\vec{e}$ additionally denote the cylinder's starting point, the connection vector between S and S_E, and the direction vector of the cylinder's axis , i.e., the edge (see Fig. 7.4(b)). At first, the normalized normal vector $\vec{n}$ of a plane that is spanned by $\vec{e}$ and $\vec{b}$ is computed with

$$\vec{n} = \vec{e} \times \vec{b} \qquad \text{with } \vec{n} = \frac{\vec{n}}{|\vec{n}|}. \qquad (7.3)$$

---

[3]In this case, the term ray is literally incorrect, as it has no end point per definition. In indoor scenarios, however, a ray is always reduced to a line segment.

Then, the closest fly-by distance d is determined by projecting the connection vector $\vec{s_E}$ on $\vec{n}$ using the dot product

$$d = |\vec{n} \circ \vec{s_E}| \qquad \text{with } \vec{s_E} = S - S_E. \tag{7.4}$$

If $d \leq r$, the ray will collide with the cylinder; otherwise no intersection can occur.

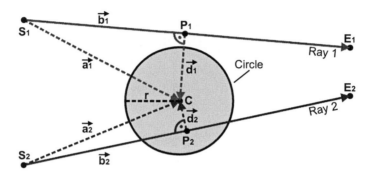

(a) Ray collision test for spheres.

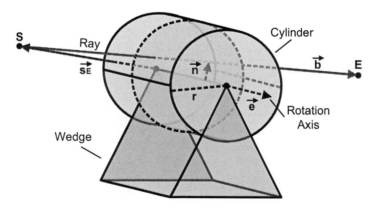

(b) Ray collision test for cylinders.

Figure 7.4: Geometrical relations between a ray and a spherical/cylindrical detector that are exploited for fast collision tests.

Chapter 8

Efficient Handling of Complex Dynamic Sceneries

"A set is a Many that allows itself to be thought of as a One."

(*Infinity and the Mind*, Rudolf von Bitter Rucker, American writer)

In multi-room environments, user interaction with portals will always result in a change of connected room groups. Therefore, concepts for a fast handling of such state changes are required, whereby the underlying simulation model has already been described in Sect. 4.3. Here, a major prerequisite is to keep computation times to a minimum by avoiding simulations of redundant and unnecessary sound propagation paths from a sound source to a receiver across the changed scene. In the following, implementation details will be given that offer a smart processing of such simulations by taking into account physical attributes of the scene during the determination of up-to-date propagation paths.

8.1 Tracking of Sound Paths

As already introduced in Sect. 4.3 and Sect. 5.5, the Acoustic Scene Graph (ASG) is the groundwork for an efficient handling of the room acoustics simulation in multi-room scenarios. In summary, each room is represented by one scene node which is interconnected to other nodes via bidirectional edges, called portals since they represent not only a logical concatenation but also a physical surface between two adjacent rooms such as doors or windows. An ASG can be implemented fairly easy by using basically two classes representing either a scene node or a portal. All scene nodes store instances of their respective portals, where the number of portals per scene node may be theoretically unlimited. Each portal saves two room IDs: (1) the room ID where it originates from, and (2) the room ID where it connects to. In addition, each portal also saves a pointer to the corresponding counter-portal of the adjacent room which connects the same scene nodes in the opposite direction. This yields the possibility to freely traverse this connected graph and, thus, use a multitude of search algorithms to find propagation paths across the scenery in the case that the sound source and the receiver are located in different rooms. Such an algorithm has to fulfill the constraints of the so-called *one-pair-all-paths* search algorithm class, where the algorithm must return *all* possible propagation paths. Here, a good choice is the so-called *depth-first search* [Sed90]. This algorithm belongs to the class of *uninformed search algorithms* that need no a priori knowledge which means that the graph structure can be changed at runtime without any false identification of propagation paths after the modification event[1].

However, if the ASG contains any cycles, a depth-first path search will end up in an infinite loop. Hence, the search algorithm must remember all visited nodes to avoid such deadlocks. It is anyway questionable whether such cycles should be included in the room acoustical simulation, as in most cases the influence of sound which cycled one or many times through the same set of rooms will be negligibly small and masked by much louder sound signals that traveled along the direct path (see Fig. 8.1).

The depth-first search is still *complete* if interception techniques for graph cycles are applied, i.e., a correct solution will always be found. Starting with the root node, i.e., the room that contains the sound source, the path search algorithm can be implemented in two ways: either iteratively or recursively. The iterative implementation yields the advantage of a limited depth, which means that possible cycle loops are automatically kept under control. Nevertheless, such approaches usually have the drawback that they use

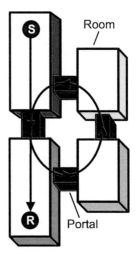

Figure 8.1: Sound propagation through a cycle of rooms that are separated by portals.

more memory, because every possible propagation path with length n that starts at the root node must be kept in memory at the same time (this is an issue only in large-scale scenarios, though). In contrast, the recursive approach uses a list of already visited nodes in the current search path; this approach can be implemented quite efficiently by using a Last-In-First-Out (LIFO) stack.

```
function PATH_SEARCH
   If (Target RoomGroup found)
      return stack    // copy stack
   For (All adjacent RoomGroups)
      If (Portal open) OR (Source audible through closed Portal)
         If (Current RoomGroup not visited yet in current path)
            push Current RoomGroup on stack
            Continue PATH_SEARCH with current RoomGroup
            pop Last RoomGroup from stack    // clean stack
```

Listing 8.1: Pseudocode of a recursive depth-first search.

---

[1]For the time of the path search itself, the graph structure is certainly assumed to be fixed.

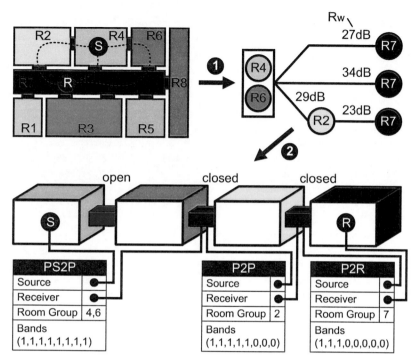

Figure 8.2: Extracting audible sound paths from the ASG: (1) Audible sound paths are determined by using a recursive depth-first path search. The algorithm decides whether a sound paths is further tracked by comparing the summed up values of R_w to the sound level of the sound source. A tree including all valid sound paths is returned from the search algorithm called PST (upper right-hand side). (2) Tree results are converted into batch commands for a convenient handling of single independent simulation steps, where additionally the complete portals' frequency response is taken into account for identifying obsolete frequency bands for the RT simulation (red numbers are skipped).

This avoids cycle loops and gives fast access to the resulting sound path in the case the target node is found, as the stack just has to be returned to acquire the completely traced propagation path from the source room to the receiver room. The recursive search is most effective with respect to its complexity in terms of time and space. To elucidate, for a recursive implementation, the space complexity is $\mathcal{O}(L)$, where L denotes the length of the longest path across the graph. Time complexity of the algorithm is proportional to the number of scene nodes n and portals p in the ASG with $\mathcal{O}(n + p)$. The algorithm is not *optimal* meaning that it does not find the shortest path first. This, however, is irrelevant for room acoustics simulation , since it is always necessary to find *all* valid sound propagation paths. The respective pseudocode of the implemented recursive depth-first search algorithm is given in List. 8.1.

The depth-first search always results in a hierarchical Path Search Tree (PST) which is depicted in Fig. 8.2 (step 1) for the same scene example that was given in Sect. 5.5, except that the portal between room $R4$ and $R6$ is now opened. The root of the PST relates to the room group which contains the sound source, while leaf nodes refer to the receiver's room group and child nodes are assigned to the traversed room groups in between the source and receiver. All nodes, except the root node, may appear multiple times in the PST, since sound can travel on various paths through the same room group via different portals. As one can see from the pseudocode above, the path search is already tweaked by checking the audibility of the current sound source. For this test, the sound reduction index R_w of the corresponding portals is taken into account in order to terminate path searches for branches where the summed up total insulation exceeds the sound level of the sound source (shown values in Fig. 8.2 are only exemplary). For RT, this concept of *source elimination* is further refined by additionally regarding the detailed frequency response of the portal, i.e., of the corresponding constructional element. In many cases, such elements feature a low-pass characteristic, meaning that higher frequencies will probably be inaudible after a single element is passed, while lower frequencies will most-likely cross several of them. Not only does the refined path search exclude inaudible sources but it also excludes frequency bands of audible sources. Hence, the RT simulation of sound sources that are not located in the receiver room group can be reduced to the simulation of only some frequency bands; this obviously reduces the computational effort significantly. This is further illustrated in Fig. 8.2 (step 2) for the propagation path that includes two portals. Here, only the three remaining frequency bands have to be simulated, since all other bands are completely damped by the portals that are included in the corresponding propagation path. From this it follows that the path search results can be seen as a specification for triggering the room acoustics simulations, whereby identical subpaths are skipped. Therefore, an appropriate and handy-to-use data structure for describing each single simulation step has to be defined, which goes along with the extracted data from the path search:

```
struct simStep{
    int type;                      // type of sub path
    void* source, receiver;        // pointer to source/receiver
    list<SceneNode*> roomGroup;    // list of involved scene nodes
    list<int> frequencyBands;}     // list of involved frequency bands
```

Using this data structure, a complete propagation path consists of a list of such simulation steps, whereby each entry contains the type of simulation (PS2R: PS to Receiver, PS2P: PS to Portal, SS2R: SS to Receiver, SS2P: SS to Portal, see Sect. 5.5), pointers to the sender (PS orSS) and receiver (listener or portal), pointers to the room group's scene nodes, and a list of all involved frequency band IDs, with

```
struct soundPath{
    list<simStep> subPaths;}       // list of involved simulation steps
```

whereby each simulation step is independent from the others. This infers that the simulation scheduler does not have to follow a certain order of path propagation.

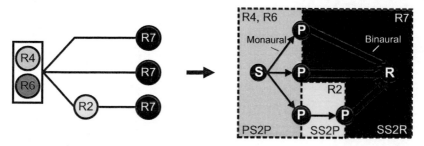

Figure 8.3: Transformation of the PST, resulting from the recursive depth-first search, into a directed acyclic PPG.

8.2 The Path Propagation Tree

After all simulations are carried out, the PST is further processed in order to extract a blueprint for a filtering network that simulates the sound propagation from the PS to the listener: the so-called Path Propagation Tree (PPG) as was already introduced in Sect. 5.5. The computation of this directed acyclic graph from a PST is fairly easy, because the PPG already contains all necessary data that are needed for constructing the corresponding filter network. This conversion is conducted in four steps: First, the PST's root node is replaced by a source node S which represents the PS. Second, all edges of the PST are replaced by nodes that represent their respective portal filters. Third, all nodes of the PST are substituted by edges that represent the sound propagation between two points, i.e., the simulated RIRs. And fourth, all leaf nodes of the PST are merged to a single summation point R, representing the receiver (an example is given in Fig. 8.3). Although the PPG is actually just a twisted version of the PST, it offers a more transparent description of the filter concatenation, which is of major importance for the real-time convolution of the complete filter network [WS09, WSPV09].

Chapter 9

Real-time Implementation of Room Acoustics Simulation Methods

'Of course I'm sane, when trees start talking to me, I don't talk back.'

(*The Light Fantastic*, Terry Pratchet, British writer)

Properly identifying simulation events and their respective input data is a basic requirement in almost any real-time application in order to avoid unnecessary computational overheads. This includes not only a logical separation of simulations events into single processes (see Chap. 5 and Chap. 6), but also an optimized storage and handling of data in terms of accessibility, demand, efficiency, and transparency. However, a complete description of all implementation details and tweaks that are applied in RAVEN is infeasible within the scope of this thesis, especially when keeping in mind that today, RAVEN has grown to roughly 70000 thousand lines of code. Therefore, only the most important details for both the IS method and RT will be further regarded that have the biggest impact on the overall implementation concept. Nonetheless, detailed descriptions can be found in [Sle04, Dro06, Pel07, Poh08, Ryb09].

9.1 Real-time Implementation of the Image Source Method

In this section, several implementation concepts for the use with ISs are described that offer three fundamental advantages: first, a significant reduction in the overall number of ISs is gained for the processing of a single simulation step. Second, a convenient handling of relationships between ISs is acquired by organizing all ISs in so-called Image Source Trees (ISTs) that support a fast expansion, update and destruction of tree nodes, i.e., ISs, which is basic necessity during modification events of the geometry. And third, concepts for the determination whether specific scene objects are visible from a certain position are introduced by the example of a tree-like data structure. This tree describes the visibility of edges among each other in order to further exclude scene elements from the simulation.

9.1.1 Plane-Polygon Map

Testing ISs for audibility (see Sect. 5.2) usually poses a bottleneck in real-time simulations due to the large amount of ISs that have to be processed within tight time frames (see Sect. 6.1). Therefore, a tweaked generation of ISs has been implemented, thereby reducing the number of generated ISs very efficiently by not mirroring on all faces of the geometry but rather on their spanned planes. This efficiently reduces the number of ISs (see below), but information of the single coplanar polygons that lie on a plane becomes lost during this plane-driven generation of ISs, e.g., two coplanar polygons may have different material data. Fortunately, it is quite easy to recover this information fast and effectively by means of a so-called Plane-Polygon Map (PPM). This map is created by searching for all coplanar polygons of a specific room geometry (static or dynamic) and storing these polygon sets under the map entries of the corresponding planes, as is exemplified in Fig. 9.1. By using the PPM in intersection tests during the IS audibility test, the produced additional computational effort for recovering the hit polygon ID is reduced to simple point-in-polygon tests of the intersection point with the plane's coplanar polygons. Thus, this overhead is negligibly small compared to the massive reduction of ISs that have to be handled at runtime. Referring back to the example in Fig. 9.1, both a polygon- and a plane-based IS-generation are compared to give an idea of the huge differences that occur already for simple geometries (here, the room represents a common wall alignment since rooms are usually quite symmetric). A closer examination of this room geometry shows that there are twelve polygons[1], four pairs of which are coplanar, as well as eight different planes. The total number of ISs N_{IS} for the respective methods is:

$$N_{IS_{poly}} = \sum_{j=1}^{i} n_{poly} \cdot (n_{poly} - 1)^{j-1} \qquad N_{IS_{plane}} = \sum_{j=1}^{i} n_{plane} \cdot (n_{plane} - 1)^{j-1} \quad (9.1)$$

---

[1]Ceiling and floor are skipped for the sake of transparency.

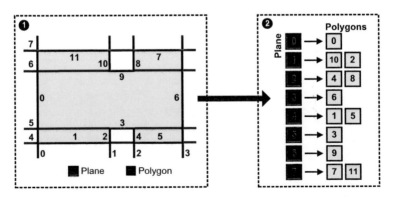

Figure 9.1: Generation of a plane-polygon map: (1) example of simple room geometry; (2) corresponding plane-polygon-map, which sorts polygons according to their coplanarity.

with n_{poly} denoting the number of polygons, n_{plane} the number of planes and i the IS order. The comparison of the total number of fourth-order ISs for both approaches reveals the advantage of the plane-based IS-method (Tab. 9.1). Instead of 17568 ISs, only 4096 ISs have to be tested on audibility at run-time, which means a reduction by a factor four and, thus, allows one to deal with higher order ISs under real-time constraints.

IS Method	Total number of generated ISs			
	1st order	2nd order	3rd order	4th order
Polygon-based	12	144	1596	17568
Plane-based	8	64	512	4096

Table 9.1: Comparison of polygon- and plane-based IS generation

9.1.2 Image Source Tree

A major problem with the large number of ISs is to efficiently gain access to specific ISs of a single source chain (see Sect. 5.2). While static indexing on data containers that simply store all ISs is probably the fastest way to generate these information, it is also the most inflexible of all solutions. If the geometry is modified, ISs have to be updated, generated and destroyed (see Sect. 6.2). This requires a dynamic linkage and update of ISs that cannot be handled efficiently on a clustered data structure – but on a tree-like one, the so-called IST. Here, tree nodes refer to ISs that are linked via edges according to their reflection path. The depth of the IST corresponds to the IS order, which means that the respective PS, SS, or DS is located in the first branch of the tree (IS of zeroth order). The subsequent branches are then created by mirroring the current IS on the room's plane, analogous to the method described in Sect. 5.2, and the newly created nodes are linked to their father via edges (see Fig. 9.2). By using this data structure, the required audibility test of ISs can be described recursively by tracking their corresponding reflection paths with:

```
function IS_AUDIBLE(TreeNode S, Point R)
  InterPoint = getIntersection(S, R)

  If(S.ISOrder != 0)          // Is TreeNode the root?
    If(InterPoint exists)     // The connection line between the
      return false;           // the last element of the source chain
    Else                      // must not intersect with the geometry
      return true;
  Else                        // Current TreeNode is an IS
    If(InterPoint hits last mirror plane of TreeNode)
      If(InterPoint lies inside one of the coplanar polygons)
        IS_AUDIBLE(getFatherNode(), InterPoint);
      Else
        return false;         // No specular reflection path exists
```

Listing 9.1: Pseudocode of a recursive audibility check of tree nodes, i.e., ISs.

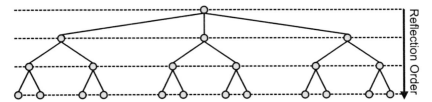

Figure 9.2: In this example, the *static* scene geometry consists of three reflection planes. ISs are generated up to third order (yellow) and stored in a tree data structure, where the tree's height denotes the maximum IS reflection order.

If a dynamic object is inserted into the scene, new ISs have to be generated that relate to the newly inserted geometry, and the IST has to be expanded accordingly. Figure 9.4(a-c) illustrates this process where a single polygon, i.e., an additional reflection plane, is added to the scene. At first, a new brother node is inserted in each subsequent branch of the root node, i.e., the IS of zeroth order (see Figure 9.4(a)). New ISs are generated by mirroring the corresponding father node's IS on the considered reflection plane of the dynamic object. In order to compute all possible ISs up to a given maximum order, the newly generated nodes have to be expanded to the full tree. Consequently, one has to distinguish between generating either a first-order subbranch or a higher order one. In the first case, only ISs of the respective brother nodes have to be taken into account for the IS mirroring process (see Fig. 9.4(b)). In the second case, all remaining and newly generated tree nodes are considered also including nodes that were generated in the first case. Thus, ISs of both brother nodes and father nodes have to be considered for computing the ISs of the newly created subbranches (see Fig. 9.4(c)). In contrast, the removal of dynamic objects from the scene is a fast and simple operation, whereby ISs are excluded from the IST again by recursively destroying all subtrees of the object's father nodes from down to top (see 9.3). The most frequent event, i.e., the object manipulation, goes along with a position update of all corresponding ISs, which is basically the reverse search operation in comparison to an object destruction. Here, the IST is traversed

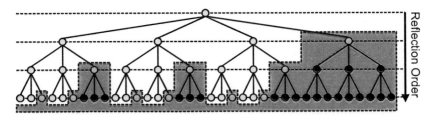

Figure 9.3: Deletion of a dynamic object and corresponding updates of the IS tree. Now, the fourth reflection plane is destroyed again and the respective ISs have to be removed from the IS tree again. Therefore, the father nodes (orange) of the destroyed object are considered, and subsequent branches are destroyed recursively (red area).

from top to down, starting from the object's father nodes (orange) and following all underlying subbranches (deep red) until the leaves of the IST are reached. Thereby, the position of each traversed IS (orange and deep red) is updated according to the modified geometry (see Fig. 9.4).

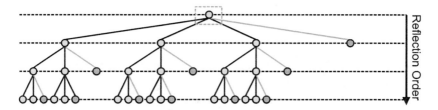

(a) A reflection plane is added to scene; this requires the computation of new dynamic ISs. These ISs are included to the IST by adding new brother nodes (orange) to all existing branches. The new ISs are generated by mirroring the respective ISs of the father nodes on the new reflection plane.

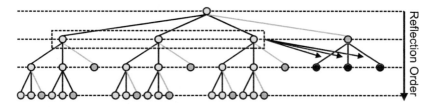

(b) ISs of brother nodes (red dashed box) are mirrored on the new inserted reflection plane and stored as child nodes (red).

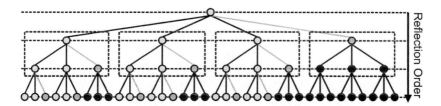

(c) Final step. All newly generated tree nodes with an order greater than one are expanded until the maximum IS order is reached. Now, ISs of both the father nodes and brother nodes have to be taken into account (deep red dashed boxes).

Figure 9.4: Insertion of a dynamic object and corresponding updates of the IS tree.

9.1.3   Tracking of Edge Diffraction Paths

In the case of diffraction simulations with the IS method, it is reasonable to add more information to the IST than just reflection paths of ISs so as to accelerate the identification of valid sound propagation paths across and in between edge sequences. Thus, all nodes of the IST that belong to a PS or SS store information on the visibility of edges, while each node of a DS's IST additionally stores information on visible receivers as well as an instance of the genuine edge that was mirrored on

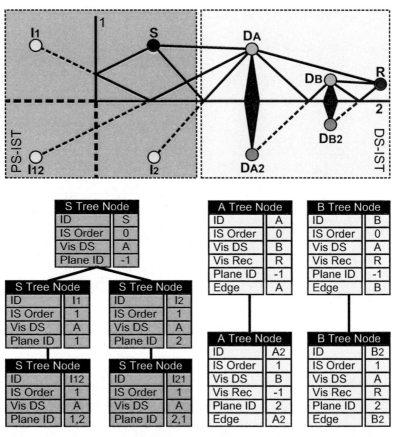

Figure 9.5: Audible propagation paths from a PS S to a receiver R across two edges, represented by their DSs D_A and D_B. Each source (S, D_A, or D_B) has independent access to its modified ISTs, where each tree node additionally contains information on the visibility of edges and, in the case of a DS-IST, also on that of receivers. By using these data structures, sound propagation paths in between and across edges can be tracked efficiently. Note that I_{21} of the PS-IST is inaudible for all potential receivers (in this example it is only D_A), which is the reason why it is not depicted above.

the node's current reflection path. In the case of edges, these visibility checks are reduced to simple point-to-point intersection tests between a starting point and the edge's starting-, center-, and end point in order to save computation times. By applying these modified ISTs, single sound propagation paths from a PS/SS to a receiver that also includes edge paths can be conveniently determined; the applied search algorithm is exemplified in Fig. 9.5). Here, the scene contains a PS S, a receiver R, and two edges represented by their DSs D_A and D_B, where the corresponding three ISTs are given below this drawing. Since the direct line of sight between S and R is blocked by the edge A, all propagation paths across and in between all involved edges are determined starting at S and ending at R. As already introduced in Sect. 5.2 and similar to the description of sound propagation paths across rooms (see Chap. 8), sound propagation paths that include edges are described by their type: either Source-to-Diffraction Edge (S2D), Diffraction Edge-to-Diffraction Edge (D2D), or Diffraction Edge-to-Receiver (D2R), with:

```
struct simStep_D{
    int type;         // Type of sub path    (S2D, D2D, D2R)
    void* source;     // Pointer to source   (PS/SS, IS, DS, DIS)
    void* receiver;}  // Pointer to receiver (R/Portal, DS).
```

The path search is performed in three subsequent steps: first, specular reflections paths from the source to all visible edges are computed (in this case to DS_A) up to a user-defined maximum reflection order by using the search algorithm given in List. 9.1 on the PS-IST with D_A as receiving point. Second, all visible edges are further processed by tracking their propagation paths along other visible edges on their way up to a maximum diffraction order, also including specular reflections in between edges. The pseudocode of the recursive search algorithm for the edge's corresponding DS-ISTs is given as follows:

```
function GET_EDGE_PATHS(list <simStep_D> path, TreeNode source)
// Save information on current path
Copy current path to stack
// Specular reflected paths to next visible edge
For(All ChildNodes)
    For(All visible DSs of current ChildNode)
        Create SimStep_D for current ChildNode// D2D
        path.push(simStep_D)                        // Add SimStep
        If(ChildNode.IS_Order <= MaxReflOrder)
            GET_EDGE_PATHS(path, ChildNode)
// Propagation paths across visible edges
For(All visible DSs of current TreeNode)
    If(Edge not already element of path)
        Create SimStep_D for current TreeNode // D2D
        path.push(simStep_D)                        // Add SimStep
        If(DiffOrder < MaxDiffOrder)
            GET_EDGE_PATHS(path, root of visible DS)// Go to next DE-IST
```

Listing 9.2: Pseudocode of a recursive search algorithm that identifies valid propagation paths across edges including specular surface reflections in between.

During the third and final step, the sound paths between the receiver and visible edges are computed, similar to step 1. Then, all propagation paths are subsequently concatenated with each other, whereby direct paths from edge to edge are skipped if there is a direct line of sight between the source edge and R. It should be noted that edge paths that were computed during step 2 do not change for static geometrical scene elements; thus, they can be preprocessed. In the case of dynamic elements, however, these paths have to be recomputed after every scene modification.

9.1.4 Powersets of Image Sources

As a matter of principle, the number of ISs that have to be generated for a multi-room scenario is quite large, even if PPMs are used to reduce this number. ISs that belong to a PS, SS, or DS have to be mirrored not only on all surfaces of the respective source room but also on the surfaces of all other rooms to cover the complete possible propagation paths through interconnecting portals. Therefore, the set of ISs has to be subdivided into smaller subsets to reduce the overall number of ISs that have to be processed at runtime. A data structure that perfectly matches this type of organization is the *power set*. The power set M of a set of n entities contains 2^n elements, whereby every subset, i.e., family set of M, refers to an n-bit number, where the m-th bit refers to activity or inactivity of the m-th entity of M. In the case of the ASG, these entities are rooms, and the room activity or inactivity is given

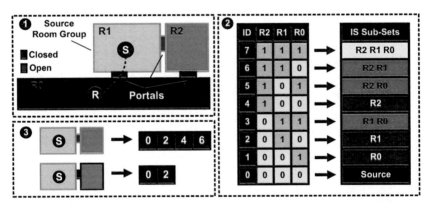

Figure 9.6: Concept of ISs handling in RAVEN: (1) Scene example: three rooms are interconnected by portals. A PS is located in the room group $\{R1, R2\}$ and the receiver is located in the room group $\{R0\}$. (2) Power set P for the three-room situation, where the room sequence is encoded in a binary code that relates to room activities (1) and inactivities (0). All ISs are sorted into encapsulated containers depending on the room combination in their reflection paths. (3) The portal between $R1$ and $R2$ becomes closed, which divides the source room group into to new room groups, each containing one room. This means that room $R2$ became inactive for the current simulation step. Therefore, ISs that where reflected inside $R2$ do not have to be taken into account for further computation of specular reflection paths in the source room group unless the portal is opened again.

by the current configuration of portal states. Thus, all ISs can be sorted into the respective family sets of M by simply gathering information on room IDs in their reflection paths. An example is given in Fig. 9.6 showing the power set for an ASG containing three rooms $R2$, $R1$, $R0$ and the linked subsets of ISs. By assuming the portal between $R1$ and $R2$ is closed in this example, $R2$ will become invalid for the first simulation step in the propagation path (see previous chapter), i.e., the source room group, which means that all IS family sets of M can be excluded from further processing that contain the room ID $R2$ – in addition to all sets that relate to a reflection path in $R0$ since this room was already blocked. This significantly drops the number of IS family sets from four to two that have to be further processed; i.e., $P(0)$ and $P(2)$ remain.

9.2 Real-time Implementation of Ray Tracing

In contrast to the IS method, RT simulations do not require any special handling to select information from a huge set of data. This type of algorithm can be implemented straight forward, whereby the underlying simulation model already includes all required data (see Sect. 5.3). Thus, the aim of an efficient RT implementation is to identify unnecessary operations, to determine termination conditions, and to maintain well-structured code that can be run in parallel by using OpenMP. It is reasonable to implement the RT-algorithm in a particle-driven way with:

```
struct EnergyParticle{
  Point  StartPoint, EndPoint;      // General stuff
  Vec    Direction;
  float  CurrentEnergy, CurrentTime, CurrentSpeed;
  // Status variables & Counters
  bool   HasDiffuseHistory;         // Particle was scattered?
  bool   AllowDetection;            // Particle detection allowed?
  int    LastHitDC_ID;              // ID of the last hit DC
  int    PreEDreflectionOrder;      // Refl. counter before 1st edge
  int    EDreflectionOrder;         // Refl. counter after 1st edge
  int    ReflectionOrder;           // Number of reflections
  int    EDOrder;}                  // Number of diffractions
```

As one can see from the pseudocode, supplemental information on the particle's reflection history is stored along with general information that describe the particle propagation, such as starting point, travel direction, energy, and propagation time. In this way, each energy particle becomes an independent data entity that carries all required information for handling the respective particle propagation during the simulation, which also includes decisions about whether the particle may be counted by a detector that intersects with the current reflection path. These decisions have to be drawn for two reasons: first, the RT is part of a hybrid simulation model, meaning that specular reflections that were already covered by the IS method have to be skipped. Second, the applied RT method unites two types of simulation methods: a common particle tracing and a secondary-particle model (diffuse/diffracted rain) that can be interpreted as a first-order radiosity dialect (see Sect. 5.3). Here, direct hits of a scattered or diffracted energy particle with detectors that cross the current propagation path ought not be counted, as this energy portion was already covered by diffuse rain and diffracted rain, respectively. The easiest way to control all status variables and reflection counters is to implement three basic functions that are executed each time the respective event occurs:

```
function REFLECTED( )
   allowDetection  = true;         // Allow detection
   lastHitDC_ID    = −1;           // Set to dummy ID

   ReflectionOrder++;              // Counter increment
   If(EDOrder == 0)  PreEDreflectionOrder++;
   Else              EDreflectionOrder++;

function SCATTERED( )
   HasDiffuseHistory = true;       // Diffuse history
   allowDetection    = false;      // Forbid detection
   lastHitDC_ID      = −1;         // Set to dummy ID

   ReflectionOrder++;              // Counter increment
   If(EDOrder == 0)  PreEDreflectionOrder++;
   Else              EDreflectionOrder++;

function DIFFRACTED(int cylinderID )
   EDOrder++;                      // Increment Diffraction Order
   allowDetection = false;         // Forbid detection
   lastHitDC_ID   = cylinderID;    // Set to cylinder ID
```

Listing 9.3: Pseudocode of energy particle functions that set status variables and counters according to the occurred event.

The final decision whether the particle is allowed to be detected is then made by a logical comparison of all relevant counters and states, with

```
// Check if current path is already covered by the IS method
function DETECTION_ALLOWED_HYBRID
   If(EDOrder!=0)
     return (
       HasDiffuseHistory ||
       (PreEDreflectionOrder > MaxPreEDISOrder )||
       (EDreflectionOrder > MaxEDISOrder )||
       (EDOrder > MaxEDOrder ));
   Else
     return (reflectionOrder > MaxISOrder );

// Check if diffuse/diffracted rain was already detected
function DETECTION_ALLOWED_PARTICLE( )
     return allowDetection ;
```

Listing 9.4: Pseudocode of logical functions that evaluate the particle's states and counters in order to return whether the particle is currently valid for detection.

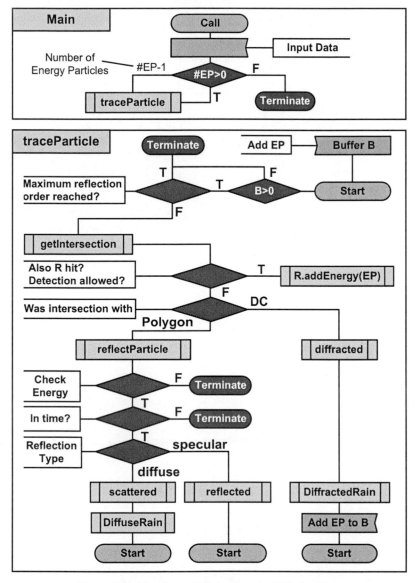

Figure 9.7: Flowchart of the implemented RT algorithm.

In addition to these logical comparisons that guarantee a correct energy balance among the simulation methods, physical-related information can be further evaluated to terminate the particle propagation:

Particle Energy If the particle's energy underruns a user-defined energy threshold, it is terminated.

Propagation Time If the particle's propagation time exceeds the histogram length or the particle cannot reach a detector within the given maximum propagation time, it is terminated.

Reflection Order If the particle's reflection order is greater than a user-defined maximum, it is terminated in order to kill algorithmic deadlocks, as particles may become trapped between polygons[2]. However, this break condition ought not interfere with the RT model, which means that a number in the magnitude of thousands should be set to avoid errors in the late part of the RIR.

The current implementation features a particle buffer where energy particles that hit a DC are temporarily stored until they are further traced. This avoids recursive calls of the RT's main routine and enables a clear and transparent implementation, whereby a flowchart is given in Fig. 9.7.

---

[2]This can happen for two reasons: (1) floating point imprecision on the dedicated working machine, and (2) inaccurate modeling of the room geometry.

Part IV

Evaluation

Chapter 10

Analytical Validation

"The logic of validation allows us to move between the two limits of dogmatism and skepticism."

(Paul Ricœr, French philosopher)

This chapter serves to investigate both the accuracy of the presented simulation concept and the quality of the corresponding implementation, whereby three crucial parts can be identified: first, the hybrid simulation model itself that takes into account specular and diffuse reflections; second, the simulation of sound transmission through structural elements into adjacent rooms; and third, the computation of sound propagation into shadow zones of edges. All three parts are assessed simply and transparently in order to reduce the number of simulation uncertainties that usually come from imprecise input data. Thus, the focus of this chapter lies more in validating the overall simulation concept than in showing that simulation results match real-word measurements of some specific setups. However, the latter has already been shown in various publications, where, for instance, a car interior [ANVS09, Jau10, AJ10] or a recording studio [AM10] were chosen as test scenario. In addition, more comparisons either with reference simulations or real-world measurements can be found in [Dro06, SDV07, VS09a, VS09b, PS].

10.1 Hybrid Simulation Model

An appropriate and simple test for validating the hybrid simulation model is the analysis of the room's reverberation time in comparison with the scattering coefficients of the applied surface materials. A complete diffuse sound field relates to a scattering coefficient of 1, whereby the simulated reverberation time has to match calculations according to Sabine[1] and Eyring[2], respectively. In addition, it is also a well-known fact that the reverberation time increases in less diffuse environments and reaches a maximum for a scattering coefficient of 0, i.e., purely specular IS-modeling. In between these two extremes, the reverberation time falls exponentially with an increasing diffuseness of the sound field, i.e., increasing scattering coefficients [Vor08]. Thus, investigating reverberation times with variable scattering coefficients ought to reveal if the two energy models of deterministic ISs and stochastic RT are combined correctly with one another.

Test Model & Simulation Parameterization

A simple shoebox-shaped room with a volume of $1344\,m^3$ was chosen as test model featuring a calculated reverberation time of 0.43 s and 0.58 s according to Eyring and Sabine, respectively. Here, the equation according to Eyring is more accurate, since it is not based on the assumption of low-absorbing surfaces as in Sabine's approach. The room's side walls were modeled with an absorption factor of 0.05, while a factor of 0.8 was assigned to both the floor and the ceiling. In contrast, the same scattering coefficient was used for both materials and varied in steps of 0.05 during the simulations. A sound source was positioned in one half of the room, and 36 in-plane receivers were evenly distributed outside the source's critical distance in the opposite half of the room (see Fig. 10.1(a)). Room acoustical simulations were carried out by taking into account ISs of up to order 4, performing RT simulations with 25000 particles per frequency bands (octave band resolution), and averaging the results of all 36 receivers (more details are given in Fig. 10.1(b)).

Reverberation Time vs Scattering Coefficient

Figure 10.1(c) shows a comparison of the simulation results, whereby reverberation times (T30) were either calculated according to DIN EN ISO 3382 [ISO07], i.e., for the center frequencies 500 Hz and 1 kHz (red line), or by evaluating all center frequencies between 30 Hz and 16 kHz (orange line). In addition, the values of reverberation times are given that were calculated according to Sabine (green line) and Eyring (blue line).

Taking a closer look, one can see that the simulated reverberation times show the typical exponentially decreasing behavior with increasing diffuseness of the sound field, where simulated reverberation times start to match the prediction of Sabine for scattering coefficients of greater than 0.6. For a scattering coefficient of exactly one, the simulations according to DIN EN ISO 3382 exactly match the reverberation time according to Eyring, whereas the value derived from all 10 octave-band just missed that point by a very narrow margin. From this it follows that the transition from pure specular reflections to a diffuse sound field is covered correctly by the applied hybrid simulation.

---

[1]Wallace C. Sabine, American physicist, 1868 - 1919.
[2]Carl F. Eyring, Mexican physicist, 1889 - 1951.

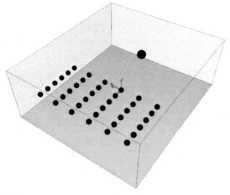

Sound Sources:	1
Receivers:	36
Maximum IS-order:	4
Particles/Band:	25000
Detector Radius:	0.25 m
Volume:	1344 m³
Temperature:	20 °C
Humidity:	50 %
Pressure:	101325 Pa

(a) CAD-model of the test scenario.   **(b)** Specifications.

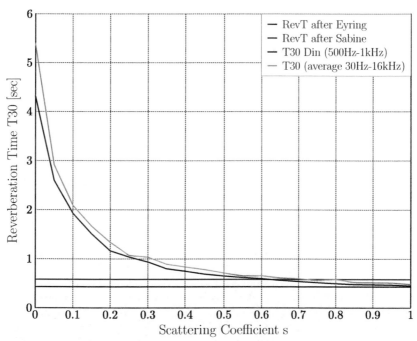

(c) Reverberation Time T30 in comparison with the scattering coefficient *s*.

Figure 10.1: A simple shoebox-shaped room was chosen as test model. Sound source and receivers are denoted by red and blue spheres, respectively.

10.2   Sound Transmission

A transparent way to prove the simulation concept of coupled rooms (see Sec. 5.5) is to model a virtual test facility for measuring the performance of a structural element and carry out simulations in compliance with the DIN EN ISO standard 140-3 in order to compute the respective building acoustics parameters from the results. As described in Sect. 2.4, the sound reduction index R can be directly derived from the average sound levels L_S and L_R in the source and receiving room, respectively. Thus, when simulating these two input values and computing the respective sound reduction indices, a good agreement with the actual portal transfer function would indicate a proper working simulation model.

Test Model & Simulation Parameterization

Figure 10.2(a) shows the model of the simple test facility for measuring the performance of the connecting partition, i.e., portal (red area). Here, the volume of each room added up to $90\,\mathrm{m}^3$, and the partitioning element had an area of $16\,\mathrm{m}^2$. An absorption factor of 0.1 and a scattering coefficient of 0.3 was assigned to all surfaces in order to create a quite diffuse sound field inside the rooms. Thirty-six in-plane receivers were evenly distributed in both rooms (18 receivers each) for measuring the corresponding averaged sound level pressures, while the sound source (red sphere) was located in the source room only. Room acoustical simulations were carried out by taking into account ISs of up to order 3 and performing RT simulations with 20000 particles per frequency band (one-third octave band resolution) and averaging the results of all 18 receivers located in the source room (L_S, green spheres) and the receiving room (L_R, blue spheres), respectively. More details are given in Fig. 10.2(b)).

Simple Room-to-Room Situation

A comparison of the portal's frequency-dependent sound reduction indices with the corresponding simulated values is shown in Fig. 10.2(c). In general, the simulation shows good agreement with the portal's reference curve, which indicates that the applied simulation model for coupled rooms is appropriate for describing sound transmission through structural elements. Here, the values fit best in the frequency band of between $2\,\mathrm{kHz}$ and $16\,\mathrm{kHz}$, where estimation errors decrease to an average error of less than $1.5\,\mathrm{dB}$. Below $2\,\mathrm{kHz}$, one can see that the simulated parameters become imprecise yet still show similar slopes as the reference curve with an average offset below $2.5\,\mathrm{dB}$. The estimation worsens for very low frequencies ($<125\,\mathrm{Hz}$), which is not so surprising, since these frequencies are far below the respective Schroeder frequency of roughly $250\,\mathrm{Hz}$. An error of $8\,\mathrm{dB}$ also occurs at $20\,\mathrm{kHz}$, which implies that not enough particles were used for the RT simulation of this frequency band due to the massive absorption by air during the particle propagation. Nevertheless, a refinement of this specific simulation was regarded as unnecessary, since human adults cannot perceive frequencies above $16\,\mathrm{kHz}$.

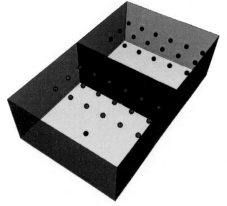

Sound Sources:	1
Receivers (Room):	18
Maximum IS-order:	3
Number of Particles:	20000
Detector Radius:	0.25 m
Volume (Room):	90 m^3
T30 (Room):	1.1 s
Area (Room):	126 m^2
Area (Partition):	18 m^2

(a) CAD-model of the test scenario.   (b) Specifications.

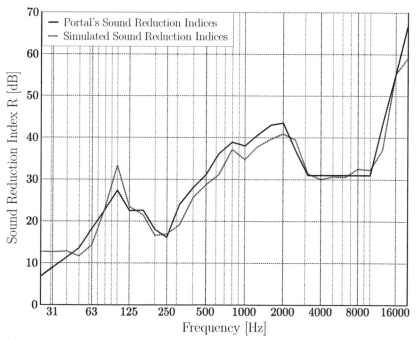

(c) Comparison of simulated sound reduction indices (red dashed line) with the input portal transfer function (black solid line).

Figure 10.2: A simple room-to-room situation was chosen as test model. The sound source is denoted by a red sphere, while receivers in the source and receiving room are represented by green and blue spheres, respectively.

10.3   Sound Diffraction

As described earlier, the implemented hybrid approach for simulating edge diffraction
from finite edges is based on Stephenson's DAPDF (stochastic RT, see Sect. 5.3.3)
and Svensson's secondary source model (IS-model, see Sect. 5.2.3), where in various
comparisons both approaches proved to work very well in either 2D (Stephenson)
[SS07, Ste10a] or 3D (Svensson) [SW00, SSV10, SE10]. Here, especially the latter is
appropriate as a reference model, since it is today one of the most accurate simulation
methods utilizing GA for computing edge diffraction from finite edges. However, the
implemented extension of Stephenson's stochastic model to 3D still has to be verified.

It was shown in Sect. 2.5 that the sound phenomenon of edge diffraction is a quite
complex process already in the theoretical case of sound diffraction from a semi-
infinite edge. Since infinite edges do not exist in reality, a simple test scenario of a
single, but finite wedge was chosen, where the analytical solution is still well known.
In the following, the test setup is described in all detail, and simulation results are
compared and discussed that were obtained either by RAVEN's simulation methods
of edge diffraction (IS-model and RT) or Svensson's Open Source Edge Diffraction
MATLAB toolbox [Sve10].

Test Model & Simulation Parameterization

Similar to the test scenario presented in [Ste10a], Fig. 10.3 shows the investigated
model of a single wedge with an inner angle of $10°$ – though this time completely in 3D
and with fix receiver positions[3]. The edge length was set at $100\,\mathrm{m}$ to prevent an early
cut-off of the edge diffraction impulse responses (see Fig. 5.8) to better investigate
the accuracy of their overall decay. As in the original test case, all surfaces were
modeled as fully absorbent to suppress any sound reflections but the direct sound,
all material parameters were set accordingly. The sound source (red sphere) and all
receivers (blue spheres) were positioned in-plane on a circle having a radius of $10\,\mathrm{m}$
and with center on the edge, whereby the sound source was exactly located at the
height of the diffracting edge. Meanwhile, receivers were distributed around the edge
in increments of $12°$ (seen from the edge), i.e., at $-84°$, $-72°$, ... , $+72°$, $+84°$. This
resulted in a total number of 15 receivers with the same distance of $10\,\mathrm{m}$ to the edge
as the sound source, where a positive and negative angle corresponded to receivers in
the view and shadow zone, respectively.

As only the direct sound path over the edge was investigated in the original test
series, room acoustical simulations had to be carried out separately, since the direct
sound is covered solely by the accurate IS-model in the case of hybrid simulations (see
Sect. 5.4). Consequently, the first simulation series was carried out with ISs of up to
order 0 (direct sound) and no RT, whereas in the second series RT simulations were
performed with 100000 particles per frequency band (one-third octave band resolution), a detection sphere radius of roughly $1\,\mathrm{m}$, and no ISs (all important simulation

---

[3]In the original test scenarios, the receivers were positioned at multiples of the regarded wavelengths in a 2D scenario.

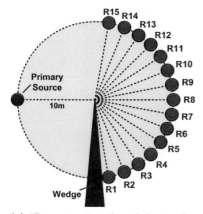

(a) 2D construction plan of the simula-   (b) CAD-model of the test scenario.
tion model.

Sound Sources:	1	Maximum IS-order:	0
Receivers:	15	Particles/Band:	100000
Angle Steps Receiver [deg]:	12	Wedge Angle [deg]:	10
Detector Radius [m]:	1.05	Edge Length [m]:	100

(c) Specifications.

Figure 10.3: A simple wedge (red area) with an inner angle of $10°$ and a length of $100\,\mathrm{m}$ was chosen as test model for validating the hybrid simulation model of edge diffraction. The sound source (red sphere) is located on one side of the edge at the same height as the edge, while 15 receivers (blue spheres) are distributed in-plane in angle steps of $12°$ on the edge's opposite side. Both, sound source and receivers are located $10\,\mathrm{m}$ from the edge.

parameters are summarized in Fig. 10.3(c)). Here, it should be noted that the large number of particles was only chosen to acquire the best possible results under these anechoic test conditions. However, tests with a lower particle count down to 10000 per frequency band showed no significant influence on the simulation results. For a better extraction of the edge's influence on the sound field, also known as the *transmission level*, all results were additionally scaled by the reciprocal of the theoretical values of corresponding free-field simulations without edge. In addition, air absorption was neglected in all cases, since it is not covered by the Edge Diffraction Toolbox.

Sound Diffraction from a Single Finite Wedge (Image Sources)

RAVEN's implemented IS-model separately handles receivers that are located either in the view or shadow zone of the wedge. Here, it was argued that the influence of the wedge in the transition zone is small and, thus, these wave effects were not considered in further conceptual aspects of the simulation model for the sake of a fast handling

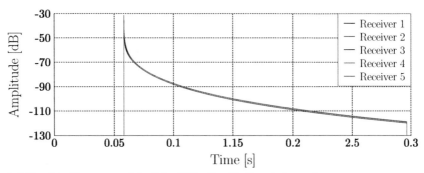

(a) Simulated by means of the Edge Diffraction Toolbox (reference).

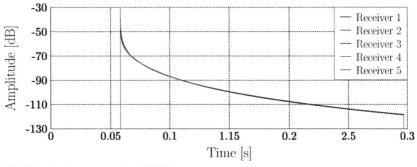

(b) Simulated by means of RAVEN.

Figure 10.4: Time domain edge diffraction impulse response calculated by means of both, (a) the Edge Diffraction Toolbox (reference) and (b) RAVEN's IS-method.

of ISs at run-time. In order to solely validate RAVEN's deterministic IS diffraction model, the first five receivers are further discussed, as they are located deep in the wedge's shadow zone (see Fig. 10.3(a)) and, therefore, ought to give exact simulation results.

Figure 10.4 shows simulated edge diffraction impulse responses that were obtained by both the Edge Diffraction Toolbox and RAVEN. In the time domain, both methods seem to provide identical results with correct onset and cut-off sample at first, but a transformation to frequency domain (see Fig. 10.5) reveals small discrepancies that come from slightly different maximum amplitudes and slopes of the impulse responses' decays. These errors can be explained by floating point imprecision on the test machine[4] and RAVEN's less accurate integration method in comparison to the numerical integration solver used in the Edge Diffraction Toolbox. Here, simulation errors start to grow up to 2 dB for frequencies of above 12 kHz due to the less accurate fine structure of the impulse responses. However, with an overall transmission level

---

[4]For fast computations at run-time, most variables are stored only with floating point precision.

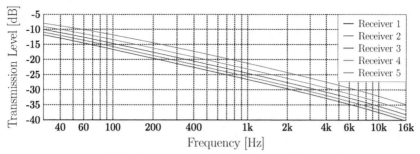

(a) Simulated by means of the Edge Diffraction Toolbox (reference).

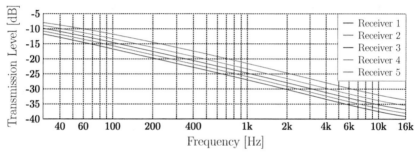

(b) Simulated by means of RAVEN.

Figure 10.5: Frequency domain edge diffraction transfer functions calculated by means of both, (a) the Edge Diffraction Toolbox (reference) and (b) RAVEN's IS method.

of over -35 dB for these high frequencies, it can be assumed that these deviations are not perceptible. Below 12 kHz, the mean error of less than 0.5 dB is negligible. Thus, the implemented diffraction model based on IS was proven to give quite accurate results for receivers located in the shadow zone of a finite wedge, at least for the more important low and middle-range frequencies that feature much higher transmission levels than high frequencies.

Sound Diffraction from a Single Finite Wedge (Ray Tracing)

Since the wave phenomenon of edge diffraction is directly integrated in the applied RT simulation method (see Sect. 5.3), no separation between view and shadow zone is necessary and, thus, all receivers are taken into account for further considerations. Here, one ought not forget that two totally different simulation models are compared with each other, where one is based on a deterministic IS-model and the other on a stochastic RT method. In addition, the applied DAPDF, which is the basis for the diffracted rain method and which describes the frequency-dependent diffraction of sound particles, is only an approximation and has never yet been tested in 3D.

In the following, the same type of plot is used for assessing the accuracy of the RT method as proposed in [Ste10a], where transmission levels are plotted for one frequency over all receiver angles; e.g., a receiver angle of $-84\,^{\circ}$ then relates to Receiver 1 (see Fig. 10.3). Two example plots are shown in Fig. 10.6 – one for a very low frequency (50 Hz) and one for a high frequency (10 kHz). Sound transmission levels from RT simulations were directly extracted from the receiver histograms by summing up the detected energy of each inspected frequency band, taking the square root, and normalizing the values as described above. Taking a closer look at both plots, one can see that the simulation results match each other quite well. Here, errors occur for low frequencies in the deep shadow zone of the edge, which is a known problem

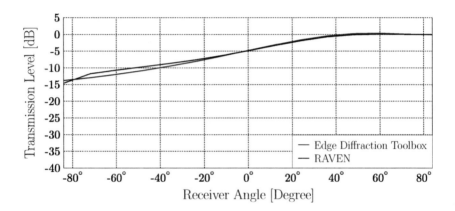

(a) Sound transmission levels at 50 Hz.

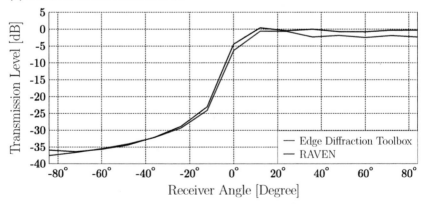

(b) Sound transmission levels at 10000 Hz.

Figure 10.6: Transmission levels with respect to receiver angles calculated by means of both (a) the Edge Diffraction Toolbox (reference) and (b) RAVEN's RT method.

of the DAPDF, especially if the distance from the source to the edge is smaller than a few wavelengths [Ste10a]. Besides Receiver 1 at $-84°$ (deepest shadow zone), the simulation at 10 kHz matches very well the results of the Edge Diffraction toolbox in the wedge's shadow zone, but other errors of about 2 dB occur in the view zone that are attributed to wave effects not covered by the simplified simulation method based on RT. Nonetheless, the overall good agreement shows that the 2D-DAPDF has been successfully ported to 3D by using the diffracted rain method.

Chapter 11

Performance

'You may delay, but time will not, and lost time is never found again.'

(Benjamin Franklin, American politician and scientist)

This chapter investigates the performance of RAVEN's core simulation concepts with respect to real-time capability, since a complete analysis of all involved algorithms would go far beyond the scope of this thesis. It was proven in various publications that the entire simulation concept is able to work within the dictated real-time constraints given in Chap. 6, where detailed performance analyses of single algorithms can be found in [SL06, SDV07, Pel07, LSVA07, Poh08, Ryb09, Sch09a]. Therefore, the focus of this chapter is rather the overall speed-up that can be gained by utilizing spatial data structures in room acoustics simulation.

After introducing five room models that were used as input data throughout the tests, the performance of both BSP- and SH-based search algorithms is analyzed with respect to the two main simulation functions – the IS method and RT. Afterwards, computation times caused by operations on dynamic geometric objects are further discussed in order to reveal issues of both types of data structures and prove the overall concept of handling dynamic scene modifications (see Chap. 6).

All results are compared to that of BF approaches, which helps to better rate the gained speed-ups by the use of spatial data structures. It should be noted that the simulation of edge diffraction was omitted in all tests for three reasons: first, no additional information on the performance of spatial data structures is gained from including diffraction to the simulation algorithms. Second, the exclusion of edge diffraction leads to simple and comprehensive test scenarios. And third, a detailed performance analysis of edge diffraction simulations is already given in [Poh08].

11.1 Test Models

Five different geometrical scenes of different complexity and size were considered for analyzing the performance of simulation algorithms. All models were constructed after real-existing rooms, where material parameters were chosen accordingly [Sta09]. In particular, the rooms were constructed after the following locations:

Living Room The floor plan was modeled after typical room geometries of living rooms. The small room contains typical furniture in a living room, such as a sofa and bookshelves, and the floor is covered with carpet.

Lecture Room The floor plan was modeled after the 4G lecture room at the Institute of Communication Systems and Data Processing, RWTH Aachen University, Aachen, Germany. The medium-size room contains typical furniture of a lecture room, such as tables and chairs, and the floor is covered with parquet, while the ceiling features absorbing elements.

Classroom The floor plan was modeled after a classroom at the Alfred-von-Reumont elementary school in Aachen, Germany. The medium-size room contains typical classroom furniture, such as tables, bookshelves and chairs, and the respective scattering coefficients were measured by using scale models [VS09b].

Concert Hall The floor plan was modeled after the Europa-Saal concert hall which is part of the Eurogress Convention Center, Aachen, Germany. The large room contains typical furniture in concert halls, such as a theater style seating, and the floor is covered with parquet. The gallery is connected to the ground floor via two stairways.

Metro Station The floor plan was modeled after a metro station in Warsaw, Poland. The large room contains typical objects of a metro station such as benches, columns, ticket machines and rails. The side walls feature absorbing elements that significantly reduce the reverberation time. All tunnel entries are modeled as fully absorbent.

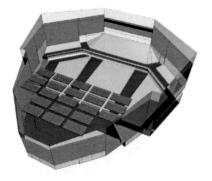   

(b) CAD-model of the concert hall.   **(a)** CAD-model of the metro station.

Figure 11.1: Exemplary computer models that were applied for benchmarking the room acoustics simulation methods.

Scene Model	Polygons	Planes	AEL[m]	Volume[m^3]	T(S)[s]
Living Room	67	31	1.43	90	0.53
Lecture Room	147	28	2.89	418	0.57
Classroom	391	81	0.79	283	0.69
Concert Hall	348	142	3.93	14372	1.3
Metro Station	272	129	4.03	16500	2.14

Table 11.1: Information on geometry and reverberation times of the applied test scenarios. Here, AEL denotes the *average edge length*, which is relevant for algorithms based on SH, and $T(S)$ relates to the reverberation time according to Sabine.

Basic information on the models' geometry and reverberation time are summarized in Tab. 11.1, and two exemplary models are shown in Fig. 11.1. More details on these room models and respective screen shots are given in Appx. A.

11.2 Performance of the Image Source Method

In the following, the performance of the IS audibility tests is analyzed with respect to spatial data structures. At first, results of a brute-force IS-method are compared to the BSP-based method, which is the core acceleration algorithm in all parts of the real-time simulation of ISs where no dynamic objects are involved. As described in Chap. 6, RAVEN switches to a SH-based IS-method to maintain a fast responding auralization during modification events. Since these geometrical operations are the most time-critical processes of all simulation events, optimization techniques for SH are first discussed before evaluating the performance of specific modification events. For a better performance rating of IS audibility tests, information on the total number of ISs are given in Tab. 11.2, which have to be processed during the simulation of each room model. It should be noted that IS-shading techniques were always disabled in order to carry out the performance tests in a more general way. IS-shading is based on evaluating the visibility of ISs from certain observation points which usually leads to a significant reduction in the overall number of ISs (examples are given for third-order ISs in Tab. 11.2). However, this acquired reduction is only valid for a certain source position, and therefore not generalizable for all possible source positions. Since these techniques were not explained in the course of this thesis, more details can be found in [Mec02].

11.2.1 Binary Space Partitioning

To give a better idea of the achieved speed-up by the use of BSP trees, a brute-force IS audibility test was implemented for comparison purpose. The latter tests every scene polygon on intersection instead of testing only a few spatial sub-partitions of the room by means of a BSP-tree structure. When using the concept of BSP for accelerating search operations, best performance is gained by using a balanced tree,

Scene Model	IS Order			
	up to 1st	up to 2nd	up to 3rd	(shaded)
Living Room	32	962	28862	(13676)
Lecture Room	29	785	21197	(7993)
Classroom	82	6562	524962	(186360)
Concert Hall	143	20165	2843267	(1873294)
Metro Station	130	16642	2130178	(633174)

Table 11.2: Information on the total number of ISs for the applied test scenarios. The values relate to the total amount of ISs, i.e., all ISs of lower-order are always taken into account, too. For third-order ISs, the reduced number of ISs as a result of IS shading for a random source position is given in parentheses.

i.e., a tree of minimum height, where the implemented method for constructing BSP-trees already optimizes this process (see Sec. 4.2). Although this subdivision is not optimal, it has always yielded a reliable and fast generation of quite balanced BSP-trees for a large variety of geometry shapes, which makes a detailed investigation rather obsolete. Therefore, this subsection only focuses on the overall performance of IS audibility tests exemplified by three test models (small, medium and large room volume).

Test Environment

All computations were performed on an off-the-shelf desktop personal computer featuring an Intel Core i7 2.8 GHz multi-core CPU (4 cores), Windows 7 (32-bit) operating system and Visual Studio 2005 SP1 as development environment. Process priorities were always set to normal in order to run the tests under ordinary system conditions. Computation times relate solely to the algorithmic test of ISs on audibility, as all necessary input data were preprocessed. Measurements were obtained by performing 100 iterations of each simulation method and averaging the respective results.

Computation Time vs. Image Source Order

Figure 11.2 shows measured computation times of IS-audibility tests up to third IS order, where the BSP-based tests are compared to the results of the brute-force approach (detailed results are given in Tab. 11.3). Three room models were taken into account, whereby each represented a certain room size. In particular, these were the models of the living room (small room), the classroom (medium-sized room) and the metro station (large room). As expected, the computation time of the brute-force method rises exponentially with the exponentially increasing number of ISs, whereas the BSP-based approach only has a rather linearly increasing computation time demand due to the drop in search complexity up to $\mathcal{O}(logN)$, with N denoting the number of polygons. With the assigned time slot of 550 ms for the simulation process (see Chap. 6), real-time capability for a room acoustical simulation with all

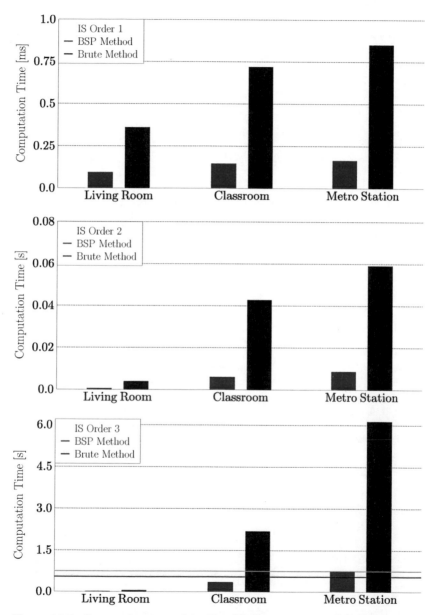

Figure 11.2: Computation times of the IS audibility test based on BSP in comparison with a BF approach. The solid red and orange lines in the third-order plot, parallel to the x-axis, denote the overall real-time constraint of 550 ms and 750 ms, respectively.

degrees of freedom such as moving sound sources, moving receiver, was reached for
all test models up to an IS order of three, with the exception of the metro station
that slightly missed this time constraint. However, computation times of the latter
room model for determining audible third-order ISs still satisfy the more moderate
constraint of 750 ms, whereby 70% of the translational movements greater than 25 cm
are covered. In addition, it should be kept in mind that the computing cluster that
is assigned to the real-time VR-system at RWTH Aachen University features eight
CPU cores per worker instead of four as in the test system.

11.2.2   Spatial Hashing

The following further investigates the three most crucial factors that directly influence
the performance of search algorithms based on SH: the voxel size, the hash table size
and the hash function. Here, the voxel size directly affects the number of polygons
that are hashed to a single voxel, whereas the hash table size and the hash function
itself affect the occurrence of hash collisions. Thus, optimized parameter settings have
to be found that yield the best possible performance. Consequently, the performance
of IS audibility tests with varying SH-parameterization is analyzed and compared to
the computation times of both the BF- and the BSP-algorithm (see Sec. 4.2).

Test Environment

All computations were performed on an off-the-shelf desktop personal computer featuring an AMD Athlon 2.7 GHz single-core CPU, Windows XP (32-bit) operating
system and Visual Studio 2005 SP1 as development environment. Although many
functions are usually computed in parallel using OpenMP, multi-core CPUs were
omitted in this analysis for the sake of comparability – some methods (especially SH)
would have gained more from the usage of parallel computing than others. Process
priorities were always set high in order to prevent an interference with other system
processes during the optimization. Computation times were measured by performing
10 iterations of each simulation method and averaging the respective results, whereby
all necessary input data was preprocessed.

Scene Model	IS Order		
	up to 1st [ms]	up to 2nd [ms]	up to 3rd [ms]
Living Room (BSP)	0.094	0.572	11.665
Living Room (BF)	0.361	3.942	48.607
Classroom (BSP)	0.146	6.003	344.324
Classroom (BF)	0.720	42.772	2187.852
Metro Station (BSP)	0.166	8.672	739.027
Metro Station (BF)	0.851	59.121	6129.158

Table 11.3: Detailed computation times of the IS audibility test based on BSP in comparison with a BF approach.

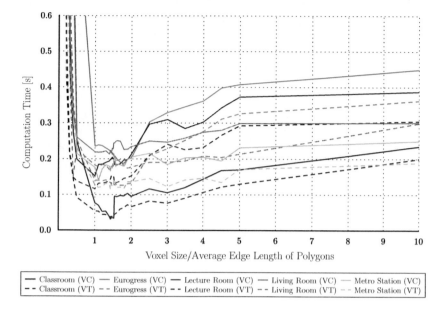

Figure 11.3: Computation times for IS audibility tests based on the two SH concepts, VC and VT, for all considered test scenarios, fixed image source order, fixed hash table size and varying voxel size in relation to the average edge length of the scene's polygons. In all cases best results are achieved by the VT approach with a relative voxel size of between [1, 2].

Computation Time vs. Voxel Size

The IS audibility tests based on SH were carried out for both methods, VT and VC (see Sec. 7.2), in both cases with a fixed hash table size. Being scene-dependent, the hash table size was always set to the number of scene polygons. The voxel size s was manipulated in relation to the average edge length of all scene polygons a_a resulting in a factor f, with $f = s/a_a$. Here, f was varied in steps of 0.1 for $f \in [0.1, 2.0]$ and in steps of 0.5 for $f \in [2.0, 10.0]$. During first measurements, the interval $f \in [1.425, 1.575]$ turned out to yield good results and the step size was therefore refined to $s = 0.025$ for this short interval. Figure 11.3 shows the computation times of IS audibility tests for both hashing approaches. For all scene models the plot shows a significant drop in computation time in the interval of $f \in [0.5, 4]$, where best results are achieved for the VT method with voxel sizes of between the single and double average edge length of the scene polygons, i.e., $f \in [1, 2]$. Table 11.4 summarizes the best results for both approaches, whereby the chosen values for f are given in parentheses. Moreover, the computation times of the BF- and the BSP-algorithm are given to better assess the computation times. Here, one can see that the BSP-based method always outperformed all other approaches, where the BF approach performed

Scene Model	IS-Order	Hash(VC)[ms]	Hash(VT)[ms]	BSP[ms]	Brute[ms]
Living Room	up to 3rd	218.3 (1.23)	174.2 (1.44)	66.7	215.4
Classroom	up to 2nd	33.3 (1.47)	37.6 (1.46)	26.7	193.0
Lecture Room	up to 3rd	177.1 (1.45)	129.2 (1.29)	62.1	293.7
Concert Hall	up to 2nd	195.9 (1.80)	126.7 (1.63)	76.1	510.2
Metro Station	up to 2nd	165.0 (1.33)	118.2 (1.50)	59.5	346.3

Table 11.4: Averaged measurement results of IS audibilty tests based on VC and VT, compared to the computation times of both the BF- and the BSP-algorithm. The corresponding average ratio between voxel size and average edge length of the scene polygons is given in parentheses.

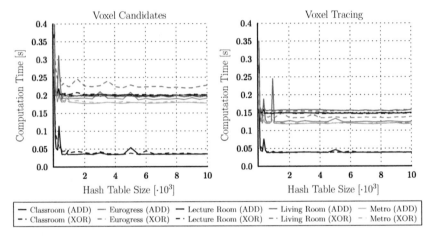

Figure 11.4: SH computation times for audibility tests as a function of selected hash table size and hash function. No significant difference in computational effort is observed in all cases.

by far the slowest. In further investigations, the voxel size was always set to one and one-half of the average edge length of the scene's polygons, since it provided good results for all five room models.

Computation Time vs. Hash Table Size/ Hash Functions

In this measurement series, the hast table size and the hash function were manipulated in order to investigate the implication of hash collisions on the computation time. Two different hash functions h_1 and h_2 were considered (see Eq. 4.11). Both functions multiplied an arbitrary point (x, y, z) with the large prime numbers $p_1 = 73856093$, $p_2 = 19349663$, and $p_3 = 83492791$, as recommended in [THM+03], but differed in the way how these numbers were combined. The first hash function h_1 performed a bitwise addition using the logical XOR operator, while the other hash function h_2

simply added the numbers. In both functions the modulo operation was referred to the current size of the hash table.

As hash functions are most efficient if the hash table has a size of a prime number [CLR90], the hash table size was always set to prime numbers which were closest to the quantized points of investigation. Here, numbers in the magnitude of 10^2 and 10^3 were varied in steps of 100, while the step size was set to 500 for larger ones. Figure 11.4 shows the measurement results for all five test models, both hash functions, and varying hash table size. As aforementioned, the hash table size or the type of hash function can only decrease or increase the number of occurring hash collisions. Single irregularities in the curves indicate such an increase in hash collisions. Regarding hash table sizes it can be assumed that the computation times are more stable for larger numbers. Hence, a hash table size of 10^4, in particular the prime number 10009, was chosen for further investigations. The variation of the hash function showed no real effect on the simulation times, except for the concert hall model. Therefore, the less complex hash function h_2 was regarded as the best candidate, as it performed slightly better than the other function, especially for the concert hall model.

Summary

The measurement results showed that the fastest IS audibility test by means of SH-methods were achieved by VT, where the hash table size was set to the prime number 10009 and the hash function h_2 was applied. As for the voxel size, a size of one and one-half of the average edge length of the scene polygons turned out to be a good rule of thumb in all room models. In real-time applications, however, the best-performing voxel size should always be used to save valuable computation time during modification events of scene geometry. With respect to other intersection tests, the SH approach was always outperformed by the BSP-based method, but still provided a much faster processing of IS audibility tests in comparison to the BF approach.

11.2.3   Handling of Dynamic Objects

In this subsection, the performance of the three basic operations on dynamic objects is analyzed: in particular, the object insertion, object destruction, and object manipulation. During all test series, a rectangular box with six reflection planes was considered as test object for the five room models. Not only did all operations include the update of the scene geometry and their corresponding spatial data structures, but they also included the creation, destruction and manipulation, i.e., translation, of ISs together with the required test on audibility. The method of VT was applied with an optimized parameterization discussed in the previous section and compared to the performance of the BSP-tree approach. Here, it should be kept in mind that each object manipulation requires the regeneration of the scene's corresponding BSP-tree resulting in further non-negligible computational costs, whereas the hash table updates come almost for free. On the other hand, audibility tests on BSP-trees are computed much faster and could thus compensate for this integral advantage of SH.

Test Environment

All computations were performed on an off-the-shelf desktop personal computer featuring an AMD Athlon 2.7 GHz single-core CPU, Windows XP (32-bit) operating system and Visual Studio 2005 SP1 as development environment. Thus, the use of multi-core CPUs was omitted again in this analysis for the same reason as described above. Process priorities were always set to normal in order to run the tests under ordinary system conditions. Computation times were measured by performing ten iterations of each simulation method and averaging the respective results. Due to memory issues on this outdated computing machine, performance tests on third-order IS audibility tests for the largest two room models, i.e., concert hall and metro station, had to be waived.

Computation Time vs Modification Events

Figures 11.5 and Fig. 11.6 depict the computation times for handling dynamic objects with both types of spatial data structures, i.e., SH and BSP. Here, the relation between the overall computation time of modification events and the computation time of audibility tests reflects the concept of handling ISs in RAVEN's dynamic mode:

Creation Only little computational effort is expended for audibility tests when creating a new dynamic object, since only static and newly generated ISs have to be tested. Thus, most computing time is required to generate the new ISs.

Destruction If the dynamic object is removed from a scene, no ISs have to be further checked, as already audible ISs stay audible at any case and no other dynamic objects exist. Thus, computation times are rather dominated by the destruction of ISs.

Manipulation If a dynamic object is manipulated, the relation is the other way around. Here, the position update of all dynamic ISs is a relatively inexpensive operation. Testing all ISs on audibility, however, is a more complex computational effort, since no ISs can be excluded from that test with the exception of initial inaudible ISs as described in Chap. 6.

As one can see from the measurement results, the handling of dynamic objects with SH proved to be generally more efficient compared to the results of the BSP with the exception of the two modification events 'creation' and 'manipulation' upon considering third-order ISs. The latter comes from faster BSP audibility tests that start to compensate for the lag created by regenerating the BSP-tree upon testing a large number of ISs. In general, the computation time for testing ISs on audibility with methods of SH exceeds the computation time of the BSP-based algorithm (roughly by a factor two), while the overall computation time for handling a modification event with BSP algorithms is dominated by the update of the corresponding tree

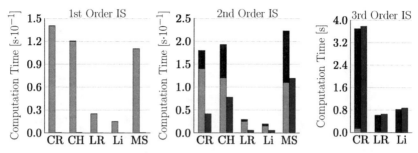

(a) Creation: a box with 6 faces is added to the scene.

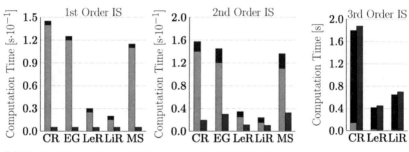

(b) Manipulation: a box with 6 faces is manipulated by the user.

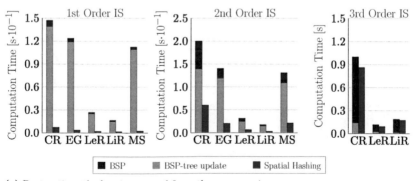

(c) Destruction: the box is removed from the scene again.

Figure 11.5: Overall computation time for insertion/manipulation/removal of dynamic object based on BSP and SH for all five test scenarios and generated ISs up to the third order. This figure focuses on the computational load caused by BSP-tree updates.

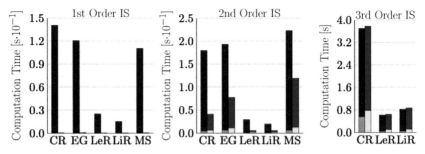

(a) Creation: a box with 6 faces is added to the scene.

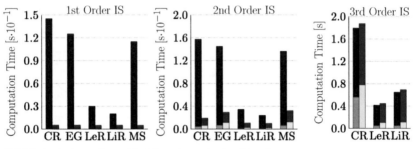

(b) Manipulation: a box with 6 faces is manipulated by the user.

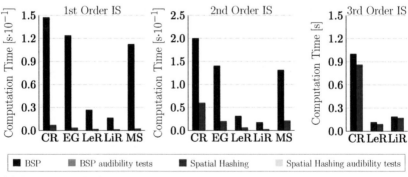

(c) Destruction: the box is removed from the scene again.

Figure 11.6: Overall computation time for insertion/manipulation/removal of dynamic object based on BSP and SH for all five test scenarios and generated ISs up to the third order. This figure focuses on the comparison of computation times for IS audibility tests based on BSP and SH.

data structures. Here, especially manipulative operations such as the translational displacement of an object gain from SH.

The recursive regeneration of a BSP-tree limits the possibilities of computing in parallel, which thus results in a fixed minimum computation time for the BSP-based algorithmic variant. By contrast, the SH approach significantly gains performance from any additional CPU core, since the hash table data structure is perfectly qualified for parallel computing in that all entries are independent from one another. On a state-of-the-art multi-core CPU (four or more cores), the SH approach thus outperforms the BSP-based method in all situations where the geometry is modified – also for the exceptions during this test series. As for the overall rating of computation times, one must keep in mind that the handling of dynamic ISs – namely generation, manipulation, removal, and audibility tests – is usually computed in parallel, too.

11.3 Performance of Ray Tracing

For measuring the performance of the implemented RT algorithms, simulations were carried out for all five test models using using both the BSP-based and the brute-force algorithm. A comparison with SH was omitted, as this type of spatial data structure is never applied for RT (see Chap. 6). During the tests, the particle number n_f per frequency band was increased by increments of 1000 particles within the interval of $n_f \in [0, 15000]$, whereby all simulations were carried out with octave-band resolution. In general, the overall computation time of RT is mainly influenced by three parameters: the mean reflection density of the room, absorption by air[1], and the room's mean absorption and scattering characteristics. Here, a high reflection density results in a high number of intersection tests per time and vice versa, while material parameters significantly influence the overall energy decay and, thus, the moment of particle destruction in the case that the particle energy has lost more than $60\,\mathrm{dB}$[2] compared to its initial value.

Test Environment

All computations were performed on an off-the-shelf desktop personal computer featuring an Intel Core i7 2.8 GHz multi-core CPU (4 cores), Windows 7 (32-bit) operating system and Visual Studio 2005 SP1 as the development environment. Process priorities were always set to normal in order to run the tests under ordinary system conditions. Computation times related solely to the actual RT, whereby all necessary input data were preprocessed. Measurements were obtained by performing 5 iterations of each simulation method and averaging the respective results.

---

[1] Air absorption starts to dominate the overall energy decay above 4 kHz.
[2] The value of 60 dB is motivated by the definition of the reverberation time.

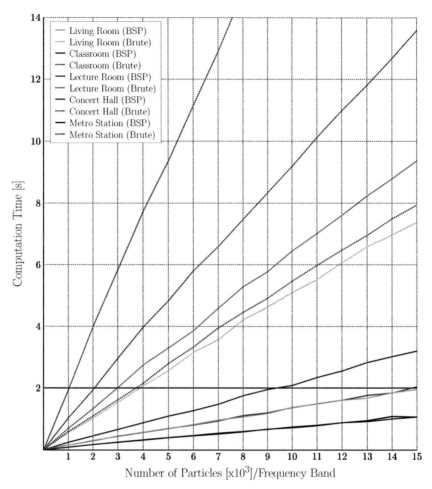

Figure 11.7: Computation times for RT methods based on both BSP and BF, whereby performance tests were carried out for all five test models. Here, the classroom model can be seen as the worst-case scenario, since it features both a high reflection density and a high polygon count. The solid red line parallel to the x-axis denotes the real-time constraint of 2 s for executing a complete RT.

Computation Time vs. Number of Particles

Figure 11.7 shows the measurement results for all room models and both RT methods, whereby, as expected, the BSP clearly surpassed the brute-force approach. Both methods scale quite linearly with the increasing particle count, whereby slight fluctuations in the measurement results are attributed to the stochastic nature of RT. Here, a maximum speed-up of roughly a factor ten was regarded for the the classroom model, which can be seen as an algorithmic worst-case scenario , since this medium-sized room combines two aspects: a quite high reflection density and a high polygon count.

When taking a closer look at the plots' respective slopes, one can see that the actual order of curves from top to down varies for both methods, which reveals more information on the overall behavior of RT. Whereas computation times for the brute-force approach are dominated by the models' respective polygon count, no significant influence of this model parameter can be observed in the case of the BSP-based method due to the decrease in search complexity to $\mathcal{O}(logN)$. In the latter case, computation times mostly depend on the room's mean reflection density, as one can see in Fig. 11.7 when comparing the results for the metro station, the concert hall and the classroom. Although these models have roughly the same number of polygons, the first two models scale best, whereas the classroom scales worst due to the much higher reflection density.

With the assigned time slot of 2 s for RT simulation (see Chap. 6), all models can be simulated in real-time, especially when using small numbers of rays at first to generate a low-resolution histogram. If the listener stays at one place for a longer period of time, the ray tracer can update the corresponding histogram with more rays to acquire a higher resolution and determine a longer impulse response, respectively. Apart from this, listening tests have shown that the required number of energy particles can be generally kept at a quite low level (usually in the range of 5000 (small room) and 15000 particles (large room) per frequency band), which will be further described in the next chapter.

Chapter 12

Optimization of Input Parameters

"Everybody experiences far more than he understands. Yet it is experience, rather than understanding, that influences behavior."

(Marshall McLuhan, Canadian media theorist)

It was mentioned earlier that the quality of a VR-system is assessable by the user's degree of immersion that improves with the number of simulated coherent stimuli and the level of both the plausibility and interactivity. At any rate, immersive environments should thus aim at simulating opto-acoustical scenes in a plausible way, since it is a well-known fact that the visual perception is significantly augmented by matching sound stimuli. Auditory information helps to assign meaning to visual information and vice versa.

As shown in the previous two sections, methods of GA can provide quite accurate results at interactive rates. However, computational costs should always be kept to a minimum to enable complex simulations also on less powerful computing machines. Such a lowering of processing power is typically achieved by reducing the order of ISs and/or the number of traced energy particles, as these parameters strongly influence the computational costs. Nonetheless, they also influence the perceptual quality of the auralization. Fortunately, a degradation of simulation accuracy is not necessarily audible, where a Parameter Threshold (PT) can be seen as a measure for an optimum parameterization in that no perceptible improvement can be achieved above this threshold. Consequently, several series of listening tests were performed described in the following. Here, a criterion-free 3-Alternative Forced Choice (AFC)-paradigm with two different assessment methods is applied in order to experimentally determine the respective PTs for different room types, where a 3x2-design revealed the interaction of relevant technical and perceptual conditions.

12.1 Listening Tests

Five series of listening tests were carried out for the same five room scenarios (living room, classroom, lecture room, concert hall and metro station) that were already

used in the previous section for doing performance tests on the applied simulation algorithms, as these models significantly differ in size and reverberation time and, thus,
comprise five very different sound characteristics. As for the visual scene representation, five detailed and textured models of the corresponding rooms and avatars were
created in order to also reproduce plausible visual stimuli (more details are given in
Appendix A). Each listening test series consisted of two sub-series: one mono-modal
series that stimulated only the subject's aural sense and one multi-modal series including both aural and visual stimuli. The mono-modal listening tests (denoted as
Lab in the following) were performed in a darkened room, and subjects were asked
to close their eyes in order to avoid any distraction. The second test series was carried out by additionally presenting stereoscopic images of the simulated scene using
the CAVE-like environment at RWTH Aachen University (denoted as *CAVE* in the
following), where each simulated scene was projected from outside onto five screens,
and the subjects were asked to look at the musician's avatar during the tests (see Fig.
12.1).

However, before these listening
test series could be performed, appropriate aural stimuli had to be
identified. At first, the overall number of stimuli was limited to a moderate amount in order to not over-
strain the subjects later on, thereby
avoiding false stimuli classifications
resulting from a gradually increasing lack of concentration. Here, preliminary tests showed that an overall duration of 20 min for one listening test sub-series could be seen
as reasonable (one room, one subject, one type of modality, i.e., ei-

Figure 12.1: Subject performing listening tests
in a virtual environment.

ther mono-modal or multi-modal). Then, an appropriate range for the investigated
parameters had to be determined. As already explained in Sect. 5.1, scattering becomes a dominant effect in the temporal development of typical RIRs, even for reflections of the order two or three. Thus, only low-order ISs (specular reflections)
were taken into account for further investigations, whereby their range was set from
order 1 to 3. To find a reasonable range for the number of energy particles (RT), two
things had to be considered: first, it can be shown that the deviation in the envelope
of the impulse response relates to the overall number of particles [Vor08], where a
variance of less than 1 dB was regarded as sufficient for the use as reference stimuli
called *anchor stimuli*[1]. Second, to maintain the subject's motivation during the tests,

---

[1]It should be mentioned that the formulas for estimating the variance in the energy envelope of
the RIR in relation to the number of particles are based on the traditional stochastic RT model,
which implies that algorithmic improvements such as the diffuse rain method, which significantly

distorted sounding stimuli had to be created that were clearly discriminable from the anchor stimuli by using a very low number of particles. All other stimuli with particle numbers in between these two extremes were created according to preliminary experiments that were carried out prior the core listening tests in order to find first PTs. This means that simulation parameters were used that lay in the direct neighborhood of these estimated PTs.

The listening tests were performed according to the method of constant stimuli following a 3-AFC-paradigm, as this type of test avoids a response bias [Gel04]. During these tests, the subjects had to evaluate series of stimuli triples in which each triple consisted of two identical stimuli and a differing stimulus that had to be identified. The overall sequence of stimuli triples was played back in a randomized order, and each triple was repeated once (at a later time, but during the same sub-series) in order to improve the listening test's reliability. Furthermore, instructions for performing the tests were given in written form, and a Graphical User Interface (GUI) that was displayed on a laptop guided the subjects through the tests to avoid any influence by the test director. All stimuli were played back using a calibrated reproduction system that consisted of a RME Hammerfall audio device and a closed Sennheiser headphone with an average damping of exterior noise by 18 dB. Although the use of closed headphones is not ideal, this headphone type was favored over open headphone variants to reduce disturbing fan noise that was unfortunately produced by the CAVE's beamers. Thus, this type of headphone was also used during the mono-modal listening tests (Lab) for the sake of comparability of test results. After completing a listening test sub-series, each subject had to fill out an evaluation questionnaire for assessing additional subjective information on the listening test itself, such as the perceived difficulty, but also on the subject's seeing and hearing capabilities, where serious physical handicaps such as hearing impairment and color blindness led to an exclusion of the subject. In the following, an exemplary evaluation of test results is further discussed on hand of the example of the virtual concert hall, since all test series showed – mostly noticeable – similar behavior. Detailed information on all performed listening tests can be found in [Sch09b, Sta09, SSM10].

12.2 Example Evaluation of Listening Tests

Due to the promising results of the preliminary studies [Sch09b] and the continuing master thesis by Starke [Sta09], additional mono-modal listening tests were accomplished in collaboration with the Audio Communication Group (ACG) at TU Berlin [SSM10], Germany, where the final results of all three studies are summarized in this section. In these test series, a room model of a concert hall (volume $14372\,m^3$, T(Sabine) 1.3 s, see Appx. A) was examined, and 21 stimuli were created from convolving differently simulated impulse responses with a dry recording. As described above, the listening tests were performed either mono-modally or multi-modally (see Fig. 12.2), according to a 3-AFC-paradigm, where the overall test design is shown

---

lowers the overall particle count and reduces the variance of the energy envelope in rooms with many scattering surfaces, are not covered by these equations.

(a) Mono-modal listening tests.   (b) Multi-modal listening tests.

Figure 12.2: Listening tests were carried out in two sub series: (a) mono-modal by presenting the aural stimuli only (Lab), and (b) multi-modal by adding the corresponding visual stimuli (CAVE).

in Tab. 12.1. To facilitate the detectability of potential artifacts, a slowly picked acoustic guitar was chosen as audio content in contrast to the smooth sounding saxophone that was used in the preliminary study. For the simulation parameterization, the settings of the preliminary study were refined by focussing on the PTs that were obtained at that time. Thus, models based on 3 orders of ISs and, at a time, 7 numbers of particles per simulated frequency band (100, 4000, 7000, 9000, 12000, 20000, 40000) were applied to generate the stimuli. The numbers ranged from a level causing an easily detectable distorted sound (100 particles) to a state-of-the-art simulation which was defined as the reference (40000 particles).

To determine the respective PTs, the test results were analyzed in two ways: 1) by using the psignifit MATLAB toolbox[2] by Wichmann and Hill [WH01a, WH01b], and 2) by analyzing the cumulative distribution function and applying a 25% paradigm [Gel04]. Figure 12.3 exemplary shows the computed functions for both methods where the IS order was fixed (order 3) and the number of particles was varied. Here, the

---

[2]This toolbox is a free multi-platform software package that performs maximum-likelihood fitting and significance testing for psychometric functions.

Measure: PT to Reference [# Particles]		Factor I (Repeated Measures) Fixed IS Order		
		1	**2**	**3**
Factor II (Grouping Variable) Stimulus Modality	**Acoustical** **(Lab)**	N=19		
	Opto-Acoustical **(Cave)**	N=14		

Table 12.1: Overview of the test design. N denotes the number of subjects.

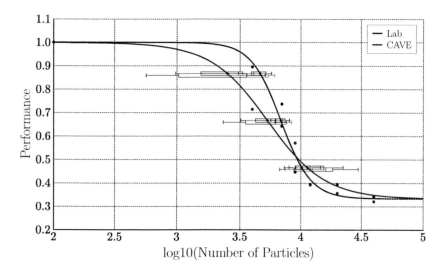

(a) Psychometric functions fitting the results of the test series. A performance of 1 means that the subjects always found the differing stimulus, whereas a performance of 0.33 shows that the subjects always guessed. Here, the PT relates to a performance of 0.66.

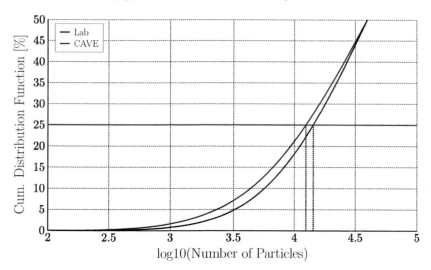

(b) Cumulative distribution function that is derived from the fitted Gaussian-distributed probability density functions. Here, the parameter threshold relates – per definition – to the 25% point of the collective psychometric function of all subjects.

Figure 12.3: Two methods of PT determination.

number of particles is always plotted logarithmically in order to stay perceptively adequate. Figure 12.3(a) depicts the psychometric functions for both test series, Lab and CAVE, obtained by the maximum-likelihood estimation method according to Wichmann and Hill. The red/black dots illustrate the average performance of the subjects in respect to the stimulus. The 68.2% and 95.4% confidence intervals are given in horizontal bars at the 0.2, 0.5 and 0.8 level of the respective psychometric functions. The PT relates to a performance of 0.66 which results for the given example in 7900 particles (Lab) and 6300 particles (CAVE), respectively. The cumulative distribution functions shown in Fig. 12.3(b) are derived from the fitted Gaussian-distributed probability density functions and represent the collective psychometric function of all subjects. Applying the 25% rule leads to a PT of 14300 (Lab) and 12400 (CAVE) particles in the given example. The higher number of particles is not surprising, since the 25% rule yields a much stronger constraint for determining PTs in contrast to the approach by Wichmann and Hill. Most noticeably, all functions showed similar behavior as in the preliminary tests, although the original stimuli of a smooth-sounding saxophone were replaced by slowly picked acoustic guitar sounds. All PTs were significantly shifted to a lower number of rays if the visual stimuli were additionally presented (again, an average of 2000 particles was observed). The total number of particles was revised according to the new assessment method, thereby resulting in 12500 particles per frequency band. This relates to a workload of only 1 s for the ray tracing (12500 particles per frequency band, octave-band resolution, see Sect. 11.3) on a standard personal computer (Intel Core i7, 2.8 GHz). However, one should keep in mind that these results are only generalizable for the presented type of room geometry and the applied simulation algorithms. Nonetheless, all test series showed that a lowered accuracy, hence faster computation time of the simulation, is not noticeable when a convergent opto-acoustical stimulus is presented.

Part V

Summary & Outlook

Chapter 13

Summary and Discussion

'Master Control Program: End of Line.'

(*Tron*, Steven Lisberger, American filmmaker)

This thesis described the concept and the implementation of the real-time room acoustics simulation framework RAVEN which is today a vital part of the interactive 3D sound rendering system of RWTH Aachen University's immersive VR-environment. After a brief excursus about the fundamentals of acoustics and the description of a concept for the multi-modal representation of natural sound sources, a physically based hybrid simulation method was introduced that took into account all important sound phenomena, i.e, sound transmission, sound diffraction, and sound scattering. Here, a deterministic IS-model for the exact computation of early specular sound reflections was combined with a stochastic ray tracer that was able to model late reverberation with a correct energy distribution over time (diffuse and late specular reflections). The real-time performance was achieved by introducing a flexible simulation framework that enabled real-time modifications of sound sources, receivers and the scene geometry. Consequently, the concept of scene graphs was adapted for a dynamic linkage of autonomously operating room groups, i.e., rooms that were connected through open portals and encoded in optimized spatial data structures for fast geometrical operations. Particular features of RAVEN were the following:

Hybrid Simulation Model The hybrid simulation model was not based on any assumption of ideal diffuse sound fields but on a full room acoustics simulation. In this way the simulation framework was able to process any kind of room shape and volume except small rooms at low frequencies. Specular and scattered components of the impulse response were treated separately, whereby the decision with regard to the amount of specular and diffuse reflections was exclusively room-dependent and purely based on physical sound field aspects. Novel concepts for simulating sound diffraction were incorporated into the simulation framework: as for the IS-model, an efficient method for handling sound diffraction across an edge sequence was described, whereby Svensson's deterministic secondary source model of edge diffraction from a finite wedge was utilized for computing time-domain edge diffraction impulse responses of reflection paths via edges. Furthermore, Stephenson's frequency-dependent 2D-diffraction model of energy particles passing an edge was ported to 3D resulting in a new RT-method for distributing diffracted scattered energy among receivers, called 'diffracted rain'. This name was chosen in analogy to the 'diffuse rain' method by Heinz, which allows a significant lowering of the number of necessary particles without producing errors in the energy envelope of the RIR (an improved version was also featured by the applied ray tracer). Methods for constructing both monaural and binaural RIRs were described with special focus on the binaural synthesis. Here, spatial cues were not only added to the direct sound and early reflections, but also to the late reverberation by introducing a spatial detector that selected appropriate HRTFs with respect to the energy distribution on the detector's surface over time. In this way, spatial cues were added in a more plausible way to BRIRs, since the common assumption of random impacting energy for later times of the impulse response holds only in an ideal diffuse sound field[1].

Coupled Rooms Regarding the simulation of complex virtual indoor scenarios, an efficient approach for the auralization of sound transmission from adjacent and indirectly-connected room groups was developed on the basis of standardized building acoustics quantities and room acoustics simulations. This included an appropriate data structure for the scene representation and an analysis of sound transmission paths in typical room-to-room situations. For the exclusion of inaudible sound sources and frequency ranges, respectively, a search algorithm of valid sound paths was designed that took into account the current states (opened or closed) and sound insulation values of all involved portals. In addition, a command structure was implemented that converted audible sound transmission paths into single simulation steps that directly controlled the application flow of the subsequent filter synthesis (monaural and binaural).

Scene Representation The simulation framework required only CAD room models as input data, where several data formats of commercial 3D modeling tools could be imported. However, some constraints regarding the scene modeling were required for the sake of an efficient processing of geometry at runtime, e.g., the use of convex polygons for fast point-in-polygon tests. Surface properties were set solely according to standardized material parameters, i.e., frequency-dependent absorption-, scattering- and sound reduction coefficients/indices. The framework then adjusted all relevant runtime parameters automatically and inherently, such as the division of the RIR into specular and scattered components. The topological structure of the scene was represented by a graph-structure called ASG. Here, each node stored the spatial representation of a single room, including the polyhedral model (encoded as both the BSP-tree and spatial hash table for accelerating geometry-related operations), material data, temperature, humidity and air pressure. The ASG's edges represented polygonal portals that

---

[1]Example auralizations are available for download under www.ravenaudio.de.

connected adjacent rooms, i.e., nodes. The connectivity between nodes was steered by the state of the respective portals, whereby the state 'closed' and 'opened' dissociated and pooled two room groups, respectively.

Interactive Environments Another important design aspect for enabling an interactive room acoustics simulation was the creation of highly flexible interaction interfaces that provided a maximum degree of freedom in terms of supported user modification events. While code adjustments for operations such as the exchange of material parameters and the manipulation of portal states were relatively easy to implement, the requirements of a modifiable geometry turned out to be quite an algorithmic challenge. After first test implementations, it became clear that RAVEN's acceleration algorithms based on hierarchical BSP did not meet the criteria of dynamically manipulable geometry, since any modification called for a time-consuming recalculation of at least large parts of the corresponding BSP-trees. It was therefore decided to introduce two different modi operandi for geometrical scene objects: static and dynamic. Whereas static objects were not modifiable during the simulation and therefore processable in a quick and efficient way, the size, shape, position, and orientation of dynamic objects were manipulable by the user at runtime. This unconditioned modification of dynamic objects was enabled by switching from BSP-trees to a slower, but more flexible approach of spatial subdivision – that of SH. Spatial Hashing (SH) is based on the idea of subdividing the 3D space by primitive volumes called voxels and mapping the infinitely voxelized subspaces to a finite set of one-dimensional hash indices. Whereas the concept of SH was easily embeddable to the applied ray tracing algorithm, a dynamic handling of ISs turned out to be more complicated as ISs had to be generated, destroyed and updated (audibility and position) at runtime. Consequently, a hierarchical tree data structure was introduced that efficiently organized ISs for a convenient and fast processing.

Parallel Computing Since the top-level interface of RAVEN was unified, the underlying computation hardware was transparent and could be either a single computer or a computation cluster of varying size. The latter was driven by a master scheduler that distributed simulation events by passing messages via network to dedicated (multi-core) worker clients using the concepts of OpenMP and MPI for parallel processing. This made the approach very scalable so that the hardware could be chosen to match the complexity of the scenery.

The accuracy of the presented room acoustics simulation model was evaluated by means of three simple test scenarios, each testing one specific simulation event. In particular, these investigations encompassed the hybrid model itself, the simulation of sound transmission between two coupled rooms, and the computation of sound diffraction from a single wedge, where simulation results were compared to analytical solutions. In all cases, RAVEN provided quite accurate results and, thus, showed the high capabilities of the underlying simulation framework.

Furthermore, several test series were carried out, where RAVEN had to prove its real-time performance in a large variety of application events. Five different scenarios were chosen for further investigation, whereby the corresponding room models differed strongly with respect to room volume and polygonal complexity ranging from a small living room to a large metro station. In the case of static geometry, computation times showed that RAVEN's BSP-based simulation acceleration enabled a quite plausible auralization of all room types within the given real-time constraints of 550 ms and 2 s for the IS-method and RT, respectively[2]. In more detail, ISs of up to order three and RT with a sufficient number of energy particles that related to a standard deviation of less than 1 dB in the energy envelope of the corresponding impulse responses, were computable on an off-the-shelf multi-core PC for almost any room type in real-time.

In addition, investigations were carried out on a single-core standard PC regarding the real-time modification of dynamic geometrical objects when applying acceleration methods based on BSP and SH to the IS-method. Before the actual test series were begun, intersection tests based on SH were analyzed, thus revealing a strong dependency of the achieved performance on the chosen voxel size. Here, good results were obtained for all scene models by setting the voxel size to one and one-half of the average edge length of the corresponding scene polygons. In general, the performance tests showed that BSP-accelerated intersection tests were much more efficient than the two introduced methods based on SH. Yet they also showed the strong disadvantage of hierarchical spatial data structures, because each object manipulation required an update of the corresponding BSP-tree, resulting in additional computation time that – in combination with the IS audibility test – was unable to compete with the performance of SH during modification events such as the creation, manipulation, and destruction of dynamic geometrical objects. However, in cases of more complex room geometries and ISs of up to order three, a large number of audibility tests had to be performed, where the combination of BSP-tree regeneration and fast BSP-based intersection tests could keep up with the performance of the SH approach.

In a subsequent series of listening tests, room acoustical simulations were regarded from a perceptual point of view in order to further optimize their parameterization for audio-visual applications. Here, listening tests were carried out by using a criterion-free 3-AFC-paradigm with two different assessment methods and with the participation of expert listeners. The subsequent evaluation of test results showed that a lowered accuracy, hence faster computation time of the simulation, was not noticeable as long as a convergent opto-acoustical stimulus was presented.

In conclusion, a unique auralization framework was presented that relied on present-day knowledge of room acoustical simulation techniques and enabled a physically accurate auralization of sound propagation in complex environments, including the important wave effects of sound scattering, sound transmission and sound diffraction. Despite this realistic sound field rendering, not only were spatially distributed

---

[2]The decision regarding the update rate and depth of impulse response simulation was based on the interaction and speed of movement of the user when operating in the immersive environment at RWTH Aachen University.

and freely movable sound sources and receivers supported at runtime, but also real-time modifications and manipulations of the geometrical environment itself were made possible.

Chapter 14

Outlook

> 'Look, I want you to know what we're talking about here. This isn't like TV only better. This is life. It's a piece of somebody's life. Pure and uncut, straight from the cerebral cortex. You're there. You're doing it, seeing it, hearing it ... feeling it.'

> (*Strange Days*, James Cameron, American filmmaker)

Despite the good performance of the whole simulation framework, there are certainly many aspects that still have to be investigated. This includes improvements in the applied room acoustics simulation model as well as new simulation strategies and algorithmic concepts that further reduce the overall computation time. Outlined here are some important ideas for future changes that will further enhance the range of RAVEN applications:

Numerical Simulations The frequencies below the Schroeder frequency could be simulated by combining wave-based and ray-based simulation methods in order to obtain realistic broadband RIRs, at least for small rooms. Here, several case studies were already carried out by Aretz et al., whereby RAVEN was combined with a fast finite element method FEM-solver [Fra08] for computing room impulse responses of small rooms [ANVS09, AJ10, AM10]. Although computation times of the FEM-solver by far exceeded the given real-time constraints, the combination of both methods significantly enhanced the overall quality of the auralization and should therefore be added to RAVEN's simulation framework in the future, but then in a real-time capable version. Until then, low-frequency RIRs could be preprocessed by the FEM-solver and combined with RAVEN's on-line simulation results. Although physically not absolutely correct, this combination would still result in a quite plausible auralization also of low-frequencies.

Diffracted Rain Recent investigations by Stephenson revealed several issues regarding the DAPDF [Ste10b]. It was shown that the basic reciprocity-principle was not fulfilled when applying the DAPDF. This infers that simulation results differed if the positions of source and receiver were simply exchanged, which in

the worst case could lead to deviations in the transmission level of up to several
decibels. Here, Stephenson proposed introducing a new term to the mathematical description of the DAPDF that compensated for this error, but then other
issues occurred. However, these problems do not directly affect the simulation
model of the 'diffracted rain' RT-method, since values of the DAPDF are read
in from a database with a resolution of one degree. Thus, the only thing to do
is to regenerate this DAPDF-database as soon as an improved description of
the DAPDF exists.

Time- and Frequency-Dependent Room Models An interesting idea for en-
hancing the quality and speed of room acoustics simulations at the same time
was introduced by Pelzer who has already added this concept to RAVEN's simulation framework in a first stage [PV10]. The approach uses a set of room
models with graduated level of detail of the same scene geometry, where every
single room model is optimized for a certain frequency range, i.e., low details
for low frequencies and vice versa. Moreover, the level of detail is also decreased
with increasing sound propagation time during the simulation, since accurate
reflection patterns are not so important in the late part of the RIR, where many
sound reflections from different directions overlap at the same time. Thus, a
total simulation speed-up of a factor of six can be achieved when combined with
the speed-up due to frequency-matched geometries.

Improved Sound Transmission Simulation The introduced approach for the
auralization of sound transmission is certainly more a rough approximation
than a physically correct simulation in aspects of building acoustics. However,
regarding the continuously increasing computation power, future versions will
be able to account for more and more sound transmission paths until the real-
time simulation finally reaches and maybe outstrips the simulation quality of
commercial off-line building acoustics software. These tools are usually based
on the same concepts as applied in RAVEN and typically simulate the sound
transmission up to first-order junctions. Although RAVEN's auralization concept of sound transmission proved to work quite well, a validation including
systematic listening tests should be performed to gather more information on
the importance of sound transmission paths and the positioning of secondary
sources.

Perceptual Culling By considering the perceived sound of a source located in a
neighboring room and damped by a closed portal, the sound impression is mostly
influenced by the portal's transfer function and the impulse response of the room
where the user is located in. Especially two sound sources at different positions
in the separated sender room will have very similar impulse responses for the
total sound propagation to the receiver. Hence, it is actually unnecessary to
render two individual impulse responses, as they would sound nearly the same.
In addition, Tsingos et al. introduced a technique called Perceptual Culling,

Figure 14.1: Emotiv EPOC system. Wireless headset for neuro-signal acquisition and processing. Images by permission of Emotiv [Emo].

which takes into account that even sound sources which are located in the same room as the receiver can share a common impulse response provided that they are in close quarters [TGD04]. With both techniques combined, a large number of sound sources could be simulated with a quite low computational effort. This would significantly improve the overall liveliness of the immersive simulation, since one is usually faced with a multitude of sounds in real-life situations.

Hardware Acceleration The utilization of graphic cards for computations apart from graphic rendering came into focus in recent years, since Graphics Processing Units (GPUs) are highly-integrated processing units with 256 and more cores. Today high-level programming interfaces, such as NVIDIA's CUDA and ATI's Stream technology have considerably simplified the development of GPU-based algorithms than some years ago. However, one should keep in mind that the enormous computation power of GPUs can only be unleashed, if algorithms meet the specific characteristics of the graphic hardware, meaning that general purpose computing is not the ultimate answer in all situations. Most suited for this type of parallel computing are so-called stream algorithms which perform the same set of operations on large data sets, such as RT algorithms. More information on general purpose computing in the field of room acoustics simulation can be found in [Tsi07]. For real-time GPU-based convolution, a highly optimized and promising solution was already presented by Wefers et al. in [WB10], which will soon be added to the 3D audio rendering system of RWTH Aachen University's immersive virtual environment.

Upon recalling Heilig's Sensorama and the improvements that were applied to VR-systems since then, one might start to wonder what another 60 years of development will bring. Recently commercially launched Brain Computer Interfaces (BCIs) aim at detecting user thoughts, feelings and expressions by using a set of sensors to tune into electric signals produced by the brain (see Fig. 14.1). Maybe one day, such a system can also work in a reverse way by inducing multi-modal stimuli directly to the cerebral cortex, either for augmenting or totally cutting-off real-world perception – a state of mind where frontiers will fade between realism and simulism, i.e., the birth of the ultimate medium. Certainly it is going to be a long and difficult road until that day and improvements are only gained in tiny little steps.

Perhaps this thesis has been one of them.

Part VI

Appendix

Appendix A

Room Models

The following briefly describes the five room models used within the scope of this thesis:

Living Room The floor plan was modeled after typical room geometries of living rooms. The room contains typical furniture in a living room, such as a sofa and bookshelves, and the floor is covered with carpet.

Classroom The floor plan was modeled after a classroom at the Alfred-von-Reumont elementary school in Aachen, Germany. The room contains typical classroom furniture, such as tables and chairs, and the floor is covered with parquet.

Lecture Room The floor plan was modeled after the 4G lecture room at the Institute of Communication Systems and Data Processing, RWTH Aachen University, Aachen, Germany. The room contains typical furniture of a lecture room, such as tables and chairs, and the floor is covered with parquet.

Concert Hall The floor plan was modeled after the Europa concert hall, which is part of the Eurogress Convention Center, Aachen, Germany. The room contains typical furniture in concert halls, such as a theater-style seating, and the floor is covered with parquet.

Metro Station The floor plan was modeled after a metro station in Warsaw, Poland. The room contains typical objects of a metro station such as benches, columns, ticket machines and rails. All tunnel entries are modeled as fully absorbent.

Scattering coefficients of geometric textures were measured by using scale models [VS09b]. More information on material parameters are given in [Sta09].

Living Room

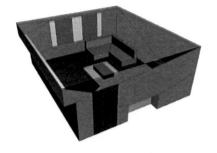

Number of polygons:	67
Number of planes:	31
Volume $[m^3]$:	89.50
Surface $[m^2]$:	147.85
T (Sabine) [s]:	0.53

(a) CAD-model of the living room.   (b) Specifications of acoustical room model.

(c) Subject performing a listening test inside a virtual living room.

Classroom

Number of polygons:	391
Number of planes:	82
Volume $[m^3]$:	283
Surface $[m^2]$:	332
T (Sabine) [s]:	0.69

(a) CAD-model of the classroom.   (b) Specifications of acoustical room model.

(c) Subject performing a listening test inside a virtual classroom.

Lecture Room

Number of polygons:	147
Number of planes:	28
Volume $[m^3]$:	418
Surface $[m^2]$:	513
T (Sabine) [s]:	0.57

(a) CAD-model of the lecture room.   (b) Specifications of acoustical room model.

(c) Subject performing a listening test inside a virtual lecture room.

Concert Hall

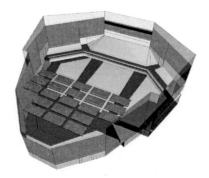

Number of polygons:	348
Number of planes:	146
Volume $[m^3]$:	14372.40
Surface $[m^2]$:	4450.82
T (Sabine) [s]:	1.30

(a) CAD-model of the concert hall.

(b) Specifications of acoustical room model.

(c) Subject performing a listening test inside a virtual concert hall.

Metro Station

Number of polygons:	272
Number of planes:	129
Volume $[m^3]$:	16499.90
Surface $[m^2]$:	7989.29
T (Sabine) [s]:	2.14

(a) CAD-model of the metro station.   (b) Specifications of acoustical room model.

(c) Subject performing a listening test inside a virtual metro station.

Appendix B

RAVEN

As described in the course of this thesis, RAVEN relies on present-day knowledge of room acoustical simulation techniques and enables a physically quite accurate auralization of sound propagation in complex environments supporting spatially distributed and freely movable sound sources and receivers, as well as modifications and manipulations of the geometrical environment at runtime.

Particular features of RAVEN are:

- Only standardized input data required.

- Hybrid simulation model that combines deterministic ISs with stochastic RT for a complete physically based simulation of room acoustics including important wave effects such as sound scattering, airborne sound insulation between rooms and sound diffraction.

- Real-time room- and building acoustics auralization of dynamically-coupled rooms.

- Real-time modification of sound sources, receivers, and geometrical objects.

- Support of parallel computing on both, distributed- and shared-memory machines.

- Powerful GUI and visualization toolbox for off-line use (see below).

- Special batch mode for the use with other applications such as MATLAB.

- More specific software details along with demonstration videos and sound files can be found here: `www.ravenaudio.de`

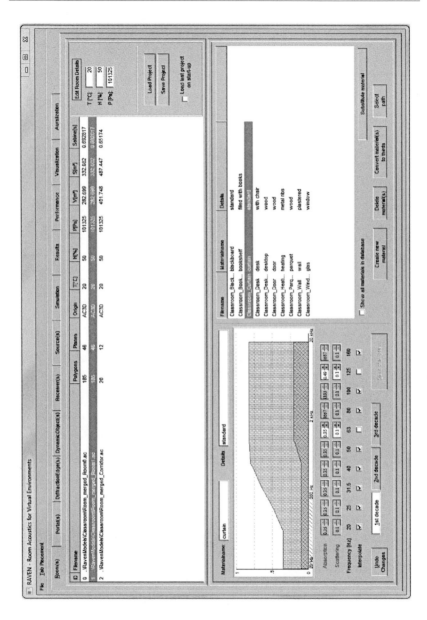

RAVEN's GUI tab 'Rooms' gives full control of all room-related data that are defined in a project file. Information on the rooms' geometrical complexity, reverberation times, and involved materials are given, whereby the latter can be modified by means of an integrated material editor.

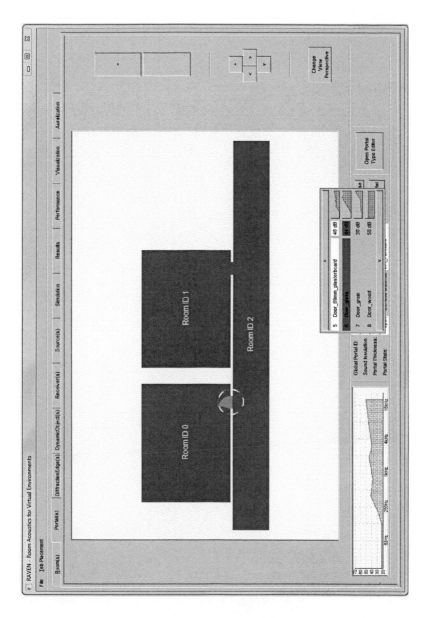

RAVEN's GUI tab 'Portals' gives an overview of all rooms that are interconnected by portals. Portal states can be changed by simply clicking on the respective portal symbol. In addition, the portals' transfer functions can be replaced or edited on-the-fly.

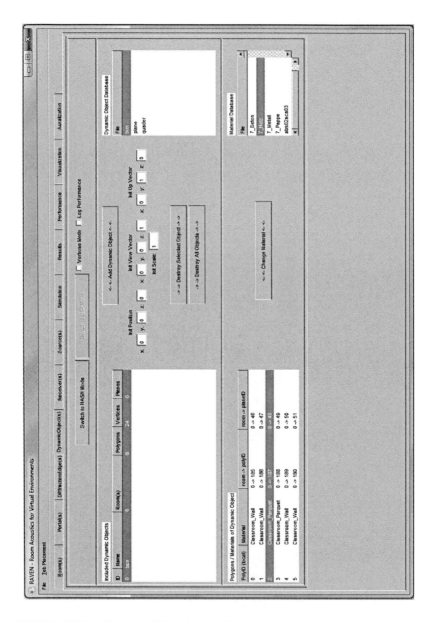

RAVEN's GUI tab 'Dynamic Objects' gives the user the opportunity to add, manipulate and destroy geometrical objects, whereby the basic objects are imported from a database.

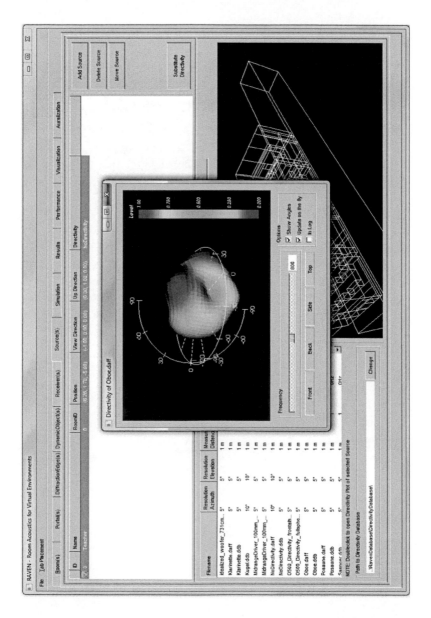

RAVEN's GUI tab 'Sources' gives an overview of all PS-related data (all secondary sources are handled by RAVEN automatically). Sound sources can be arbitrarily added, moved, and destroyed, and corresponding directional patterns can be changed on-the-fly.

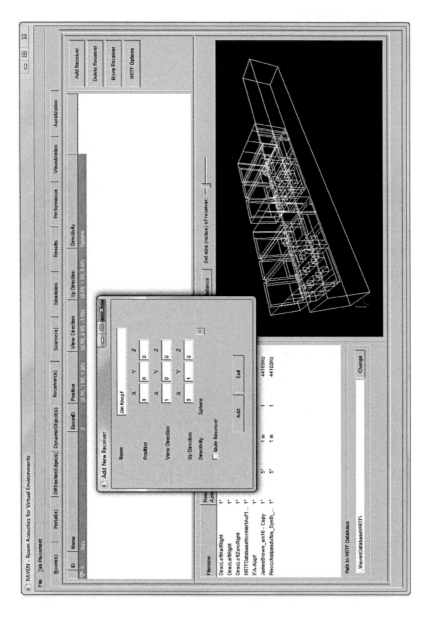

RAVEN's GUI tab 'Receivers' gives an overview of all receiver-related data. Receivers can be arbitrarily added, moved, and destroyed and corresponding directional patterns (HRTFs) can be changed on-the-fly.

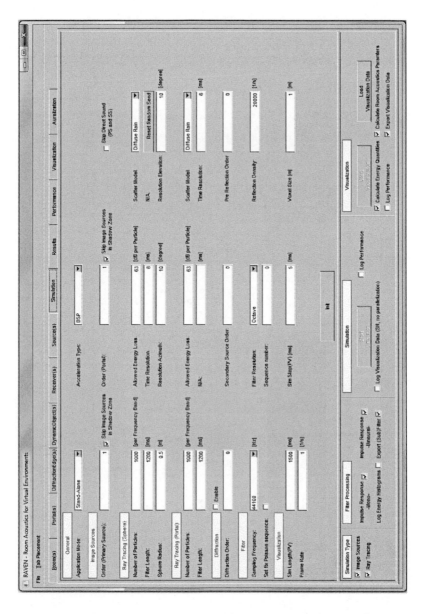

RAVEN's GUI tab 'Simulation' enables the complete parameterization of RAVEN's core algorithms for simulation and filter synthesis such as IS-order, number of RT particles, histogram interval size, sampling rate, or frequency resolution.

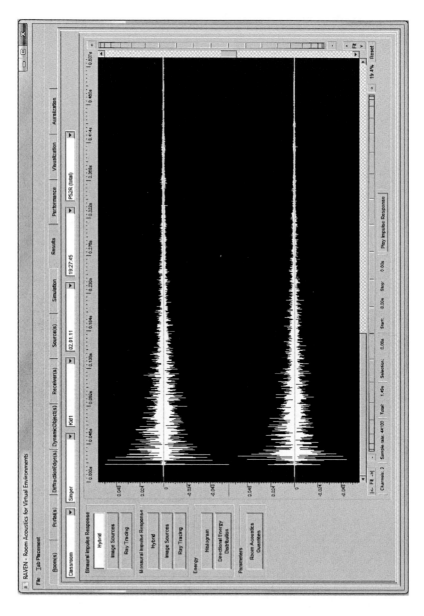

RAVEN's GUI tab 'Results' offers a convenient view of project-wise sorted simulation results such as RIRs and BRIRs (specular and diffuse parts plus their hybrid combinations),
Schroeder plots, energy histograms, and room acoustical quantities.

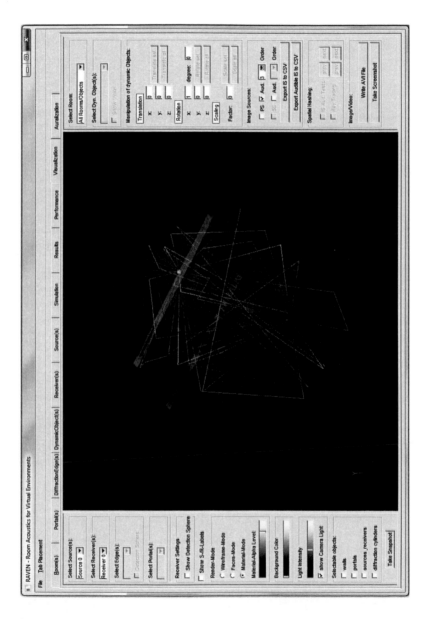

RAVEN's GUI tab 'Visualization' gives an overview of the complete scene and is updated each time a modification event was carried out by the user. Various visualization techniques and export functions are supported.

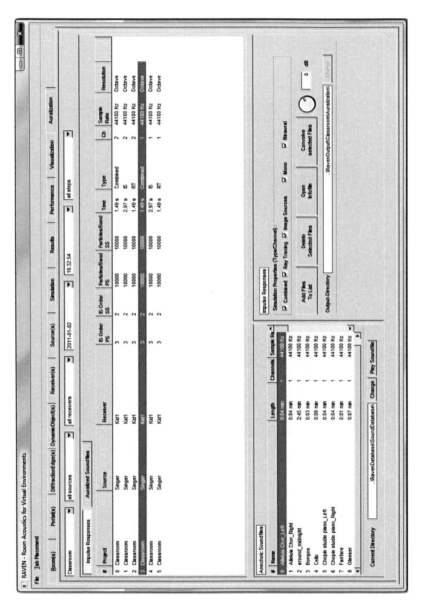

RAVEN's GUI tab 'Auralization' enables a handy management of auralization tasks. Here, impulse responses are sorted project-wise, while dry signals can be chosen from a database.

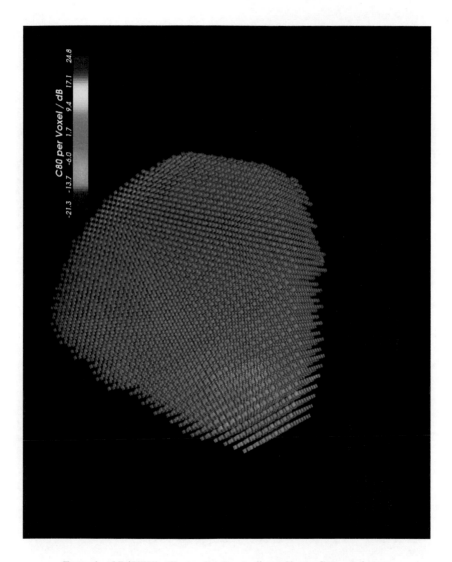

Example of RAVEN's 3D visualization toolbox. Clarity C80, voxel view.

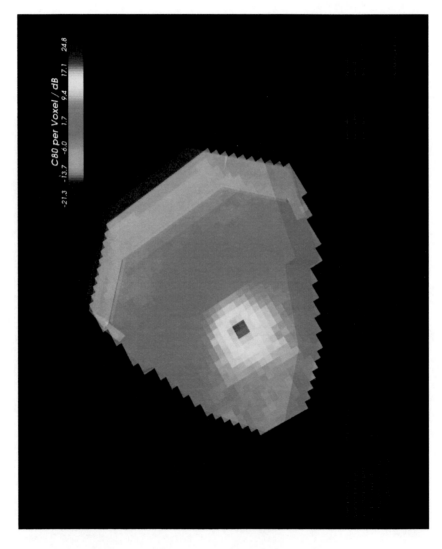

Example of RAVEN's 3D visualization toolbox. Clarity C80, cross-sectional view.

Bibliography

[AB79]   J. B. Allen and D. A. Berkley. Image Method for Efficiently Simulating Small-Room Acoustics. *Journal of the Acoustical Society of America*, 65:943, 1979.

[AB95]   R. Azuma and G. Bishop. A frequency-domain analysis of head-motion prediction. In *Proceedings of the 22nd annual conference on Computer Graphics and Interactive Techniques*, New York, NY, USA, 1995.

[AJ10]   M. Aretz and L. Jauer. Perceptual comparison of measured and simulated sound fields in small rooms. In *Proceedings of the DAGA*, Berlin, Germany, 2010.

[AK08]   I. Assenmacher and T. Kuhlen. The VISTA Virtual Reality Toolkit. In *Proceedings of the IEEE VR SEARIS*, Reno, USA, 2008.

[AM10]   A. Aretz and P. Maier. Simulation based Auralization of the Acoustics in a Studio Room using a combined Wave and Ray based Approach. In *Proceedings of the 26th Tonmeistertagung*, Leipzig, Germany, 2010.

[AMH02]   T. Akenine-Möller and E. Haines. *Real-Time Rendering, 2nd edition*. A.K. Peters, 2002.

[ANVS09]   M. Aretz, R. Nöthen, M. Vorländer, and D. Schröder. Combined broadband impulse responses using fem and hybrid ray-based methods. In *Proceedings of the EAA Auralization Symposium*, Espoo, Finland, 2009.

[Arv91]   J. Arvo, editor. *Graphics Gems II*. Academic Press, 1991.

[Ass09]   I. Assenmacher. *Low latency technology for interactive virtual environments*. PhD thesis, RWTH Aachen University, 2009.

[BC03]   G. C. Burdea and P. Coiffet. *Virtual Reality Technology, 2nd edition*. John Wiley & Sons, 2003.

[Ber80]   B. Bernfeld. Absorption of Sound by Air: A Personal Calculator Program. In *Proceedings of the 66th AES Convention*, Los Angeles, USA, 1980.

[Bla96]   J. Blauert. *Spatial Hearing – The Psychophysics of Human Sound Localization, revised edition*. MIT Press, 1996.

[Bor84]   J. Borish. Extension of the Image Model to Arbitrary Polyhedra. *Journal of the Acoustical Society of America*, 75:1827, 1984.

[Bor00]   I. Bork. A comparison of room simulation software – the 2nd Round
               Robin on room acoustical computer simulation. *Acta Acustica United
               with Acustica*, 86:943, 2000.

[BPS08]   G. K. Behler, M. Pollow, and D. Schröder. Messung und Simulation von
               Raumimpulsantworten für eine realistische Auralisation. In *Proceedings
               of the 25th Tonmeistertagung*, Leipzig, Germany, 2008.

[BS95]   J.S. Bradley and G.A. Soulodre. The influence of late arriving energy
               on spatial impression. *Journal of the Acoustical Society of America*,
               97:2263, 1995.

[BSM+04]   D. S. Brungart, D. D. Simpson, R. L. McKinley, A. J. Kordik, R. C.
               Dallman, and D. A. Ovenshire. The interaction between head-tracker
               latency, source duration, and response time in the localization of vir-
               tual sound sources. In *Proceedings of ICAD 04 - 10th Meeting of the
               International Conference on Auditory Display*, Sydney, Australia, 2004.

[BT57]   M. A. Biot and I. Tolstoy. Formulation of wave propagation in infinite
               media by normal coordinates with an application to diffraction. *Journal
               of the Acoustical Society of America*, 29:381, 1957.

[BW99]   M. Born and E. Wolf. *Principles of Optics, 7th Edition*. Pergamon
               Press, 1999.

[CDD+06]   T. J. Cox, B.-I. L. Dalenbäck, P. D'Antonio, J. J. Embrechts, J. Y.
               Jeon, E. Mommertz, and M. Vorländer. A Tutorial on Scattering and
               Diffusion Coeffcients for Room Acoustic Surfaces. *Acta Acustica United
               with Acustica*, 92:1, 2006.

[CHV02]   L. Chai, W.A. Hoff, and T. Vincent. Three-dimensional motion and
               structure estimation using inertial sensors and computer vision for aug-
               mented reality. *Presence: Teleoperators and Virtual Environments*,
               11:474, 2002.

[CLR90]   T. Cormen, C. Leiserson, and R. Rivest. *Introduction to Algorithms*.
               MIT Press, 1990.

[CLT+08]   A. Chandak, C. Lauterbach, M. Taylor, Z. Ren, and D. Manocha.
               AD-Frustum: Adaptive Frustum Tracing for Interactive Sound Propa-
               gation. *IEEE Transactions on Visualization and Computer Graphics*,
               14:1707, 2008.

[CNSD+92]   C. Cruz-Neira, D. Sandin, T. DeFanti, R. Kenyon, and J. Hart. The
               cave: Audio visual experience automatic virtual environment. *Com-
               munications of the ACM*, 35:64, 1992.

[CP69]   M. J. Crocker and A. J. Price. Sound Transmission using Statistical
               Energy Analysis. *Jounal of Sound and Vibration*, 9:460, 1969.

[CP70]   M. J. Crocker and A. J. Price. Sound transmission through double pan-
            els using statistical energy analysis. *Journal of the Acoustical Society
            of America*, 47:683, 1970.

[CR05]   C. L. Christensen and J. H. Rindel. A new scattering method that
            combines roughness and diffraction effects. In *Proceedings of the Forum
            Acousticum*, Budapest, Hungary, 2005.

[Cra93]   O. Cramer. The variation of the specific heat ratio and the speed of
            sound in air with temperature, pressure, humidity, and CO_2 concen-
            tration. *Journal of the Acoustical Society of America*, 93:2510, 1993.

[Dal95]   B.-I. L. Dalenbäck. *A New Model for Room Acoustic Prediction and
            Auralization*. PhD thesis, Chalmers University if Technology, Gothen-
            burg, Sweden, 1995.

[Dal96]   B.-I. L. Dalenbäck. Room acoustic prediction based on a unified treat-
            ment of diffuse and specular reflection. *Journal of the Acoustical Society
            of America*, 100:899, 1996.

[Dro06]   P. Dross. Real-time capable reverberation estimator for virtual environ-
            ments. Master's thesis, RWTH Aachen University, Aachen, Germany,
            2006.

[Emo]   Emotiv. www.emotiv.com.

[EN97]   European Standard EN. 12354: Building acoustics - estimation of
            acoustic performance of buildings from the performance of products,
            1997.

[Far95]   A. Farina. RAMSETE - a new Pyramid Tracer for medium and large
            scale acoustic problems. In *Proceedings of the Euronoise*, Lyon, France,
            1995.

[FCD]   ISO/IEC FCD. 19774:200x: Information technology - Computer graph-
            ics and image processing - Humanoid animation (H-Anim), www.hanim.
            org/.

[Fra08]   A. Franck. *Finite-Elemente-Methoden, Lösungsalgorithmen und
            Werkzeuge für die akustische Simulationstechnik*. PhD thesis, Institute
            of Technical Acoustics, RWTH Aachen University, Aachen, Germany,
            2008.

[FTC+04]   T. A. Funkhouser, N. Tsingos, I. Carlbom, G. Elko, M. Sondhi, J. E.
            West, G. Pingal, P. Min, and A. Ngan. A beam tracing method for
            interactive architectural acoustics. *Journal of the Acoustical Society of
            America*, 115:739, 2004.

[FvDFH96]   J. D. Foley, A. van Dam, S. K. Feiner, and J. F. Hughes. *Computer
            Graphics, Principles and Practice, 2nd edition*. Addison-Wesley, 1996.

[Gel04]   S. A. Gelfand. *Hearing. An Introduction to psychological and physio-logical acoustics, 4th edition.* Dekker, 2004.

[Ger79]   E. Gerretsen. Calculation of sound transmission between dwellings by partitions and flanking structures. *Applied Acoustics*, 12:413, 1979.

[Ger86]   E. Gerretsen. Calculation of airborne and impact sound insulation between dwellings. *Applied Acoustics*, 19:245, 1986.

[GHW+04]   A. Gerndt, B. Hentschel, M. Wolter, T. Kuhlen, and C. H. Bischof. VIRACOCHA: An Efficient Parallelization Framework for Large-Scale CFD Post-Processing in Virtual Environments. *IEEE Computer Society*, page 50, 2004.

[Gir96]   F. Giron. *Investigations about the directivity of sound sources.* PhD thesis, Ruhr Universität, Bochum, Germany, 1996.

[Gla89]   A. Glassner. *An Introduction to Ray Tracing.* Academic Press, 1989.

[Gla93]   A. Glassner, editor. *Graphics Gems.* Academic Press, 1993.

[Hec94]   P. Heckbert, editor. *Graphics Gems IV.* Morgan Kaufmann, 1994.

[Hei62]   Morton L. Heilig. Sensorama simulator, August 1962.

[Hei93]   R. Heinz. Binaural room simulation based on an image source model with addition of statistical methods to include the diffuse sound scattering of walls and to predict the reverberant tail. *Applied Acoustics*, 38:145, 1993.

[Hei94]   R. Heinz. *Entwicklung und Beurteilung von computergestützten Methoden zur binauralen Raumsimulation.* PhD thesis, RWTH Aachen University, Aachen, Germany, 1994.

[Hol02]   J. Holländer. *Improvements on an algorithm for insulation of airborne sound insulation.* Institute of Technical Acoustics, RWTH Aachen University, Aachen, Germany, 2002.

[ISO03]   DIN EN ISO. 354: Acoustics – Measurement of sound absorption in a reverberation room, 2003.

[ISO04a]   ISO. 17497: Acoustics – Measurement of sound scattering of surfaces, 2004.

[ISO04b]   DIN EN ISO. 140: Acoustics – Measurement of sound insulation in buildings and of building elements, 2004.

[ISO07]   DIN EN ISO. 3382-2: Acoustics – Measurement of room acoustic parameters – Part 2: Reverberation time in ordinary rooms, 2007.

[Jau10]   L. Jauer. Schallfeld Simulation im Fahrzeuginnenraum mittels kombinierter wellen- und strahlenbasierter Simulationsverfahren. Master's thesis, RWTH Aachen University, Aachen, Germany, 2010.

[JNW06]   D. Jackèl, S. Neunreither, and F. Wagner. *Methoden der Computeranimation.* Springer, 2006.

[KDS93]   M. Kleiner, B. I. Dalenbäck, and U. P. Svensson. Auralization - An Overview. *Journal of the Audio Engineering Society,* 41:861, 1993.

[Kel62]   J. B. Keller. Geometrical theory of diffraction. *Journal of the Optical Society of America,* 52:116, 1962.

[Kir92]   D. Kirk, editor. *Graphics Gems III.* Morgan Kaufmann, 1992.

[KJM05]   B. Kapralos, M. Jenkin, and E. Milios. Acoustical diffraction modeling utilizing the huygens-fresnel principle. In *Proceedings of the IEEE International Workshop,* Ontario, Canada, 2005.

[Kom07]   L. Komzsik. *Approximation Techniques for Engineers.* CRC PRess, 2007.

[KP74]   R. G. Kouyoumijan and P. H. Pathak. A uniform geometrical theory of diffraction for an edge in a perfectly conducting surface. *Proceedings of the IEEE,* 62:1448, 1974.

[KSS68]   A. Krokstad, S. Strøm, and S. Sørsdal. Calculating the acoustical room response by the use of a ray tracing technique. *Journal on Sound and Vibration,* 8:118, 1968.

[Kut95]   H. Kuttruff. A simple iteration scheme for the computation of decay constants in enclosures with diffusely reflecting boundaries. *Journal of the Acoustical Society of America,,* 98:288, 1995.

[Kut00]   H. Kuttruff. *Room Acoustics, 4th edition.* Elsevier, 2000.

[KvdPvEJ06] A.G. Kohlrausch, S. L. J. D. E. van de Par, R. L. J. van Eijk, and J. F. Juola. Human performance in detecting audio-visual asynchrony. *Journal of the Acoustical Society of America,* 120:3084–3085, 2006.

[Lam96]   Y.W. Lam. A comparison of three reflection modelling methods used in room acoustics computer models. *Journal of the Acoustical Society of America,* 100:2181, 1996.

[LCM07]   C. Lauterbach, A. Chandak, and D. Manocha. Interactive Sound Rendering in Complex and Dynamic Scenes using Frustum Tracing. *IEEE Transactions on Visualization and Computer Graphics,* 13:1672, 2007.

[Len07]   T. Lentz. *Binaural Technology for Virtual Reality.* PhD thesis, RWTH Aachen University, Aachen, Germany, 2007.

[Lew93]   P. Lewers. A combined bream tracing and radiant exchange computer model of room acoustics. *Applied Acoustics,* 38:161, 1993.

[LJ03]   J. J. LaViola Jr. A testbed for studying and choosing predictive track-
            ing algorithms in virtual environments. In *Proceedings of the 7th Inter-
            national Immersive Projection Technologies Workshop, 9th Eurograph-
            ics Workshop on Virtual Environments*, Zurich, Switzerland, 2003.

[LM62]   R. H. Lyon and G. Maidanik. Power flow between linearly coupled
            oscillators. *Journal of the Acoustical Society of America*, 40:7, 1962.

[LSVA07]   T. Lentz, D. Schröder, M. Vorländer, and I. Assenmacher. Virtual
            reality system with integrated sound field simulation and reproduction.
            EURASIP Journal on Advances in Signal Processing, 2007:19, 2007.

[Lun08]   P. Lundén. Uni-verse acoustic simulation system: interactive realtime
            room acoustic simulation in dynamic 3D environments. *Journal of the
            Acoustical Society of America*, 123:3937, 2008.

[Mae68]   Z. Maekawa. Noise reduction by screens. *Applied Acoustics*, 1:157,
            1968.

[Mec02]   F. P. Mechel. *Formulas of Acoustics*. Springer, 2002.

[Med81]   H. Medwin. Shadowing by finite noise barriers. *Journal of the Acous-
            tical Society of America*, 69:1060, 1981.

[Mey09]   J. Meyer. *Acoustics and the Performance of Music, 5th edition*.
            Springer, 2009.

[Mor05]   M. Mori. Views on the uncanny valley. In *Proceedings of the IEEE-RAS
            Humanoids Workshop*, Tsukuba, Japan, 2005.

[MPI08]   MPI. A Message-Passing Interface Standard Version 2.1, `www.mcs.`
            `anl.gov/research/projects/mpi`, 2008.

[Mös95]   M. Möser. Die Wirkung von zylindrischen Aufsätzen an Schallschirmen.
            Acustica, 81:565, 1995.

[Mös05]   M. Möser. *Technische Akustik, 6th edition*. Springer, 2005.

[Nay93]   G. M. Naylor. ODEON - another hybrid room acoustical model. *Applied
            Acoustics*, 38:131, 1993.

[NKSS08]   M. Noisternig, B. Katz, S. Siltanen, and L. Savioja. Framework for real-
            time auralization in architectural acoustics. *Journal of the Acoustical
            Society of America*, 94:1000, 2008.

[Opea]   OpenDaff. `www.opendaff.org`.

[Opeb]   OpenMeasurements. `www.openmeasurements.net`.

[Ope08]   OpenMP. Application Program Interface Version 3.0, `www.openmp.org`,
            2008.

[OR04]   F. Otondo and J. H Rindel. The influence of the directivity of musical instruments in a room. *Acta Acustica United with Acustica*, 90:1178, 2004.

[Pae95]   A. Paeth, editor. *Graphics Gems V.* Morgan Kaufmann, 1995.

[PB09]   M. Pollow and G. Behler. Variable Directivity for Platonic Sound Sources Based on Spherical Harmonics Optimization. *Acta Acustica United with Acustica*, 95:1082, 2009.

[PBS10]   M. Pollow, G.K. Behler, and F. Schultz. Musical instrument recording for building a directivity database. In *Proceedings of the DAGA*, Berlin, Germany, 2010.

[Pel07]   S. Pelzer. Real-time auralization of complex dynamic virtual environments. Master's thesis, RWTH Aachen University, Aachen, Germany, 2007.

[Pie88]   A. Pietrzyk. Computer modeling of the sound field in small rooms. In *Proceedings of the 15th AES International Conference on Audio Acoustics and Small Spaces*, Copenhagen, Denmark, 1988.

[PL10]   J. Pätynen and T. Lokki. Directivities of symphony orchestra instruments. *Acta Acustica United with Acustica*, 96:138, 2010.

[Poh08]   A. Pohl. Beugungsalgorithmen für die Echtzeit-Raumakustiksimulation. Master's thesis, RWTH Aachen University, Aachen, Germany, 2008.

[PS]   A. Pohl and D. Schröder.

[PSV11]   S. Pelzer, D. Schröder, and M. Vorländer. The number of necessary rays in simulations based on geometrical acoustics using the diffuse rain technique. In *Proceedings of the DAGA*, Düsseldorf, Germany, 2011.

[PV10]   S. Pelzer and M. Vorländer. Frequency- and time-dependent geometry for real-time auralization. In *Proceedings of the 20th International Congress on Acoustics (ICA)*, Syndey, Australia, 2010.

[RA08]   D. Rausch and I. Assenmacher. A sketch-based interface for architectural modification in virtual environments. In *Proceedings of the 5th VR/AR Workshop*, Magdeburg, Germany, 2008.

[Rab03]   R. Rabenseifner. Hybrid parallel programming: Performance problems and chances. In *Proceedings of the 45th Cray User Group Conference*, Columbus, OH, USA, 2003.

[RE01]   S. Ranta-Eskola. Binary Space Partitioning Trees and Polygon Removal in Real Time 3D Rendering. Master's thesis, Uppsala University, Uppsala, Sweden, 2001.

[Reu08]   S. Reuter. Simulation of natural sound sources in immersive virtual environments. Master's thesis, RWTH Aachen University, Aachen, Germany, 2008.

[Rin04]   J. H. Rindel. Evaluation of room acoustic qualities and defects by use of auralization,. In *Proceedings of the 148th Meeting of the Acoustical Society of America*, San Diego, CA, USA, 2004.

[Ros70]   S. M. Ross. *Applied probability models with optimization applications.* Holden-Day, 1970.

[Ryb09]   A. Ryba. Real-time auralization of modifiable rooms. Master's thesis, RWTH Aachen University, Aachen, Germany, 2009.

[SAB62]   M. R. Schroeder, B. S. Atal, and C. Bird. Digital computers in room acoustics. In *Proceedings of the 4th International Congress on Acoustics*, Copenhagen, Denmark, 1962.

[Sav99]   L. Savioja. *Modeling Techniques for Virtual Acoustics*. PhD thesis, Helsinki University of Technology, Helsinki, Finland, 1999.

[SBGS69]   R. Shumacker, R. Brand, M. Gilliland, and W. Sharp. Study for Applying Computer-Generated Images to Visual Simulations, AFHRL-TR-69-14. Technical report, U.S. Air Force Human Resources Laboratory, 1969.

[Sch09a]   M. Schlütter. Parallelisierung von Algorithmen für die Echtzeit-Raumakustiksimulation. Master's thesis, RWTH Aachen University, Aachen, Germany, 2009.

[Sch09b]   D. Schröder. Optimization of input parameters for real-time room acoustics simulations. In *Proceedings of the International Conference on Acoustics NAG/DAGA*, pages 1456–1458, Rotterdam, The Netherlands, 2009.

[SDV07]   D. Schröder, P. Dross, and M. Vorländer. A fast reverberation estimator for virtual environments. In *Proceedings of the 30th AES International Conference*, Saariselkä, Finland, 2007.

[SE10]   U. P. Svensson and H. El-Bann Zidan. Early energy conditions in small rooms and in convolutions of small-room impulse responses. In *Proceedings of the 129th AES Convention*, San Francisco, USA, 2010.

[Sed90]   R. Sedgewick. *Algorithms in C*. Addison-Wesley, 1990.

[SFV99]   U. P. Svensson, R. I. Fred, and J. Vanderkooy. An analytic secondary source model of edge diffraction impulse responses. *Journal of the Acoustical Society of America*, 106:2331, 1999.

[Shi62]   M. Shimrat. Algorithm 112: Position of point relative to polygon. *Communications of the ACM*, 5:434, 1962.

[SHLV99]   L. Savioja, J. Huopaniemi, T. Lokki, and R. Väänänen. Creating inter-
            active virtual acoustic environments. *Journal of the Audio Engineering
            Society*, 47:675, 1999.

[SL06]   D. Schröder and T. Lentz. Real-time processing of image sources using
            binary space partitioning. *Journal of the Audio Engineering Society*,
            54(7/8):604–619, 2006.

[Sle04]   K. Slenczka. *Simulations of natural sound sources for binaural synthe-
            sis*. PhD thesis, RWTH Aachen University, Aachen, Germany, 2004.

[SLKS07]   S. Siltanen, T. Lokki, S. Kiminki, and L. Savioja. The room acous-
            tic rendering equation. *Journal of the Acoustical Society of America*,
            122:1624, 2007.

[SN99]   J. S. Suh and P. A. Nelson. Measurement of transient response of
            rooms and comparison with geometrical acoustic models. *Journal of
            the Acoustical Society of America*, 105:2304, 1999.

[SRA08]   D. Schröder, S. Reuter, and I. Assemnacher. Multimodale Darstellung
            natürlicher Schallquellen in virtuellen Umgebungen. In *Proceedings of
            the DAGA*, Dresden, Germany, 2008.

[SS07]   U. M. Stephenson and U. P. Svensson. An improved energetic approach
            to diffraction based on the uncertainty principle. In *Proceedings of the
            19th International Congress on Acoustics*, Madrid, Spain, 2007.

[SSM10]   D. Schröder, B. Starke, and H.-J. Maempel. Optimization of input
            parameters for the real-time simulation of room acoustics - revisited.
            In *Proceedings of the DAGA*, Berlin, Germany, 2010.

[SSV10]   D. Schröder, U. P. Svensson, and M. Vorländer. Open measurements
            of edge diffraction from a noise barrier scale model. In *Proceedings of
            the International Symposium on Room Acoustics (ISRA)*, Melbourne,
            Australia, 2010.

[Sta09]   B. Starke. Investigation of the influence of acoustical simulation pa-
            rameters on the perception in virtual environments. Master's thesis,
            RWTH Aachen University, Aachen, Germany, 2009.

[Ste96]   U. M. Stephenson. Quantized Pryamidal Beam Tracing - a New Al-
            gorithm for Room Acoustics and Noise Immission Prognosis. *ACTA
            ACUSTICA united with ACUSTICA*, 82:517, 1996.

[Ste04]   U. M. Stephenson. *Beugungssimulation ohne Rechenzeitexplosion:
            die Methode der quantisierten Pyramidenstrahlen; ein neues Berech-
            nungsverfahren für Raumakustik und Lärmimmissionsprognose; Ver-
            gleiche, Ansätze, Lösungen*. PhD thesis, RWTH Aachen University,
            Aachen, Germany, 2004.

[Ste10a]   U. M. Stephenson. Simulation of diffraction within ray tracing. *Acta
            Acustica United with Acustica*, 96:516, 2010.

[Ste10b]   U. M. Stephenson. Some further experiments with the beam diffraction model based on the uncer tainty relation - is it valid also with double diffraction? In *Proceedings of the DAGA*, Berlin, Germany, 2010.

[SV07]   D. Schröder and M. Vorländer. Hybrid method for room acoustic simulation in real-time. In *Proceedings of the 20th International Congress on Acoustics (ICA)*, Madrid, Spain, 2007.

[Sve10]   Edge Diffraction Matlab Toolbox by U. Peter Svensson. www.iet.ntnu.no/~svensson/software/index.html, 2010.

[SW00]   U. P. Svensson and K. Wendlandt. The influence of a loudspeaker cabinet's shape on the radiated power. In *Proceedings of Baltic Acoustic 2000*, Vilnius, Lithuania, 2000.

[TGD04]   N. Tsingos, E. Gallo, and G. Drettakis. Perceptual audio rendering of complex virtual environments. *ACM Transactions on Graphics (SIGGRAPH Conference Proceedings)*, 3, 2004.

[Tha05]   R. Thaden. *Auralisation in Building Acoustics*. PhD thesis, RWTH Aachen University, Aachen, Germany, 2005.

[THM+03]   M. Teschner, B. Heidelberger, M. Müller, D. Pomeranets, and M. Gross. Optimized Spatial Hashing for Collision Detection of Deformable Objects. In *Proceedings of the VMV*, Munich, Germany, 2003.

[Tsi07]   N. Tsingos. Using programmable graphics hard-ware for auralization. In *Proceedings of the EAA Auralization Symposium*, Espoo, Finland, 2007.

[Val07]   J. T. Valvoda. *Virtual Humanoids and Presence in Virtual Environments*. PhD thesis, RWTH Aachen University, Aachen, Germany, 2007.

[vdPK00]   S. van de Par and A. Kohlrausch. Sensitivity to Auditory-Visual Asynchrony and to Jitter in Auditory-Visual Timing. In *Proceedings of the Human Vision and Electronic Imaging V*, San Jose, USA, 2000.

[vE00]   O. von Estorff. *Boundary Elements in Acoustics: Advances and Applications*. WIT Press, 2000.

[VM00]   M. Vorländer and E. Mommertz. Definition and measurement of random-incidence scattering coeffcients. *Applied Acoustics*, 60:187, 2000.

[Vor89]   M. Vorländer. Simulation of the transient and steady-state sound propagation in rooms using a new combined ray-tracing/image-source algorithm. *Journal of the Acoustical Society of America*, 86:172, 1989.

[Vor95]   M. Vorländer. International Round Robin on room acoustical computer simulations. In *Proceedings of the 15th International Congress on Acoustics*, Trondheim, Norway, 1995.

[Vor08]   M. Vorländer. *Auralization - Fundamentals of Acoustics, Modelling, Simulation, Algorithms and Acoustic Virtual Reality*. Springer, 2008.

[VRC]   VRCA. www.vrca.rwth-aachen.de.

[VS09a]   R. Vitale and D. Schröder. Investigation of scattering coefficient of everyday furniture. In *Proceedings of the International Conference on Acoustics NAG/DAGA*, Rotterdam, The Netherlands, 2009.

[VS09b]   R. Vitale and D. Schröder. Measurements of scattering coefficients for classroom acoustics computer simulation. In *Proceedings of the EURONOISE*, Edinburgh, UK, 2009.

[VT00]   M. Vorländer and R. Thaden. Auralisation of airborne sound insulation in buildings. *Acustica united with Acta Acustica*, 86:70, 2000.

[VvM86]   J. Vian and D. van Maercke. Calculation of the room impulse response using a ray-tracing method. In *Proceedings of the ICA Symposium on Acoustics and Theatre Planning for the Performing Arts*, Vancouver, Canada, 1986.

[Wal80]   J. P. Walsh. The design of Godot: A system for computer-aided room acoustics modeling and simulation. In *Proceedings of the 10th International Conference on Acoustics*, Sydney, Australia, 1980.

[WB10]   F. Wefers and J. Berg. High-performance real-time FIR-filtering using fast convolution on graphics hardware. In *Proceedings of the DAFX*, Graz, Austria, 2010.

[WD07]   I. Witew and P. Dietrich. Assessment of the Uncertainty in Room Acoustical Measurements. In *Proceedings of the 19th International Congress on Acoustics*, Madrid, Spain, 2007.

[Wef07]   F. Wefers. Optimizing segmented realtime convolution. Master's thesis, RWTH Aachen University, Aachen, Germany, 2007.

[WH01a]   F. A. Wichmann and N. J. Hill. The psychometric function: I. fitting, sampling and goodness-of-fit. *Perception and Psychophysics*, 63:1293, 2001.

[WH01b]   F. A. Wichmann and N. J. Hill. The psychometric function: Ii. bootstrap-based confidence intervals and sampling. *Perception and Psychophysics*, 63:1314, 2001.

[Wil99]   E.G. Williams. *Fourier Acoustics: Sound Radiation and Nearfield Acoustical Holography*. Academic Press, 1999.

[Wit04]   I. Witew. Spatial variation of lateral measures in different concert halls. In *Proceedings of the 18th International Congress on Acoustics*, Kyoto, Japan, 2004.

[WO95]   J. R. Wu and M. Ouhyoung. A 3D tracking experiment on latency
            and its compensation methods in virtual environments. In *Proceed-
            ings of the 8th annual ACM symposium on User interface and software
            technology*, New York, NY, USA, 1995.

[WS09]   F. Wefers and D. Schröder. Real-time auralization of coupled rooms.
            In *Proceedings of the EAA Auralization Symposium*, Espoo, Finland,
            2009.

[WSPV09]   F. Wefers, D. Schröder, S. Pelzer, and M. Vorländer. Real-time filter-
            ing for interactive virtual acoustic prototyping. In *Proceedings of the
            EURONOISE*, Edinburgh, UK, 2009.

[Zie00]   O.C. Zienkiewicz. *Finite Element Method Volume 1 - The Basis, 5th
            edition*. Elsevier, 2000.

[ZS06]   F. Zotter and A. Sontacci. Virtual Game-Lan Graz, IEM Report 35/06.
            Technical report, Institute of Electronic Music and Acoustic, University
            of Music and Performing Arts, Graz, Austria, 2006.

Curriculum vitae

Personal Data

Date of Birth:	22th of June, 1974
Place of Birth:	Cologne, Germany
Filiation:	Ursula and Friedhelm Schröder

Education

01/2005–02/2011	**Ph.D. Studies at the Institute of Technical Acoustics**
	RWTH Aachen University, Germany
	Concentration: Virtual Acoustics/Immersive Audio
10/1997–10/2004	**Master Degree in Electrical Engineering (Dipl.-Ing.)**
	RWTH Aachen University, Germany
	Concentration: Communication- and Information Technology

Professional Experience

05/2011–today	**Research Fellow (ERCIM Scholar)**
	Centre for Quantifiable Quality of Service in Communication Systems, Centre of Excellence, NTNU Trondheim, Norway
01/2005–03/2011	**Research/Teaching Assistant**
	Institute of Technical Acoustics, RWTH Aachen University, Germany
08/2009–12/2009	**Research/Teaching Assistant**
	Centre for Quantifiable Quality of Service in Communication Systems, Centre of Excellence, NTNU Trondheim, Norway
10/2003–02/2004	**Internship**
	Philips Research, Aachen, Germany
06/2003–08/2003	**Internship**
	Intelligent Systems and Control (ISAC) Research Group, Belfast, United Kingdom